"Ancient monastic authors
use to readers. Like them, Michael Casey has written a useful
volume, a volume to live by. Drawing on a wealth of sources,
and reading deeply in the book of experience, he shows what a
vast perspective is indicated in the 'little Rule' of Benedict, what
fullness of life is in store for those who follow it with courage
and coherence."

—Eric Varden, OCSO
Mount Saint Bernard Abbey

"*Seventy-Four Tools for Good Living* is Michael Casey's ingenious
way of rendering the wisdom of St. Benedict for our times. As a
master teacher, he weaves together sources from the monastic
tradition and contemporary insights through these seventy-four
tools. If this is not his best book, it is certainly his most readable
and gracious offering to his students and readers. This is a book
that comes from his personal *lectio* and living the monastic way
of life in Australia. It is also a book I can use for *lectio* and living
my monastic way of life here in Indiana. Lay contemplatives,
especially oblates, will find this a cut above the books published
in most bibliographies on monastic spirituality. This book matters!"

—Meg Funk, OSB
Our Lady of Grace Monastery

"Michael Casey brings a deep lived knowledge of the monastic
tradition to this splendid set of reflections on Benedict's Rule. He
manages to marry faith commitment to pastoral common sense
in such a manner that monks and laity as well can find answers
to that request made to the old desert dwellers: Give me a good
word. Casey, in fact, gives us many good words."

—Lawrence S. Cunningham
John A. O'Brien Professor of Theology (Emeritus)
The University of Notre Dame

"In my regular university course on the Rule of St. Benedict as a mirror to present-day culture there is close reading of some chapters of the Rule. To my shame I tended to neglect chapter four a bit. Michael Casey's deep reflections in this remarkable book are nourished by a half century of monastic reading and deep psychological and existential insight. I can now draw from nearly 300 pages of wisdom on the fourth chapter of Benedict's Rule. Just to quote from Fr. Michael's preface: 'There is much more in Benedict's Rule than meets the superficial eye.'"

—Wil Derkse
    Andreas van Melsen Chair for Science,
      Society and Worldviews (retired)
    Catholic Radboud University of Nijmegen
    The Netherlands

Seventy-Four Tools for Good Living

Reflections on the Fourth Chapter of Benedict's Rule

Michael Casey, OCSO

LITURGICAL PRESS
Collegeville, Minnesota

www.litpress.org

Imprimi potest: Abbot Steele Hartmann, OCSO, 26 January 2014.

Cover design by Ann Blattner. Illustration: *Thebaid*, attributed to Gherardo Starnina (1335–1413), Uffizi Gallery, Florence, Italy. Courtesy of Wikimedia Commons.

1   2   3   4   5   6   7   8

Library of Congress Cataloging-in-Publication Data

Casey, Michael, 1942–
    Seventy-four tools for good living : reflections on the fourth chapter of Benedict's Rule / Michael Casey, OCSO.
        pages   cm
    ISBN 978-0-8146-3720-3 — ISBN 978-0-8146-3745-6 (ebook)
    1. Christian life—Catholic authors.   2. Christian life—
Meditations.   3. Benedict, Saint, Abbot of Monte Cassino.
Regula. Caput   4. Quae sunt instrumenta bonorum operum.
I. Title.

BX2350.3.C373   2014
255'.106—dc23   2014001609

For Richard Franklin

After fifty years

Contents

Abbreviations

CC	*Corpus Christianorum: Series Latina*
CCCM	*Corpus Christianorum: Continuatio Medievalis*
Dil	Bernard of Clairvaux, *De diligendo Deo* in SBOp 3
Div	Bernard of Clairvaux, *Sermones de diversis* in SBOp 6A
DSp	*Dictionnaire de Spiritualité* (Paris: Beauchesne, 1937–95)
EM	*Exordium Magnum*
Hum	Bernard of Clairvaux, *De gradibus humilitatis et superbiae* in SBOp 3
PL	J.-P. Migne, *Patrologia Latina*
RB	The Rule of Saint Benedict
RM	The Rule of the Master
S.	Aelred of Rievaulx, *Sermo*
SBOp	*Sancti Bernardi Opera*, 8 vols. (Rome: Editiones Cistercienses, 1957–77)
SC	Bernard of Clairvaux, *Sermones super cantica canticorum* in SBOp 1–2
SChr	Sources Chétiennes (Paris: Cerf)

Unless otherwise noted, all translations are my own.

Preface

Half a century ago, when I was a novice, a venerable old monk (whom I now realize was only in his late forties) held up a diminutive copy of the Rule of Saint Benedict and proclaimed, "You will find all the wisdom you will need to live a good monastic life in this Rule." At the time I thought he was exaggerating. Fifty years later I am of a different opinion. There is much more in Benedict's Rule than meets the superficial eye.

To begin with, as Benedict's final chapter indicates, the Rule does not stand alone. It was intended as a practical gateway to the more extensive and richer tradition that preceded it and that animated most of its provisions. By living according to Benedict's Rule, we not only move into the world of John Cassian and Saint Basil but also are invited to go further back to the scriptural basis of all Christian and monastic living. Benedict's hope is that ultimately we pursue our spiritual journey by the guidance of the Gospel (RB Prol 21).

The more time I spend with the Rule the more I become convinced that it yields its deepest meaning only to those who are prepared to engage with it through close reading. This means reading very slowly; considering every word, every phrase, and every sentence; and trying to comprehend not only what is expressed but also the hidden meanings that lie beneath the words, in the space between authorial intent and written text.

For close reading to be more than arid pedantry, we need to allow the text to enter into dialogue with our lives. Drawing from our experience, we learn to appreciate more fully what Benedict is saying and, sometimes, why he is saying it in the way that he does. Conversely, the text may illuminate our own experience by helping us to understand elements of our unique past and to offer guidance concerning our future. If we so choose, reading the Rule of Saint Benedict can be life-changing and life-enhancing.[1] These are the principles that have guided this presentation of Benedict's fourth chapter: "The Implements: Good Works."

This is not a commentary but a book of reflections, written sequentially over the space of a year. As reflections, each individual section not only mirrors the part of Saint Benedict's text under discussion but also draws together different strands from more than fifty years of monastic reading. It has also been modified by my experiences around the time of writing, including the thoughts that happened to come to me from the liturgy and from whatever I was reading around that time. In particular the reader will note the strong influence of the *Sermones* of Saint Aelred of Rievaulx, which I was reading during the same period that these reflections were composed.

As with some of my other writings, I recommend that this book be read slowly one section at a time. Its purpose is not only to communicate my reflections on a given topic but to encourage readers to continue the process of reflection for themselves, applying what is written to their own lives and drawing on the wisdom and insight that the years have brought them.

The book was not written by following a master plan but created from moment to moment, following Saint Benedict's text. This means that there is some contingency in my comments. If I were writing the book today, my thoughts may well have drifted in a different direction. This also means that repetition is inevitable, partly caused by the repetition in the text of the Rule and partly from my own thoughts spontaneously revisiting a topic already raised. The astute reader will notice that there are parallels with what I have written in other books and articles. Sometimes I have added a reference to these in the notes.

In writing this book I have been compelled by Saint Benedict's text to venture into some areas of monastic *conversatio* that were relatively unfamiliar to me, and so my understanding of monastic spirituality has been broadened in the process. It is my hope that the reader will have a similar broadening experience.

It is my hope also that these reflections will be useful beyond the context in which Saint Benedict has written. Nevertheless, in sections of the book in which I am offering an interpretation of Benedict's teaching, I have usually done so in the context of a monastery of men. This happens to be the situation with which I am most familiar. In reading ancient texts all of us have to work hard to apply it to our own different situations. I am confident that readers will be able to take the lessons that Benedict gives beyond their gendered and cloistral origins into their own world of experience and still find them profitable. Where possible, however, I have tried to keep my writing gender neutral.

I am happy to acknowledge that, as I wrote these pages, I have kept Terrence Kardong's commentary open nearby and, to my profit, have often referred to it, though, obviously, he is not to blame for any inadequacies in my interpretation of the Rule.

The Implements: Good Works

¹In the first place, to love the Lord God from the whole heart, the whole soul, the whole strength, ²then, to love the neighbor as himself. ³Then, not to kill. ⁴Not to commit adultery. ⁵Not to steal. ⁶Not to lust. ⁷Not to speak false testimony. ⁸To honor all people. ⁹Let him not do to another what he does not wish to be done to himself. ¹⁰To deny himself to himself in order to follow Christ. ¹¹To restrain the body. ¹²Not to embrace delights. ¹³To love fasting. ¹⁴To improve the lot of poor people. ¹⁵To clothe a naked person. ¹⁶To visit a sick person. ¹⁷To bury one who is dead. ¹⁸To come to help in trouble. ¹⁹To console one who is feeling pain. ²⁰To make himself a stranger to the actions of the world. ²¹To put nothing before the love of Christ. ²²Not to go all the way with anger. ²³Not to prolong a time of rage. ²⁴Not to hold deceit in the heart. ²⁵Not to give a false peace. ²⁶Not to abandon charity. ²⁷Not to take an oath in case one breaks it. ²⁸To bring forth truth from the heart and from the mouth. ²⁹Not to return evil for evil. ³⁰To do no injury, but to endure patiently injury done to oneself. ³¹To love enemies. ³²Not to return curses to those who curse but rather to bless. ³³To endure persecution for righteousness. ³⁴Not to be proud. ³⁵Not to drink much wine. ³⁶Not to eat much. ³⁷Not [to be] sleepy. ³⁸Not [to be] lazy. ³⁹Not [to be] a murmurer. ⁴⁰Not [to be] a detractor. ⁴¹To commit his hope to God. ⁴²When he sees something good in himself, to attribute it to God and not to himself. ⁴³But let him know that evil done is always from

himself, and let him attribute it to himself. [44]To fear the Day of Judgment. [45]To be terrified of hell. [46]To desire eternal life with all spiritual yearning. [47]To have death present before one's eyes every day. [48]At every hour to keep guard over the actions of his life. [49]To know for certain that in every place the Lord is watching him. [50]Immediately to crush the evil thoughts coming into his heart on the rock of Christ and to manifest them to a spiritual senior. [51]To guard his mouth from evil and depraved speech. [52]Not to love much speaking. [53]Not to speak empty words or those leading to laughter. [54]Not to love much or violent laughter. [55]To listen willingly to holy readings. [56]To engage in prayer frequently. [57]To confess to God daily in prayer with tears and groaning his past evil actions. [58]Also, to avoid these evil actions. [59]Not to go all the way with the desires of the flesh. [60]To hate self-will. [61]To obey the instructions of the abbot in all things, even if he himself should act otherwise. (May it not happen.) [Let the monk be] mindful of the Lord's instruction, "What they say, do; what they do, do not do." [62]Not to be willing to be spoken of as holy before he is; but first to be so that it may be said more truly. [63]Daily to fulfill by deeds the instructions of God. [64]To love chastity. [65]To hate nobody. [66]Not to have jealousy. [67]Not to give scope to envy. [68]Not to love contention. [69]To flee elation. [70]To venerate the seniors. [71]To love the juniors. [72]In Christ's love to pray for enemies. [73]Before the sunset, to return to peace with those with whom there has been a quarrel. [74]And never to despair of God's mercy.

[75]Behold, these are the implements of the spiritual craft. [76]When they are used by us, unceasingly, night and day, and given back on the Day of Judgment, we will be paid the reward from the Lord which he himself promised. [77]"What God has prepared for those who love him, eye has not seen, nor ear heard, nor has it arisen in the human heart." [78]The workshop where we diligently work at all these is the cloister of the monastery and stability in the community.

Introduction
The [Monk's] Implements: Good Works

The tools of the monk's trade are good works.[1] The monastic enclosure is his workshop. Because a monastic rule has as its principal focus the practicalities of daily life, Saint Benedict begins his presentation of monastic virtues and values by an ample list of dos and don'ts. Saint Benedict is promulgating his moral catalogue with monks in mind. Most of the precepts he offers come from standard lists found in earlier Christian writings and are applicable to almost anybody, but Saint Benedict is thinking mainly of how these values and practices are lived out within the context of a monastery. This, of course, does not prevent present-day readers from interpreting this chapter for themselves in a more general context.

There are very few surprises in the content of this chapter. What is unexpected is that a man of Saint Benedict's spiritual stature should have included such a long and sometimes banal catalogue for the guidance of his monks. We know of other such lists. To begin with, there are the Ten Commandments. Saint Paul offers us a series of some twenty-six pungent precepts in Romans 12:9-21. And, of course there are the 613 commandments of rabbinic Judaism. Who, we may ask, can get their heads around a list of seventy-four admonitions? The brain cannot handle so many different items. Overwhelmed,

xviii *Seventy-Four Tools for Good Living*

most of us are inclined to set our minds on cruise control and simply glide through the list without paying too much attention to its details. This is a pity, because the evidence suggests that, although Benedict borrowed most of his content from previous lists, he made sufficient changes in both substance and style to indicate that he had thought through his material very carefully, and, presumably, he wants us to take it seriously.

I would like to say a little about my approach to the sources of this chapter. It is possible to spend a lot of time examining the pedigree of each of the recommendations that Benedict makes, tracing them back to their original formulation. This research can be useful to the extent that it may throw light on the primitive meaning or context of a particular item. The fact remains, however, that the primary determinant of meaning must be its inclusion in a rule written for monks living under a rule and an abbot. For one as habitually economical with words as Saint Benedict, drawing attention to these various elements of behavior may well indicate that there is danger that their importance may be overlooked. Why include an admonition if it is completely self-evident or always observed?

Benedict's principal and immediate source in this chapter, as it is through much of his Rule (especially in the opening sections), is the so-called Rule of the Master. There are, however, important differences. While taking over much of the Master's third chapter on the art of holiness, Benedict completely omits his supplementary fourth chapter on the spiritual tools to be used in the practice of the divine art. More important, Benedict severely summarizes the seventeen verses of the Master's extravagant eschatological conclusion into four short verses with a distinctly different flavor. Benedict's view of the final reward of a life dedicated to good works is much more sober and restrained than that of his source. There are around thirty other significant changes that

Benedict makes to the Master's list: additions, omissions, and variations, including the exclusion of the opening profession of faith in the Trinity, although this may have been a later addition to the Master's text.[2] It is clear that Benedict, while borrowing extensively from his major source, did so with a great deal of freedom, determined to make his text say exactly what he wanted it to say. Researchers have identified further sources behind the Rule of the Master. These are important because they serve as reminders that these precepts are paralleled in the writings of earlier fathers of the church, particularly Cyprian of Carthage and Basil of Caesarea.[3]

To give concreteness to his description of the art of spiritual living, Benedict uses the images of workshop and tools. The first thing about a workshop is that it is a place to work. In the Prologue, Benedict demonstrates that he is fully aware of the crucial role played by grace in the spiritual life, but he is equally conscious that to make progress we need to exert ourselves. That is why the image of a workshop is apposite. It would be nice if monastic life were simply a matter of sitting under a shady tree by a babbling brook, contemplating eternal verities. We know that it is not. It is a place of work and effort and struggle; it is a war zone in which the need for spiritual combat repeatedly reasserts itself. And it is a long war. This is why Benedict emphasizes, at the end of this chapter, the need to keep at our task, to persevere, to put into practice the crucial monastic virtue of stability. We will need to keep investing effort in the spiritual craft over a long period if we are to have much hope for any real progress.

One of the great dangers faced by monastic practitioners is that, after a few months or a few years or a few decades, we become weary of investing so much effort in the spiritual pursuit with so little evidence of having made very much progress. We need to be encouraged to keep plodding forward in the lifelong task of acquiring the virtues we still lack. John Cassian gives us these words of Abba Theodore:

We must always extend ourselves with unceasing care and solicitude to acquire the virtues, and we must constantly occupy ourselves in these exercises, lest when forward motion suddenly ceases, loss occurs. For, as we have said, the mind is not able to remain in one and the same state—that is, so that it does not experience either growth or diminishment in virtue. Not to increase is to decrease, because when the pursuit of going forward ceases, there will be a danger of going back.[4]

In a workshop there is usually an array of tools; the artisan knows when to use one and when to exchange it for another. Not all the tools are used simultaneously but only when the particular task demands it. In the same way, we will not be confronted with the need to engage in all the various good works at every hour of every day. Most often the need for one or another of them will manifest itself from time to time. Today may be relatively free of challenge. Tomorrow I may be overwhelmed by feelings of envy so that I can barely think of anything else. Then is the time for the struggle against envy to commence. But at some point, envy too will cease its harassment, and I will be forced to turn my attention in another direction. I cannot clothe the naked or feed the hungry or welcome the stranger if nobody around me is naked, hungry, or foreign. The challenge is to recognize the call of the moment and to respond to it rather than seeking to impose on the reality of daily life a preprogrammed assortment of good deeds.

Such a long list may seem intimidating. Even more daunting is the fact that it is not exhaustive. For example, although it uses the imagery of work, the list does not include any reference to daily work or to the more characteristic work of the Liturgy of the Hours. Between them, these two signature activities occupy more than half of the monk's waking hours, and Benedict himself devotes many chapters to them. Even so, here they pass unremarked. This omission may serve as a reminder that any list of good works will be ultimately incomplete because no list can envisage all possible opportunities for doing the right thing.

It would be wrong, however, to conclude from the title of the chapter that Benedict's workshop is dominated by a concern with manufacturing virtues. From a total of seventy-four recommendations, thirty-eight—over half—detail courses of action to be avoided.[5] "Not to be proud, not to drink much wine, not to eat much, not [to be] sleepy, not [to be] lazy, not [to be] a murmurer, not [to be] a detractor" (4.34-40). Of course, resistance can sometimes be a highly active process, but strictly speaking, it has no external product. To be a good and virtuous monk it is not necessary to be always and visibly engaged in good works; often it is a call to a more interior virtue that consists in refusing to give consent to a particularly harrowing temptation. There will be times when the inclination to sin will be so strong that simply doing nothing may well be considered high virtue. Sometimes monastic life consists more in deliberately turning aside from evil than in positively doing good. Even then, that is not the whole story; once a solid quota of virtue is attained, "being good" may consist simply in being fully attentive to spiritual reality by a kind of disconnectedness with observable behavior, working by rote while interiorly engaged elsewhere.

If I were asked to draw a picture of a good monk, what image would I conceive? Would he be a doer of good deeds or one who refrains from what is wrong? Maybe I would portray a monk rapt in silent contemplation or fervently singing the Divine Office. Perhaps I would choose to imitate the twelfth-century Cistercian miniaturists who painted jolly portraits of monks engaged in all sorts of rustic tasks. All of these options successfully show an aspect of what a good monk is and does—but not the whole reality. For this I would turn to a painting in the Uffizi Gallery in Florence, attributed to Fra Angelico (1395–1455), titled *Thebaid*, reproduced on the cover of this book.

In this canvas one can see multiple expressions of the monastic ideal through around fifty vignettes of monks engaged in a variety of activities: ecstatic prayer, manual work, hospitality, fraternal communion, and all sorts of mutual service. This painting is a great reminder that to be a good monk we have to be prepared to do all sorts of things—even contrary or contradictory things—as occasion demands. There is an element of unpredictability in the monk's day. As Saint Benedict says at the beginning of "On the Measure of Drink": "Each has his own gift from God: one this, another that" (RB 40.1).

When Saint Bernard speaks of the monastery as an anticipation of heaven, *paradisus claustralis*, he thinks of unity as being its characteristic constituent. The unity of which he is thinking is not the reductionist uniformity that comes from the suppression of multiplicity but the harmony that results from diverse elements working together toward a common goal.

> The monastery is truly a paradise, a region fortified with the ramparts of discipline. It is a glorious thing to have men living together in the same house, following the same way of life. How good and how pleasant it is when brothers live in unity!
> You will see one of them weeping for his sins,
> another rejoicing in the praise of God,
> another tending the needs of all,
> and another giving instruction to the rest.
> Here is one who is at prayer
> and another at reading;
> here is one who is compassionate
> and another who inflicts penalties for sins.
> This one is aflame with love
> and that one is valiant in humility.
> This one remains humble when everything goes well
> and this other one does not lose his nerve in difficulties.
> This one works very hard in active tasks,
> the other finds quiet in the practice of contemplation.[6]

The list is, of course, illustrative rather than exhaustive. The point is that, at a particular time, any one of these activities is appropriate to the good monk, even though others in the community are engaged in different occupations. It is not expected that anyone engage in all of them—especially at the same time.

Of course, a similar variety is witnessed in every community with different members performing different functions, but it is also realized in the life of each individual who, at different times, may be called on to be involved in a variety of services or ministries alongside the basic activities of monastic *conversatio*. Thus, in the course of a lifetime, we will probably experience different seasons—periods in which the graces and challenges will differ substantially, and our primary fidelity will be to respond to the reality of each moment rather than trying to hold on to what has passed or look forward to what may be reasonably expected of the future. This is why we tell newcomers: "You don't have to wait for profession or ordination or graduation; you can start living a full monastic life from the very beginning."

This chapter on the implements of good works can serve as a checklist of whether we are making the effort to do the deeds that follow from our commitment to the Gospel and resisting behavior that is contrary to the Gospel. It can serve as a kind of examination of the integrity of our conscience. Do we see only those faults or omissions where we can claim to be blameless by some form of rationalization? Are we becoming one of those who will say to the Lord, "When did we see you hungry or thirsty or naked?" This inventory of good works is meant to prod our consciences to see possibilities for virtue that we habitually overlook. For Benedict's list to be effective, however, we have to have acquired a certain level of self-knowledge and a capacity for radical self-honesty. Those who are complacent and self-righteous, who never admit to making mistakes or to being governed by weakness or blind to opportunities, will inevitably find in this chapter no incentives to purer and more generous living. They may even begin to purr: "All these things I have kept since my youth." Let us remember the warning, "Let those who are still standing take care lest they fall" (1 Cor 10:11).

I note that there are seventy-four items on the list. This means that if every day we took time to ponder a single one of the first seventy-three items we should traverse the whole list five times in a year. The final point, "never to despair in God's mercy," is worth recalling every day. Such an exercise, seriously undertaken, would provide abundant matter for a thorough examination of conscience and perhaps move us out of our usual interior preoccupations into a more objective self-scrutiny.

Above all, we should not regard this list as something trivial and elementary that we may safely pass over without reflection. This facile dismissal cloaks a more somber reality. There is an ingrained resistance to much that is prescribed here, coming from both nature and nurture. We do not want to live in this way. We want to be left alone to live our life as we please, to fill our cup with every enjoyment available to us, and to avoid anything that might occasion effort on our part. We already do plenty of good deeds, though mostly of our own choosing. We do not want someone coming along to ask us to do more or to take us out of our comfort zone. We don't want to be stretched. It is even possible for us to begin to rationalize this position in the manner of David Hume, seeing too much virtue as unnatural and unattractive. This is what the Scots philosopher of the eighteenth century wrote:

> Celibacy, fasting, penance, mortification, self-denial, humility, silence, solitude and the whole train of monkish virtues; for what reason are they everywhere rejected by men of sense, but because they serve to no manner of purpose, neither advance a man's fortune in the world, nor render him

a more valuable member of society; neither qualify him for entertainment of company, nor increase his power of self-enjoyment? We observe, on the contrary, that they cross all these desirable ends; stupefy the understanding and harden the heart, obscure the fancy and sour the temper. We justly, therefore, transfer them to the opposite column, and place them in the catalogue of vices.[7]

The instinctive sympathy we feel for such a standpoint indicates that to put this chapter into practice will pose a great challenge for us. Taken as a whole, Benedict's list is indicative of a viewpoint that many good people of our own time would regard as foolish, excessive, inhuman, and even scandalous. Such a life is unthinkable without a radical conversion—a total change in the way we see things and evaluate the issues that confront us. This profound conversion is expressed in the fundamental reorientation of our life and, more especially, through a diligent and detailed determination to implement Gospel values not only in the major matters of life but also in situations that are superficially insignificant. Fidelity in little things is a means by which we signal our wholehearted commitment to God. As so often in human relations, it is the little things that matter most. "Quantitative judgements don't apply."[8] Just as our genetic signature permeates every cell of our body, so our basic will to serve God expresses itself not only in the major decisions that shape our life but also in small gestures that often pass below the threshold of public awareness. We do not have to express our following of Christ in heroic feats of achievement or endurance; often the giving of a cup of cold water suffices. Benedict's list announces that everything matters. Nothing is unimportant.

Saint Paul's reminder in the second chapter of the Letter to the Romans can serve as an incentive to the practice of virtue: "Are you not aware that the kindness of God is leading you to conversion?" (Rom 2:4). The word he uses is *metanoia*, familiar to us from the gospel tradition. A change of thinking is required if we are to accept the truth of what he is saying. God's kindness toward us goes beyond our own self-acceptance. God sees us as capable of better and so is continually urging us to change our thinking, to reevaluate our priorities, and to upgrade our behavior. This is a theme to which Saint Benedict repeatedly returns in his Prologue, finally citing this very text, "Are you not aware that the patience of God is leading you to repentance?" (RB Prol 37).[9]

1-2

In the first place, to love the Lord God from the whole heart, the whole soul, the whole strength, then, to love the neighbor as himself.

Far from being an esoteric discipline, accessible to only a few high-level practitioners, monastic spirituality grounds itself on this most fundamental and universal of all precepts: the indivisible love we must have for God and neighbor. In Saint Benedict's mind, the monk is no different from the commonplace Christian—with the same ideals and the same struggles; what is distinctive is that monastic life provides a more expansive opportunity to understand and to practice Christ's new commandment in daily life. It is ordinary Christian discipleship lived in a protected environment that is designed to make discipleship simpler to practice and more difficult to avoid.

The original sources of this double commandment are Deuteronomy 6:5 and Leviticus 19:18.[1] Jesus combined them, as some of the rabbis did, to form a concise summary of human obligation. We are to love God and to love other people. In this dual precept is contained all that the law and the prophets enjoin (Matt 22:40; Gal 5:14). In this form, the double commandment is well known to us, and as a result, we are inclined to allow it to pass us by without our paying too much attention. Although Saint Benedict places it at the head of his list of tools for good living, we are inclined to do no more than register its presence and then move on.

To begin with, it is worth asking ourselves how love can be the content of a law or commandment. Laws usually concern external actions, since there is no way for interior dispositions to be accessible to external enforcement. I can be constrained to bow to the king, but I cannot be forced to have reverence for him in my heart. The law can compel me to abstain from murder and mayhem, but it cannot insist on my having a positive attitude toward others. Furthermore, as Saint Paul insists, the written law may be eloquent in telling us how to live, but it is impotent when it comes to helping us develop those dispositions that will enable us to fulfill such noble demands. We are left in the lurch; we are given ideals and expectations that are impossible to achieve with the resources that we have.

This is why it is important to insist that Christ's injunction to both vertical and horizontal love is not, strictly speaking, a commandment—whether a new commandment or an old one. It is, rather, an exhortation to transcend the order of law and obligation and to operate on a higher plane. In calling us to love one another as he loves us, Christ is calling us to be perfect—not only in the sense of being complete human beings, but also as perfect as our heavenly Father is perfect. From our vantage point, this is an impossible task, the dimensions of which we are not even able to imagine. What does it mean to be infinitely perfect in all the circumstances of our daily life? How can a necessarily imperfect human being realistically aspire to such perfection?

The very impossibility of this "commandment" indicates that the way of Christ cannot be reduced to the level of law, ethics, or morality. The "law" of Christ (Gal 6:2; 1 Cor 9:21) is not a written law given externally. It derives from the Spirit of life, and its effect is to liberate us from any written code that serves only the "law of sin and death" (Rom 8:2).

It does this by removing our innate incapacity to do good. In the phrase coined by Saint Augustine, the law of Christ gives what it commands. The freedom that Christ came to bring is not primarily a release from external obligations but the graced capacity to live under the impulsion of the Spirit of love, to live a life that would otherwise be impossible for us. It is freedom-for rather than freedom-from. Christ's gift is to endow us with the ability to live the life of love for which our nature was created and for which every human heart yearns but which is far beyond our own resources.

The distinctive love by which Christians are recognized is not merely the result of an affectionate nature or the acquisition of skills or a suitably nurturing social situation. It is a gift of God which both fulfills and simultaneously surpasses our nature's desire to be loved and to love. Christian love (or *agape*) is the infusion of the divine lovableness and love into the human spirit, repairing the damage which love's absence has wrought and lifting up the human to the level of the divine. Simultaneously, it is an upgrading of our perception so that we are able to see just how lovable our neighbor is. This gift enables us to see through the objective failings of other persons to reach the inner core of their being, where everything is beautiful. This is not a human quality or skill but a gift of God that is both sign and guarantee that we are already living on a supernatural plane.

Such love is a gift because it cannot be self-generated. It arises out of an encounter with God. It is easy for us to reduce religion to a particular mode of thinking or a particular mode of acting. In other words: to see religion merely as theology or morality. In such an approach, the kind of love about which we are speaking is thought to be the result of an act of the will. We try harder and *force* ourselves to love; love is thought to be something pushed out from us by willpower. Alternatively, love is something into which we trick ourselves, as it were, by using our intellect to move our concentration away from that which repels us and look on the bright side, hitherto hidden from us. In both of these incomplete solutions, love is seen as the fruit of human effort. On the contrary, unconditional love is a gift, and it cannot be generated by human effort. It derives its energy from the intrinsic attractiveness of the other.

True religion, although it gives birth to systems of thought and behavior, is not identified with them. The religion that leads to love derives its force from a meeting with God, from our experience of ultimate reality. In this encounter, whether conscious or below the threshold of consciousness, God is revealed and given to us. It is by this divine self-communication that the seed of love is planted in the soil of our hearts. It is as though we are born again, born from above, as St. John says (John 3:3).

Saint Bernard of Clairvaux wrote a monastic treatise that he titled *De diligendo Deo*. This is often translated as "On the Love of God" or "On Loving God." Both of these are incorrect. The title refers not to us or to our activity but to God: *De Deo*. And the quality of God that is highlighted is God's lovableness. The correct rendering is "On the God Who *Must* Be Loved" or, more loosely, "On the God Whom It Is Impossible Not to Love." To see God is to love God; to meet God is to love God. We cannot come face-to-face with God without falling in love with this essentially lovable Other.

If love for God must be taken as a commandment, then it should be seen as an obligation to put ourselves in the way of meeting God, for this is the only means by which divine love is infused into our hearts: "For the love of God has been poured forth in our hearts by the Holy Spirit who has been given to us" (Rom 5:5). The active presence of God in our hearts impresses upon us the reality that we are loved, and our response to being loved is to love in return. The Latin term for this return of love, as used by Augustine and Bernard, for example, is *redamare*: "to love back."[2]

This leads us to remember the well-known conclusion that the condition for giving our love to another is our first receiving love from someone. In the same way, we love God because we have experienced that God first loved us (1 John 4:19). The more we have experienced God's love, the more likely we are to return that love. If the monastery is considered to be a school of love, then this is because, first, those who enter monasteries do so because they have experienced something of the wonder of God's love and, second, because monastic life is an environment where we learn to experience ever more intensely the love that God has for us and the love that other persons also have for us. In this way we gradually become adept at responding to the love we have first received. This is why Saint Bernard, in discussing the skills necessary for creative community living, reverses a familiar formula of Augustine and speaks instead of the art of "being loved and loving." We learn to love by learning to accept love from others. One who never received love will never know what love is and, as a consequence, will be unable truly to love others. The most that can be achieved is the semblance of love: self-love passing itself off as concern for others. We learn love by being loved. We learn the love of God by experiencing God's unconditional love for us. When that happens, everything else in the spiritual life falls into place.

Love is undivided and indivisible because God, its source, is one God, on whom all beings depend for their existence. The human heart cannot simultaneously experience love and hate.[3] When we are touched by love, we are taken over by a force which knows no limits, draws no boundaries. "The measure of love," says Saint Bernard, "is to love without measure."[4] This can be interpreted in two ways. Objectively, nobody is excluded from our love; it embraces God and all his creation in an act which is both falling under an attraction and self-gift. Subjectively, love totally touches, engages, transforms, and elevates all of our faculties and powers. This is what it means to love "with the whole heart, the whole soul, and the whole strength." We cannot imagine a man who has fallen profoundly in love with the woman of his dreams loving her only some of the time and with only a part of his affections. Real love implies a totality of involvement; it is a case of all or nothing.[5]

To love "with the whole heart, the whole soul, and the whole strength" implies a total absence of inner division. In the monastic tradition only the monk who has, by God's grace, attained purity of heart is in full possession of his selfhood and so is able to love with such complete intensity. Such a love cannot be achieved by systematic programs of self-improvement; it can come to us only as a gift from God. This is because loving God with the undivided totality of our being is an act that is impossible for us so long as we are marooned in space and time. It is an act that belongs to eternity. This is what Romano Guardini writes on this point:

> The more a man wills the Absolute, the more he himself participates in its character. The more firmly and energetically he strives for the good, the more he grows into the nature of the Absolute—Goodness. Consequently, if a man willed a thing wholly good in itself, and willed it with complete candour and with all his heart, pouring into this willing and doing the full measure of his vital force, a mysterious thing would happen. He would have passed into eternity.[6]

What this means is that loving in this way, fulfilling this "commandment," is possible only in heaven; the nearer we are to doing this, the closer we are to entering eternal life. By God's grace even now we have been given the gift of eternal life; its capacity to transform us is, however, dependent on willingness to recognize and receive this gift and to allow it to reshape and reform our lives to the likeness of Christ.

The Letter to the Ephesians broadens the theological horizons of the commandment to love both God and neighbor.

It envisages Christians called to a double unity. We are simultaneously one with Christ and through Christ with the Father, and one with the other members of Christ's body. This unity is revealed through the use of many words to which the prefix *syn-* has been added, indicating togetherness. We come alive together with Christ; we are raised together with him and are seated at God's right hand together with him (Eph 2:5-6). But we are citizens together with other Christians, joined together with them, built up together with them, inheriting together with them, forming one body together with them, participating together with them, bound together with them by love, and held together with them (Eph 2:19, 21, 22; 3:6; 4:3, 16).[7] By being united with Christ, we are automatically united not only with the Father but with all who are in Christ.

In the commandment to love with the whole heart, the whole soul, and all one's strength, Saint Bernard of Clairvaux sees a reference to three complementary modes of love:

> O Christian, learn from Christ how you are to love Christ. Learn to love sweetly, to love prudently, and to love strongly. Sweetly, so that we are not seduced [by pleasures]; prudently, so that we are not deceived [by errors]; strongly, so that we are not turned away from love of the Lord by oppression. . . . See that whether these three [qualities] are not also handed down to you in the Law when God said, "You must love the Lord your God from your whole heart and from your whole soul and from your whole strength" (Deut 6:5). It seems to me—unless there happens to be a more appropriate meaning to this threefold distinction—that the love of the heart refers to a certain affective intensity, the love of the soul refers to the operation and judgment of reason, and love with [the whole] strength refers to constancy and vigor of spirit. Therefore, love the Lord your God with total and full affection of the heart. Love [God] with all the vigilance and caution of reason. Love [God] also with all [your] strength so that you may not be afraid to die for

love [of God] for "Love is as strong as death and passion is as harsh as hell" (Song 8:6).[8]

His conclusion is: "To love with the whole heart, the whole soul, and the whole strength is not to be led astray by pleasures, not to be seduced by falsity, and not to be broken by injuries."[9]

There is another point that can be made about the wholeheartedness of love. The rabbis interpreted this wholeheartedness to which the verse of Deuteronomy refers as meaning that we are to bless God with both good and evil impulses (*yetserim*).[10] Even the shadows in our personal history are called upon to bless the Lord. We may not exclude our sins, because in some way, these unfortunate choices belong to the integrity of who we are. They are not to be banished from consciousness. As we grow in self-knowledge we become more aware of aspects of our being that displease us. Some of these we can eliminate by industrious self-discipline. Some of them drop away as the years pass. Others remain and will remain permanently as a goad to our complacency. We never graduate from a state of being utterly dependent on God's mercy and forgiveness. In fact, the more we advance along the spiritual path, the more aware we become of our impediments, of the many ways in which we are resistant to God's love, and of the burdens we carry as a result of choices made in the past. We are not to ignore these liabilities; they also must join in our hymn of praise to the God of grace. The shadow is part of our reality, and so in a spirit of faith, we thank God also for the darkness in our life, for the mistakes we have made, for the abuse we have inflicted on ourselves. Our very unworthiness of love makes the God who loves us ever more lovable. It is only to the extent that we see God neutralizing these malign aspects of our being that we begin to grasp the height and depth, the length and breadth of God's all-embracing love. And so, in our own small way, we are able to respond in kind. And as it grows within us, this divine love creates a desire to make some reparation to those we have harmed by our selfishness, indifference, or malice.

A point well made by John Macquarrie is that love for others is not always a matter of seeking closer union; sometimes it is expressed by giving other persons as much space as they need as they advance toward a fuller humanity. Love can be a deliberate standing back in order to allow others to find their freedom. It is not an absence of care or concern but selfless desire that the other person may grow. "Most typically, 'letting-be' means helping a person into the full realization of his potentialities for being."[11]

For Saint Benedict, living by this double love, in all its various expressions, is a sign that a monk is really giving himself to the life to which he has been called. In a sense, nothing else matters much. A good monk is one who, in the course of a lifetime, keeps coming closer to God and to his fellow human beings. The opposite is one who is self-willed, self-centered, self-pitying, voluntarily isolated, and permanently disgruntled. It would be idealistic to expect that such persons are never found in monasteries.

3-8

Then, not to kill. Not to commit adultery. Not
to steal. Not to lust. Not to speak false testimony. To honor all people.

When the rich man approached Jesus with a view to
acquiring eternal life, the response he received seemed, at
first, too meager compared with his own sense of righteousness. Jesus said simply, "Keep the commandments" (Mark
10:17-19), implying, as he said in another place, "You have
Moses and the Prophets, listen to them" (Luke 16:29). Saint
Benedict seems to have the same attitude. Before you start
setting your sights on lofty mystical heights, begin by making
sure that the ordinary virtues are alive and well in you. This
means, in practice, begin by making sure that you are somewhat free from the ordinary vices. It is not within our power
to eliminate the roots from which vicious actions spring, but,
by God's grace, we can gradually learn how to prevent these
innate inclinations from finding expression outwardly.

So Saint Benedict recommends that we keep the Ten Commandments—or at least, in these opening verses of the chapter,
those precepts which concern our relations with others. Before
we become indignant because we feel that he is not taking seriously our sincere spiritual aspirations, it is good to recall the
saying of the Roman poet Terence: "I am a human being and I
am a stranger to nothing that is human." It may well be that,

up to this point in our lives, we are convinced that we have not grossly sinned against these fundamental precepts. This, however, is no guarantee that circumstances may not arise in which what is now seemingly unthinkable may occur. Worse than that, by repetition sins easily become routine practice. There are plenty of examples in history and in literature of heroes felled by a tragic flaw that had long been hidden, at least from public gaze. Moreover, we need to remember that Hitler was a born Catholic, Stalin had been a seminarian, and Pol Pot had spent time as a Buddhist monk. Be vigilant! If such reversals were not possible we would not have been instructed to pray, "Lead us not into temptation." There but for God's continuing grace go I.

It would be rash to dismiss the keeping of Ten Commandments as too elementary to concern us who are high spiritual seekers. Nor should we think the observance of these universal norms undemanding, as the rich man in the gospel seems to have done. Such a conclusion overlooks the reality that there are to be found within each one of us tendencies that may lead us to act in a way contrary to our presumed ideals. The human heart is not automatically set to pursue virtuous living. Good living is not our default condition. In the story of Noah's flood, the author of the book of Genesis affirms that "every inclination of the heart's thought is consistently evil" (Gen 6:5), and Jeremiah goes further in saying that "the heart is deceitful above all else and perverse beyond comprehension" (Jer 17:9). Qoheleth continues the tradition: "The hearts of human beings are full of evil and there is madness in their hearts as long as they live" (Eccl 9:3).

Jesus is quite explicit about this in the seventh chapter of Mark's gospel. When the Jerusalem scribes and Pharisees complained about his disciples who were observed eating with unwashed hands, Jesus responded with a statement of fundamental principle: "It is not what goes into a person from outside that defiles. . . . [I]t is what comes out of the person." He then goes on to list the actions that flow from a heart that has not yet been purified: evil thoughts, acts of fornication, acts of theft, murders, adulteries, acts of greed, and acts of malice. Applying this first list to ourselves may leave our high self-esteem relatively unscathed. But to these Jesus adds the chronic tendencies from which bad actions spring: deceit, lust, envy, slander, arrogance, and stupidity. If we are honest, we have to admit that we experience such inclinations as these often enough. This seems to indicate that until such time as the heart has been radically purified, it will foster tendencies contrary to the Ten Commandments that will be a continual source of incitement to wrongdoing.

This is certainly the position that the early monks envisaged and that served as the underlying principle of the way of life they embraced. Evagrius of Pontus spoke about the "eight evil thoughts" inherent in the human heart: gluttony, fornication, avarice, sadness, anger, acedia, vainglory, and pride. In his view, these vices are not the result of choices made by us; they preexist any act of personal choice and constitute the first movements of sin. Evagrius affirmed that it is not in our power to determine whether our peace will be disturbed by these contrary imaginations; he considered them to be innate and, therefore, preelective. They keep coming: all we can do is resist. John Cassian took up the same theme in his teaching about the "eight vices." In both of these monastic masters of the spiritual life, we see a clear awareness that living a spiritual life is not smooth sailing. It is warfare, and it requires of us ongoing and systematic effort.[1] We cannot afford to think ourselves somewhat immune to the attraction to serious sin. Once complacency sets in, the downward path toward even the most heinous crimes is not beyond the range of possibility.

The Ten Commandments provide us with an objective standard against which we can assess the seriousness of our spiritual pursuit. Are we entirely free from tendencies to do harm to others, to various forms of covetousness, and to sexual immorality? Can we honestly say that we have never taken what is not ours and never spread untruths? Most of all, can we really claim that we respect and honor all persons, including both those closest to us and strangers? And if we do make this claim, will those around us support our plea of innocence?

In the opening chapter of the Letter to the Romans, Saint Paul draws our attention to another aspect of this matter: "They had knowledge of God but did not give God glory or thanks; they became foolish in their thoughts and their unintelligent hearts were darkened. . . . Therefore God handed them over in the lusts of their hearts to uncleanness" (Rom 1:21, 24). The failure to make room for God in our lives and in our thoughts leads to a subtle degradation of our inner powers so that, progressively, we reach a situation in which no abomination is unthinkable. Not immediately, but over the course of time. Unless we exert ourselves in straining upward, natural gravity takes over and pulls us downward. The situation is, however, more dire than this. The darkening of the heart means that we are largely unaware of our loss of integrity. So gradual has been our decline that we have been able to convince ourselves that each downward step was unimportant and easily reversible. But that is not the truth.

Our resistance to vice is not confined to dramatic moments of heroic struggle against temptation. We need also to take steps to prevent the erosion of our hard-won virtues. Our natural downward drift needs to be countered all the time by a positive upward momentum, seeking the more excellent way, turning our hearts and thoughts to God, ensuring the health of our soul by making use of the means at our disposal, and building up our spiritual immune system, as it were, against the day of temptation.

In case we think this is merely pulpit rhetoric, it is good to hear confirmation from another source. Richard Sipe is a psychologist who has had much experience in helping those who have become involved in inappropriate sexual behavior. This is his conclusion:

> In studying religious celibacy for thirty-five years I have never found one exception to this fundamental rule: Prayer is necessary to maintain the celibate process. A neglectful prayer life ensures failure of celibate integration. No matter at what point in or out of the celibate process you find yourself, if you really want to be celibate, you can begin today by praying.[2]

This seems to say that even basic good living is impossible without regular prayer. It must surely be one of the more successful wiles used by the Tempter to persuade people that regular prayer is not important. Our own experience confirms that when prayer and the other essential monastic observances are allowed to weaken or fall away, our tendencies to behavior that is inconsistent with our monastic vocation become much stronger. The same erosion is noted by Abba Moses in one of Cassian's *Conferences*:

> When [vigils, acts of fasting, and prayers] cease through a return of negligence, it is necessary that the mind, curdled by the filth of the vices, immediately inclines to the fleshly part and falls to the ground.[3]

Even the minimum observance of the Ten Commandments is not possible in the long term without vigorous faith and fervent practice.

There is another consideration in this matter of keeping the commandments. Jesus denounced the teachers and strict observers of his own day because they took the trouble to strain out the gnat and yet, even so, swallowed the camel (Matt 23:24). There is always a possibility that religious professionals become so concerned about the niceties of minor matters that we ignore more crucial commandments that oblige us to such basic virtues as human kindness and compassion. We can forget the broad exigencies of the Ten Commandments while punctiliously observing minor rubrics and regulations. Again and again in history and in literature, we meet the figure of the hard-hearted religious practitioner who has no empathy for suffering, no sense of proportion, and not much common humanity. It is such as these who bring religion into disrepute, and unfortunately, as we all know, they are not confined to the pages of history or literature but can sometimes be found even in the higher echelons of religious institutions. We take some comfort when the arrogance of such persons brings about their downfall. Alas, we can—if we are honest—find the same tendencies in ourselves, and we ought to be somewhat fearful lest, unrestrained, they eventually rise up against us and bring us down. "Let those who think that they are standing firm, watch out lest they fall" (1 Cor 10:12).

Saint Benedict reminds his monks and all of us that, if we are going to embrace a spiritual life, the first thing we have to do is to observe the commonplace commandments that are binding on Christians of all degrees. To these we might add the observance of the natural law, the moral imperatives inherent in human nature: kindness, truthfulness, consistency, integrity in word and action. The distinctive observances typical of a more intense spiritual life need to be built on the foundation of ordinary goodness.

While the Ten Commandments apply to everyone, in a broader and fuller sense they apply to each person in a singular way according to his or her particular situation in life. So, if monks are to keep the Ten Commandments, they are to do so according to their monastic vocation. This means that the common commandments need to be interpreted more exigently. Jesus himself distinguished this two-stage approach to spiritual living: "Keep the commandments . . . but, if you wish to be perfect . . ." It is not enough for a person intent on living a spiritual life to refrain from murder, adultery, and theft. A greater depth of interior purity is demanded. In practice this means withholding consent from *thoughts* of murder and adultery as well as movements of covetousness, as Jesus himself noted. This is a more complete observance of the commandments than simply abstaining from the proscribed actions.

Saint Benedict, having suggested first that we observe the double commandment of love, enjoins on us the practice of those commandments that relate to our dealings with our neighbors. Let us look at each of these in more detail.

3. Then, not to kill.

It may seem a little odd to begin a list of monastic good works by instructing the monk to refrain from murder. It is good—especially for monks—to remember that embracing monastic life does not immunize people from normal human vices. The monks at Vicovaro attempted to murder Benedict himself, and he needed a miracle to escape. Saint Aelred was violently assaulted by one of his monks who, "bellowing cruelly and gnashing his teeth, seized hold of a side of the mat with the father [Aelred] lying on it, tossed them both up with all his might and hurled [him] into the fire among the cinders, saying: 'O you wretch, now I am going to kill you.' "[4] History has a plentiful supply of monastic rogues of all descriptions, and medieval monasteries were obliged to have a prison to incarcerate those who committed criminal acts.[5] Dom Gerard, the sixth abbot of Clairvaux, was murdered by a mad monk of Igny.[6] Even within living memory there have been murders, attempted murders, and violent assaults by monks.[7] Usually these crimes have been committed by persons who were mentally disturbed, but some of them have been cases in which persons have been spurred on by long-cherished anger or envy or by frustrated lust or ambition—the tragic end of a long history of self-destructive choices.

Even if, for the present, murder happens to be outside our range of realistic options, it may be that we are not strangers to the sources from which murder is likely to spring. We can still allow ourselves to be challenged by the words of Jesus in the gospel: "You have heard that it was said to the ancients, 'Do not kill and anyone who kills will be subject to judgment.' But I tell you that anyone who is angry with his brother will be subject to judgment" (Matt 5:21-22). The First Letter of Saint John says the same thing: "Whoever hates his brother" that is, whoever fails to love his brother, "is a murderer" (1 John 3:15). The ill-will expressed in murder can be expressed equally through insult, harshness, or detraction. It is not for nothing that we refer to detraction as "back-stabbing." In the eyes of the criminal justice system, such attacks are, undoubtedly, lighter forms of aggression than actual homicide or assault, but they are still expressive of an attitude which Jesus condemns and which is indefensible for his disciples.

How much more guilty of murder are those who leave the body intact but bring the soul of another to ruin. We have seen in our own times the damage done to individuals, and more indirectly to the church as a whole, by the scandalous behavior of some clerics and religious and the failure of those in authority to deal effectively with it. The same impairment of integrity can be found sometimes in monasteries. This, undoubtedly, is why Saint Benedict insists on excommunicating serious delinquents, cutting off their contact with the rest of the community, warning the abbot of the serious consequences of any failure to take decisive action to limit potential damage, especially in cases where the delinquent monk is unlikely to see the error of his ways.

4. Not to commit adultery.

Recent experience of sexual abuse in the church and many instances of boundary crossing throughout history should serve as a reminder that there is good reason to admonish

monks to avoid engaging in activities that are likely to lead
to a fully sexual relationship in any form, including adultery.
A fundamental safeguard is for a monk to take the trouble
to become aware of the needs within himself from which
such relationships arise: genital needs, intimacy needs, gen-
erativity needs, and, sometimes, the need for reassurance and
admiration. And he needs to recognize both the aphrodisiac
quality exuded by power and the weakening of resistance that
follows alcohol intake. These urgings are natural inclinations
which are far broader than sexuality. When a monk's life as
a whole fails to provide for some fulfillment of basic human
needs, their urgency increases, and the monk begins to seek
covert satisfaction without necessarily understanding the
interplay of psychic dynamics that are involved. Heedlessly
he is swept into deeper water until unknowingly he passes
the point where he is able to offer any effective resistance.

Those of us who are avid readers of the desert fathers and
John Cassian will be aware that temptations against chastity are not unknown to monks, although we may not have
needed to go to the ancient classics to have discovered that.
The fact is that thoughts against chastity are a normal part
of celibate experience. When Abba Cyrus of Alexandria was
asked a question on the topic of thinking about fornication,
he replied, "If you do not have [such] thoughts then you are
without hope, since if you do not think about fornication
you are doing it. He who does not fight against sin or resist
it in thought, sins in body. The one who sins in body is not
bothered by [such] thoughts."[8]

The transitions from thought to action and from episode
to habit are not usually sudden; the groundwork is laid by
many shortcuts and compromises over the years, by actions
and omissions that undermine commitment and render the
continuance of chastity precarious. Options become "temptations" only when there is a good possibility that their suggestion will be followed. So it is that a monk has to deal not only

with thoughts that can be brushed away like so many flies but also with those that are more persistent and may well bring him down. This outcome, however, need not be the end of the story. It may well be that the unexpected fall shocks him into awareness and repentance, and the final result will be positive, as it was in the life of a tenth-century saint, John of Beverley. More usually, alas, the experience is repeated, and any lingering uneasiness about its inconsistency with the ideals he professes is rationalized and repressed. In such a state, conversion becomes ever more difficult unless there is a great influx of grace or some external change which makes the continuance of the relationship unfeasible. In such a vulnerable state, the only way that impending adultery can be ruled out of contention is through a providential lack of opportunity.

5. Not to steal.

In describing the ritual of monastic profession, Saint Benedict makes it clear that the monk must renounce all that he possesses: "Let him know that from that day he will no longer have power even over his own body" (RB 58.25). And to make the point as plain as day, he prescribes that, during the ritual of profession, all his clothes are to be removed, and he is to be reclothed in monastery garments. In addition to this, an entire chapter of the Rule is devoted to the radical uprooting of this "most wicked vice" of private ownership (RB 37.1-8).

This being the case, it must follow that any appropriation of monastery resources must be considered as theft. The monk who does so is reserving for his own use what does not belong to him or, at least, what belongs equally to all. Here also it is good to remember that "quantitative judgments do not apply." Many monastic writers make the point that the same acquisitiveness is at work whether it is directed toward large things or small. The fact that our private possessions are paltry in comparison with what might have occupied our attention before entry does not mean that our clinging to them is less a sign of vice than our previous concern for expensive items. A story in Herbert of Clairvaux's *Book of Wonderful Happenings* describes how a novice was rebuked who hid a piece of cloth in order to repair his habit.[9] It is common experience that attachment to trivial things can be as strong, or even stronger, than that which is directed to more valuable objects. In a monastery molehills easily become mountains.

A collateral consideration arises from the fact that many monks consider that the vow of stability gives them an excuse never to throw anything out. As the years roll by, there is a proportionate increase in the contents of their rooms. Benedict seems to be aware of this possibility since he insists that when new things are acquired, the old things are to be returned (RB 55.9). And he instructs the abbot to search their beds to ensure that there is no contraband hidden there (RB 55.16). We have to recognize that hoarding can sometimes become compulsive and irrational and, as such, indicate a psychological disorder. Under a misguided banner of poverty, all sorts of obsolete and useless objects are stored away because "someday they might come in handy." Turning one's own living area into a substitute for the rubbish dump may seem harmless, but it is not. Living in the midst of external clutter is an invitation to reproduce interiorly the state of the living space one has created. Hoarding leads to accumulation, disorder, confusion, lack of simplicity, and consequent low morale.

The community in the Acts of the Apostles is described as being of "one heart and one soul" because "none claimed any possessions as their own but for them all things were in common" (Acts 4:32). John Cassian quotes the teaching of Abba Joseph that connects the absence of private ownership with good community relationships: "If he claims nothing for himself, he entirely cuts off the first cause of quarrel which habitually comes from small and worthless material things."[10]

6. Not to lust.

This seems like a useless recommendation, at least for beginners, since the struggle against the vice of covetousness, whether in the sexual area or with regard to food, recreations, opportunities, or possessions, will occupy their attention for much of this initial period. These urgent desires cannot simply be set aside with a dismissive flick of the fingers. In a sense, it is an unfair precept since desires are an intrinsic element of human nature and often reflect genuine needs.[11] Their moral quality is determined by their object. And while it is surely virtuous not to lust for unworthy objects, the fact of the matter is that these instinctual or conditioned movements of desire arise unbidden and unwelcome. We have all experienced this. If the sayings of the desert fathers are any guide, Benedict is probably thinking especially of sexual desires and cravings for food, whereas it is likely that the original Decalogue envisaged desire for the acquisition of property, but the word itself is quite general (RB 4.46). And we can see here, if we choose, an admonition to be free from the tyranny of subpersonal desires of every kind. To arrive at such a state of *apatheia*, as the ancients termed it, will require a lifetime of effort, struggle, and probably many failures along the way. It is no easy goal to suppress our tendencies to want something more. Consumerism has been the matrix in which many of us have been formed, so that it may well be that we feel good about ourselves and our situation in life only to the extent that our craving for consumer goods is satisfied. High-end labels become important for us, and we are dissatisfied with anything but the very latest version of our electronic gadgetry. Our restlessness goes further; not only do we want certain goods, but we want them yesterday. Without such accessories our life seems incomplete. Maybe as senility approaches some desires of the flesh seem to weaken, but even then, it seems, not for everyone. In any case, when some desires lose their urgency, others move in to take their place. Given the fact that at least some desires will remain active for a lifetime, it must be inferred that what this verse means is that we should not consent to unwholesome desires or act them out. Even so, as a blanket commandment it is probably most often observed in the breach. Wishful thinking is not easily quenched, and perhaps, it is not always wholesome to attempt to do so. Sometimes the best strategy seems to be to wait patiently until inappropriate thoughts wear themselves out by crashing against the rock of stability. Let these riotous imaginations and desires storm against me; with God's help, I shall not be moved.

Here, we come across this key idea in Benedict's spiritual vision: stability. Once we have made the choice of God, do not seek to annul it. We should stay where we are. Things are not always what they seem. Do not be alarmed that daily experience portends a dire future. Contrary desires will be with us always, but they are there to be resisted. By standing up to them, a solid sea wall of virtue is slowly built up in us. There is little about perfection in Benedict's Rule. As experience teaches, monastic life is not a fast track to perfection; it is more like a process by which we learn to live with manifold imperfection, trusting in the grace and mercy of God ultimately to resolve whatever issues prove intractable.

7. Not to speak false testimony.

In its original context, the Mosaic commandment is speaking of formal legal testimony and, by extension, the avoidance of the crime of perjury, about which Benedict will speak later (RB 4.27). There is, however, a ready application in everyday life. Even good people experience many situations in which telling the naked truth is awkward, and, accordingly, they seek to avoid it not only through vagueness, embroidery, equivocation, and half-truths but also through downright lies. We will have more to say about this when we speak about Benedict's recommendation that we "bring forth truth from the heart and the mouth" (RB 4.28).

It is almost impossible for human beings to speak the *whole* truth, simply because we do not know it. True, we may be able to give an objectively accurate recital of the relevant facts, but facts are like icebergs. Invisible to observation is a great mass of subjective prehistory that would give meaning and context to what we see, if only we knew it. In Dostoyevsky's *The Idiot*, Aglaya accuses Prince Myshkin of failing to take these hidden factors into consideration in making judgments about Ippolit's attempted suicide: "You have no tenderness; only truth, and that's why you are unfair."[12] Since we rarely know the whole story, more often than not it is wiser to say less than to say more, particularly when we permit ourselves to infer motivations and intentions from observable behavior.

The best way not to speak false testimony is not to speak. Permit me to offer a parody of Benedict's words concerning the drinking of wine in chapter 40 of the Rule. Although we read that silence is most fitting for monks, monks of our times cannot be persuaded of this. At least let us agree to attempt what even the children of this world, wiser in their generation, endeavor: to say nothing behind people's backs that we would not say to their faces.[13] There is a cowardly element in most false testimony. It is a matter not of speaking the truth in love but of sowing seeds of division and mistrust by spreading baseless rumors and lies, without the need to confront the one whom we are condemning. There is no chance of counterargument. Our poison goes unchallenged. Why we so much enjoy malicious gossip must be left to the psychologists to determine. If we want to avoid it, along with all other forms of calumny and detraction, then the best way is to acquire some control over our speech through the practice of silence. Surely a monk can never go wrong by upgrading his control of the tongue. Once he has made some progress in this area, he will find that he has less difficulty in reducing unkind and judgmental thoughts. He will soon discover that unwholesome thoughts are less likely to present themselves when there is a reasonable certainty that they will be ignored.

8. To honor all people.

Benedict expands the Decalogue's injunction to honor father and mother to include all people. The reason for this may be practical. For mature-age monks, filial obedience to parents is inappropriate; in any case, it may be that for many their parents have predeceased them, and so the precept is rendered bootless thereby. Also, in a monastic context, family ties can be a hindrance to or an escape from the kind of life to which the monk commits himself. This is a well-attested temptation in those cultures where family obligations are lifelong and paramount. The monk is torn between two conflicting duties. Benedict learned from experience to avoid this danger to a monastic vocation, as we can see from his chapter on the reception of children (RB 59.7). But there is more to this precept than pragmatism, as we shall see.

Murder, idolatry, and theft do not often occur in monasteries in a way that attracts the attention of the criminal justice system, but the sources from which they spring remain virulent: anger, together with a tendency to aggression, lust, and acquisitiveness. The only way to be secure in the hope that we may avoid transgressing the Ten Commandments is to be proactive in reducing the influence of these precursors of sin and replacing them with a positive regard for all people that progressively becomes more unconditional. Fundamentally, that is what monastic life is all about.

8-9

To honor all people. Let him not do to another what he does not wish to be done to himself.

Saint Benedict's expansion of the scope of the commandment, in line with 1 Peter 2:17, is typical of his attitude to life. People are to be treated well. The addition of the Golden Rule in its negative form adds specificity to the precept. To honor others is to treat them as we ourselves would like to be treated. This universal obligation stems from our nature as social animals. It is recognized in many cultures and religious traditions, and, of course, it was embraced by Jesus himself. In this single precept, he affirmed, the whole import of the Law and the Prophets is contained (Matt 7:12).

Honor is more than praise. On occasion, praise can be offered impersonally, with no emotional investment on the part of one who gives it. Praise can also be insincere. It can also be mere flattery. Seneca wrote in *Atreus*: "Even a low-born peasant can get true praise, but only the powerful can get false praise." Praising another can be a means of keeping them in bondage, always awaiting another laudatory comment to fall from our lips. In this way praise once received can be a source of ongoing anxiety, for fear that in the future it may be withheld.[1] Where there is an absence of unconditional positive regard, the giving and withholding of praise becomes a prime instrument in the art of manipulating others.

Honor is more interior than praise. It begins as an attitude within the person who honors; progressively this interior disposition shapes the way that person deals with the one honored. Honoring others is an indication of a certain nobility and generosity of spirit that sees beyond surface indicators of mediocrity or unworthiness, a perception that is not blocked by the mechanisms of repression and projection. Honor goes beyond respect, just as respect goes beyond that social virtue which is variously named courtesy, politeness, urbanity, or civility.

Rendering honor is a matter of recognizing another's inherent value or dignity[2] and, by word, deed, or attitude, communicating this recognition to the other person. When I honor others, I appreciate their uniqueness, and in consequence of that, I reduce myself and my self-assertion in order to make room for them. I step back so they have space to expand. A deep sense of humility is at the heart of honor. "I must decrease: the other must increase." When I honor others, I am offering them gracious hospitality, welcoming them into my life and my space with sincere delight. To honor is to allow others to be what they are without disguising themselves; it allows them to exercise their personal autonomy without constraining them to act as we would wish; it is to stand back and allow them to exercise an authentic personal style, to act with flair and panache. Honor is profoundly liberating for the one who receives it.

When I give honor, I am fully present to the other person, not drifting away mentally, but really listening. I do not monopolize the conversation with repetitive monologues on topics that are of interest to me and, quite possibly, to me alone. I do not fill the air with stentorian tones but speak quietly. I do not seek to impose my own will on others but engage in what Benedict includes under the heading of "mutual obedience" (RB 71), giving priority to what other persons wish. I do not procrastinate over their requests or keep them waiting unnecessarily. I do not skimp on providing for their needs under the guise of frugality, but I extend myself in being magnanimous and open-handed. I do not expect a *quid pro quo*: giving due honor is its own reward. When gratitude is offered for our service we respond with sincerity, "It has been my privilege to serve you."

Giving honor gives others permission to exist. It encourages the emergence of what is hidden, and it provides a nurturing environment in which the inner self may become more and more visible and active. For strangers, a deeply welcoming community gives them the possibility of shedding a false identity and, so, gradually learning to become what they are. If others are able to see Christ in me so that they offer to me the reverence that is his due (RB 53.7), then I am encouraged thereby to allow that hidden self to blossom. To live in a community in which the members are deeply respectful of one another and are generous in giving honor is an incentive to rapid growth in personal authenticity and integrity.

In the seventeenth century, Abbot Armand-Jean de Rancé, the reformer of La Trappe, encouraged his monks to think of their confreres in a very lofty manner. "You must consider your brothers as people who carry on their foreheads the imprint of a blessing. They belong to Jesus Christ by a very special consecration. They are destined for his service in a unique way. They are precious vessels in his house."[3] To see others in this light preempts a tendency to conflict and lays the foundation for a life lived in concord. There can be no authentic love without honor, only its pallid substitutes.

Anthropologist and philosopher Fernand Schwarz meditated on the topic of honor, following an incident involving the "honor killings" of two young men in Grenoble. This was his conclusion.

> It would be good to redefine what honor means and what it entails. To be men and women of honor is to learn to respect oneself and to respect the other, to attribute value to the intrinsic dignity of being human. It is to feel responsible not

only for oneself and one's family but also for one's town, one's country, and perhaps even the whole human family to which we belong. It is to know how to give one's word and to respect it. It is also to have a sense of service, understanding that one's own happiness comes via the service of the other, stemming from an altruistic and generous attitude.[4]

Disrespect and dishonor, perceived or factual, are at the core of many acts of violence. When a person feels slighted, whether the belittling is intentional or not, there is a reflex desire to bring equivalent pain and humiliation to the person who has inflicted the hurt. In many conflicts the accusation is often bandied back and forth by the combatants, "You started it!" The origins of a quarrel are not always easy to determine, but they often begin with a perception of disrespect. This can be found as readily in omission as in overt behavior, as much in unspoken "meta-messages" as in the actual words used. Disrespect fractures human relations, whereas honoring others encourages them to draw closer.

Persons who are honored feel better about themselves and probably are more effective in their chosen fields of endeavor. They are not afraid to make use of their talents. An article in *The Economist* in 2007 reported research which suggested that—barring physical accidents and the sudden onset of fatal illness—Nobel Prize winners and top executives live longer and healthier than their less honored peers. "It is, indeed, more stressful to be at the bottom than at the top."[5] People who are deprived of the affirmation that comes with honor often live in a state of chronic vulnerability, especially when the withholding of due recognition is spiteful or envious. They live poised for preemptive aggression—whether active or passive—ever mindful that attack is the most gratifying form of defense.

Hierarchy in organizations, including religious institutions, is a breeding ground for ambition, especially when higher posts are rewarded with visible perquisites and privileges. Members are forced to view one another as either higher or lower in terms of power and status. This creates what Alain de Botton has termed "status anxiety,"[6] which, in turn, leads to envy and competitiveness. We see this exemplified in the Rule of the Master, where monks are encouraged to compete with one another in vying to fill the vacancy when the abbot dies. Benedict will have none of this. If possible, he wants the monastery to be administered by a plurality of deans rather than by a single prior (RB 21; 65.12-13), aware perhaps of the danger of creating a multilevel hierarchy and the consequent pressure on all to keep climbing higher until they reach the top.

Honoring others and treating them as we ourselves would like to be treated demands a high degree both of empathy and self-regard. The commandment to love the neighbor as oneself can be seen as an invitation to put self and others on an equal footing. We are all members of one body; what profits one is of advantage to all. My capacity for honoring others is a reflection of the esteem in which I hold myself. When I feel good about myself, I am more likely to be caring and generous toward others. There is a recurring cycle going on here. The more persons are held in honor, the more likely they are to honor others, to treat them well, to allow and encourage them to be themselves. Those who live in an environment of mutual esteem are more likely to be fulfilled human beings, able and willing to offer to others the same recognition that they themselves have received.

Honor is based on truth. It does not consist in treating everyone in the same gracious manner, like a dignitary on a receiving line. It means recognizing others as they are and treating them accordingly. Communities are not composed of clones; each person is different and must be treated differently. This Saint Benedict affirms when he prescribes that the abbot is to be at the service of many different characters (RB 2.31). As we shall see later, he differentiates between how a senior relates to a junior and how the junior relates back:

the older man is affectionate, the younger, reverential and respectful (RB 4.70-71). Throughout the Rule there is a keen awareness that individuals have different graces (RB 40.1), talents (57.1), capacities (RB 48.24), needs (RB 37.1-3), and possibilities (RB 2.32) and that a one-size-fits-all approach to community regimen is unlikely to produce long-term benefits. Due honor must be paid to what people are: by nature, by grace, by history, and, to some extent, by personal choices.

Such is the community envisaged by Saint Benedict. It seems also to have been what the fathers of the Second Vatican Council had in mind in speaking about the role of superiors in religious communities: "They should govern those under them as sons [or daughters] of God, respecting them as human beings."[7] It is always a delight to visit a community in which all are respected and held in esteem; the atmosphere is different. Readily perceptible is a certain naturalness or assurance typical of those who are at home in themselves and in community. And there is energy and a sense of purpose found only in a house that is not divided against itself. This is the kind of community that honor and mutual esteem create.

9. Let him not do to another what he does not wish to be done to himself.

In general, we mistreat others only when the relationship is in some way asymmetrical and in our favor. I am smart enough to understand that any hardship I inflict on an equal is likely to be reciprocated. I am also smart enough to avoid starting a fight with a heavyweight bruiser who is well able to pay back any disrespect with exorbitant interest. If I wish to vent my aggression, I, like all bullies, look for someone who is weaker than I am. I do not want to cause trouble for myself. If I want to hurt another, I need to do so from a position of strength: physical prowess, higher status, greater wealth, superior intelligence, bureaucratic invulnerability, or confidence in the approval of the mob. Might is right.

Usually the unfortunate victims of my wrath are those who are not only weaker but also different: the already reprobate, outsiders, foreigners, refugees, class enemies, or members of a different tribe. To avoid cultivating any sense of solidarity with such people that may soften my attitude, I demonize them. This process of dehumanizing those whom we wish to persecute has been given the charmless name of "uglification."[8] I vilify. I create a class of people who are of lesser value, perhaps who are less than fully human. Then to reinforce my prejudice, I do everything possible to rob them of dignity and respect so that even the most gratuitous violence not only is allowable but, in some perverse way, increases my own sense of self-respect. It is as though I am honoring "us" by dishonoring "them." The unspeakable horrors of genocide are an example of how this process works on a larger scale, but even on a more domestic level, there are examples of how we can be caught up in a similar failure to recognize human solidarity.

One of the features of contemporary life is the decline of neighborhoods and a corresponding loss of any sense of neighborliness. We allow ourselves to live among permanent strangers. We neglect to create the bonds of friendliness and support with those who live around us. As a result, we lack people nearby on whom we may call in times of difficulty.

The parable of the Good Samaritan embodies a different ideal. In this story it is the class enemy who is active and magnanimous in coming to the assistance of the man who fell among thieves. We see how compassion is able to transcend the stupid boundaries placed on goodwill by social and political conditioning. The neighborliness of the Good Samaritan is the opposite of the indifference we feel toward those who are not like us and whose troubles we ignore as we pass by on the other side of the road. The Good Samaritan came near (nigh) to help; we tend to draw back to ensure that sufficient distance is maintained to allow us, with a clear conscience, to refuse help to someone in trouble.

To treat others as we ourselves would like to be treated, we must begin by seeing others as like ourselves—despite the external markers (like race, gender, age, culture) that signal difference. First, I need to change my thinking. I need to restrain the malign tendency to go around making judgments on others, as if I were the norm according to which everyone else is to be measured. Often this tendency to diminish others—at least mentally—comes from a reduced sense of self-worth. Commonly, it is not that I have such an inflated esteem for myself that others seem to be of lesser value. More usually it is because my self-regard is so fragile that I am secretly fearful that I will be found to be inferior if I do not drag others down to my own level. I denigrate others in the perverse hope that they will be judged to be lower than myself. It is, of course, a futile strategy. Dishonoring others dishonors myself, even if it is only in my innermost thoughts.

Treating others as we ourselves would like to be treated is not only evangelical virtue; it is common sense. What goes around comes around. The generosity I show to others is not only an adornment to myself; it initiates a process of change in the recipient of my benevolence. Some day that other person may be drawn to replicate my good deed, and thus a chain of goodness is created that could easily find its way back to me as someone else comes to my relief at the moment when I need it desperately. There can be little doubt that if many people followed the Golden Rule the world would be a better place. On a smaller scale, imagine what a difference it would make in a house if everyone dealt with everyone else with the same kind of compassion and generosity with which they themselves would like to be treated.

10-20

To deny himself to himself in order to follow Christ. To restrain the body. Not to embrace delights. To love fasting. To improve the lot of poor people. To clothe a naked person. To visit a sick person. To bury one who is dead. To come to help in trouble. To console one who is feeling pain. To make himself a stranger to the actions of the world.

Saint Benedict, in line with most monastic teachers, saw renunciation as an essential element of Christian and monastic living. Any firmly chosen goal demands a restriction of freedom. I cannot become a surgeon or a concert pianist unless I practice, and to make time for practice, I have to renounce other gratifying activities. Think of Olympic athletes—how much they have to invest in training and disciplined living in order to attain a perishable crown, as Saint Paul reminds us (1 Cor 9:25). To hope to make progress in any field of aspiration without sustained and disciplined investment of energy is delusional.

Furthermore, it is worth recalling that renunciation is a core requirement for community living. People who live by themselves can do what they like when they like. Those who live in a community, especially an intentional community, must renounce whatever behavior is inconsistent with the aims of that community or disturbs the harmonious coexistence of its members. A person unwilling to restrict self-will is unsuitable for community living.

10. To deny himself to himself in order to follow Christ.

Saint Benedict has joined a reflexive note to the text of the Rule of the Master, adding an important qualification not always translated: "to deny oneself *to oneself.*"[1] This addition seems to mean reducing that kind of narcissism which concentrates all its outgoing energies on self: self-gratification, self-enhancement, self-assertion, self-promotion. Concentration on self is a frustration of positive outgoing tendencies; it cannot be life-giving.

The self that is to be denied is not the deep, inner core of personality—to use the terminology favored by Thomas Merton—but the masquerading self, compounded of denials, delusions, and the unenlightened opinions of others. The false self is concerned only with its own narcissistic gratification, a "self" that can exist only as a form of enslavement to the pleasure principle and in denial of the obligations of human solidarity imposed on us by our shared humanity.

It is clear that for Benedict the kind of self-denial demanded by the Gospel is not an end in itself, nor is it pure mortification. It is imitation of Christ, expressed through self-control, practical charity, and withdrawal from the loose living of the world. "He follows Christ who, as much as he can, conforms himself to Christ by his behavior and life."[2] The objectives formulated by Saint Benedict give to renunciation a specific Christian flavor. To deny oneself to oneself is not a matter of total self-negation, but it involves, rather, the channeling of the energies of self in the service of something greater than oneself—the imitation of Christ and the improvement of the lot of those who need help.

Here, as elsewhere, it is important to be mindful of the strong Christological context in which Benedict's Rule is to be interpreted. Monastic life as a whole is to be understood as the following of Christ, and each good action is done in imitation of him and for his sake. Let us consider some examples of this. Monks are called:

- to fight/serve for Christ the true King (RB Prol 3)
- to share in the passion of Christ (RB Prol 50)
- to be one in Christ (RB 2.20)
- to practice self-denial in order to follow Christ (RB 4.10)
- to put nothing before the love of Christ (RB 4.21)
- in Christ's love, to pray for enemies (RB 4.72)
- to obey those for whom nothing is dearer than Christ (RB 5.2)
- to act in full humility from love of Christ (RB 7.69)
- to serve Christ in the sick (RB 36.1)
- to welcome guests as Christ (RB 53.1, 7, 15)
- to obey the abbot as representing Christ (RB 2.2, 63.13)
- to prefer nothing whatever to Christ (RB 72.11)
- to obey the abbot as a representative of Christ (RB 2.2; 63.13).

The recommendations which follow this general precept of self-denial divide themselves naturally into two categories: saying no to the pleasure principle and saying yes to the neighbor; both activities are animated by a desire to follow Christ. In other words, self-denial receives its motivation and meaning from a sense of being called to the imitation of Christ. It is because of his identification with Christ and his desire to enter more fully into a relationship of discipleship with him that the monk practices self-denial.

Elsewhere Saint Benedict is clear that the primary object of mortification is to limit the amount of control self-will exerts on daily behavior. Let us consider some typical texts:

- Of sarabaites, he says: "Their law is the pleasure of their desires: whatever they think or choose this they call holy: and what they do not want they consider unlawful" (RB 1.8).
- Of gyrovagues, he says: "Always wandering and never stable, serving their self-will and their unlawful appetite for food" (RB 1.11).
- "In all things, therefore, all are to follow the rule as master and nobody is to deviate from it rashly. None in the monastery is to follow the will of his own heart" (RB 3.7-8).
- "To hate self-will" (RB 4.60).
- "And so they seize the narrow path, of which the Lord said, 'Narrow is the path that leads to life.' They desire to have an abbot over them so that not living by their own judgments nor obeying their desires and pleasures, they walk by the judgment and rule of another and live in communities" (RB 5.11-12).
- "The second step in humility is if a person does not love his own will and does not delight in satisfying his desires" (RB 7.31).

The primary target of renunciation is the unredeemed human will, and the means of bringing it into submission to the deeper impulses of the self is community living "under a rule and an abbot." Wholehearted participation in community life and the acceptance of authority and the common will severely restrict the scope of self-will. Such conformity is much more challenging than self-chosen mortifications or the voluntary pursuit of actions that go against the grain. There is much less on which the ego may feed, and there is no letup in the demands that are made. Saint Benedict's teaching on mutual obedience is beautiful to ponder but exceedingly hard to keep practicing.

One of the channels by which self-will imposes its authority is, perversely enough, the choice of mortification. Monastic history and contemporary experience reveal that there is a tendency among those fervid few who consider the common way insufficient to seek out individual practices of self-denial: fasting, early rising, and penances of one kind or another. Sometimes these inclinations to self-punishment (and even self-harm) derive from unhealthy psychic energies and do no good. People who submit to these promptings forget the admonition with which Saint Benedict concludes the chapter on Lent: "What is done without the permission of the spiritual father is to be reckoned as presumption and vainglory and not as worthy of a reward" (RB 49.9).

11. To restrain the body.

Castigare, the verb used here, seems very harsh. In English the word castigate implies punishment or, at least, severe criticism. Is Saint Benedict envisaging monasticism as a lifetime program of punishing the body? Certainly not! According to Lewis and Short's *A Latin Dictionary, castigare* is a contraction of *castum agere,* to make chaste, pure, or spotless. It is rendered in English by such expressions as the following: to set right by word or deed; to correct, chastise, punish; to blame, reprove, chide, censure, find fault with. It clearly suggests correction that is "more forcible than *reprehendere* and *vituperare;* but weaker than *culpare."*[3] The treatment of the body is to be remedial rather than vindictive; it could equally be described as a process of *retraining* the body. It is inspired not by a hatred for the body or by contempt for it but from the desire to render it helpful to the spiritual pursuit, rather than have it run wild and subvert the direction the monk has given to his life. In the Middle Ages, bodily urges and particularly sexuality were often compared to the horse. Following this analogy, what is being envisaged here is that the bridle and bit be used to ensure that the horse's energy is directed toward the goal that the monk has set himself. Discretion is always needed, as Cassian notes: "Our body is to be restrained by an abstemiousness that is always reasonable and fair."[4] And restraint of bodily urges needs to be complemented by an effort at interior discipline: "It does not suffice to restrain the body [*corpus castigare*] from unlawful practices unless [the heart] is restrained from evil and unwholesome thoughts."[5]

It is worth noting that Saint Benedict has modified the text he was working with. The original read, "To restrain the body *for the sake of the soul*" (RM 3.11). As usual, Benedict seems to be avoiding a dualistic opposition between body and soul. The use of the word "body" is shorthand not so much for the material organism as for the instincts and impulses that have a stronger biological basis—the tendencies that lead us into gluttony, fornication, idleness, anger, and, perhaps, some of the other vices. These are often referred to as "sins of the flesh," though the psychological and emotional content of them is not insignificant. Overeating is the result not only of a ravenous appetite but of what is happening emotionally. Fornication is more than the satisfaction of genital needs— there are many other factors operative as well.

It was for the purpose of retraining the body that Saint Benedict set up the school of the Lord's service. The Benedictine way of life (*conversatio*) is a balanced set of external observances designed to provide an appropriate inner and outer environment for the seeking and finding of God. It is not a matter of abstract principles to be applied willy-nilly in an ambience of laissez-faire. Saint Benedict is unabashedly prescriptive. This is what he insists at the end of the Rule: "We have written this Rule in order that, by observing it in monasteries, we might show that we have some goodness of behavior and the beginning of *conversatio*" (RB 73.1). The Rule is set forth in order that it may be put into practice.

The best way for the monk to retrain the body is to keep it within the bounds of monastic observance as this is practiced in the local community. This gives monastic life the opportunity to work its magic on us. Over the years, through the conjoined exercise of body and soul, we are formed, reformed, and transformed. Saint Aelred of Rievaulx goes further than this. He considers it delusional to believe that, in some mysterious way, the goals of monastic life can be realized independently of monastic observances. In one of his *Chapter Discourses*, he notes, "What I wish to insist on is that you cannot come to this point [of contemplation] through slackness or indolence but by labors, vigils, fasts, tears and contrition of heart."[6] We live in a period of history in which there is a widespread resistance to prescriptions that limit personal freedom; we need to remember that the purpose of prescription is simply to indicate the fastest way to get to where we want to be. The goal is presupposed. This idea occurs clearly in the Prologue. "*If* you wish to have true and everlasting life," then this is what you have to do (RB Prol 17). If that is not your wish, "go away a free man" (RB 58.10).

In a monastery, as in any serious attempt at spiritual living, there must be a clear attempt to establish priorities. If one opts to live life as a spiritual journey, then bodily gratifications must often take second place. There is work to be done in reducing the role of tendencies to vice, and sacrifices will often be demanded. This is surely the experience of all who take the spiritual life seriously. Saint Aelred of Rievaulx lays the matter clearly before his monks:

> In this house fleshly banquets are not laid out for those attending, but spiritual banquets. These refresh the soul rather than the body. In this house the body is sacrificed, the flesh

is crushed, the spirit is strengthened; vices are suppressed, virtues rise up and are eagerly taken.[7]

The importance of submitting the body to retraining is illustrated by the role played by posture in prayer. Experience confirms that participation in the liturgy is greatly enhanced by adopting a good posture, by not looking around, and by breathing correctly. In meditation, especially in its simpler forms, sustained bodily stillness is essential for maintaining concentration when there is so little to entertain the mind or the imagination. The principle can be extended throughout life. Just as tension, anxiety, and depression find external expression, so the impact of interior disturbances can be softened by consciously attending to bodily stance, the way we walk, and our manner of sitting.

There is always the danger that we elevate ourselves into spiritual beings for whom any concern with the body is to be discounted. Sometimes this is mere folly stemming from spiritual vanity. At other times it seems to be the work of darker psychological forces which involve withholding recognition from genuine bodily needs. We are reminded of the scathing judgment of Blaise Pascal concerning the nuns of Port-Royal-des Champs: "In aspiring to be higher than the angels they fell lower than the beast."

Professor Peter Brown has written a masterly volume on the attitudes of early church ascetics to the body. Many of their expressions appear negative to us and are sometimes judged to be dismissive of the body. He rejects this explanation and insists that, on the contrary, the early monks took the body very seriously. "Life in the desert revealed, if anything, the inextricable inter-dependence of body and soul."[8] Most innovative of all was the assumption that spiritual goals could be achieved through bodily practice. The state of the soul could be influenced by changing what is happening at the level of the body. An example of this would be the importance of posture in achieving stillness and thus facilitating greater concentration during prayer. Body and soul are interdependent. That is a teaching that could well be imparted to many of our contemporaries.

12. Not to embrace delights.

Saint Benedict has made another change to the text he was following. The Rule of the Master has "to flee delights"— an energetic and proactive summons to avoid all that is pleasurable (RM 3.12). Benedict tones this down. We are not to be too enthusiastic in our search of pleasure; nor are we to cling to it when its time has passed. There is a certain humanity in this change which is typical of the author of the Rule, even though he notes elsewhere that "death stands near the entrance to delight" (RB 7.24). This is another instance in which an extreme statement in his source has been modified into something more reasonable.

In the Aristotelian ethics followed by Thomas Aquinas, pleasure was regarded as a sign of virtue and goodness. If we rest when we are tired, it is pleasurable because it is the right thing for us to do at that time. If we drink when we are thirsty and eat when we are hungry, we are rewarded at the level of feeling because we have done the right thing. There is a certain pleasure in virtue also since, as is sometimes said, "Virtue is its own reward." When I am kind (that is, when I act in accordance with my nature or kind) I feel good about what I have done, and, admittedly, sometimes this end-feeling is the main incentive for action, a fact that has led some to doubt the possibility of complete altruism. For the normal human being, it is impossible to avoid pleasure coming through our senses. There is much in an ordinary day that will bring delight to sight and hearing, to taste and smell and touch. In fact, the loss of pleasure in daily life is one of the crucifying aspects of the disorder known as depression. Sunsets and bird-song, friendship and a passing smile, beauty in all its forms: how can we not be touched by delight when we experience these? The existence of a fully alive human being is constantly punctuated by unsolicited spasms of delight. To tell a monk to run away from such simple pleasures is to risk creating a hard and unfeeling man with a dour attitude to life, who will be, in all probability, harshly critical of all who seem to have found any enjoyment, an attitude which we often—rightly or wrongly—associate with Puritanism.

The pursuit of pleasure becomes disordered when plea-sure is sought as an end in itself and not merely accepted as the occasional byproduct of daily life or the effect of good living. In locating pleasure at the summit of life's values, hedo-nist tendencies embody a skewed vision of human existence that will necessarily impact on the quality of choices made in the course of daily life. If it feels good, I will do it. If prayer brings me pleasure, I will pray. If service is pleasurable, I will serve. If reading is dry and challenging, I will abandon it. A life lived under such tyranny will yield no growth. Pleasure is most potent when it is unsought. A pleasant surprise is so because it is not of our own making.

It is true that in hagiography the saints are sometimes credited with a variety of penitential practices. My novice master used to insist that these examples were to be admired, not imitated. In some cases, such as the Cistercian lay brother Arnulf of Villers, who died in 1228, self-harm is practiced to the point where it is clearly pathological and does not serve any ascetical purpose. Misguided penances which are driven by an unconscious self-contempt or self-hatred are an abuse of self, no matter how pious their assumed justification. There are, alas, still people who are drawn in this direction; fortunately, only a few.

It is known that regular self-flagellation was prescribed in many religious orders of men and women in the period before the Second Vatican Council.[9] Originally a punitive measure to punish wrongdoers, flagellation began to be practiced voluntarily and devotionally from the seventh century, not only by those in monasteries, but also by clerics and laity. The first known example of such usage is in the life of Saint Kentigern, bishop of Glasgow, who died in 603. In the eleventh century the great proponent of the practice was Saint Peter Damian. He praised one of his disciples who whipped himself continually with both hands for the space of more than twelve Psalters. The rest of his time he spent devising other ways to hurt himself. The practice grew wildly. The fanatical bands of Flagellants in the fourteenth century were a bizarre example of religious practice hijacked by pathology; they were rightly but ineffectively banned by church authorities.[10]

There is something profoundly unevangelical about an asceticism which goes beyond reasonable strictness to the point of seeking pain, or a puritanism that generates a suspicion of everything that is a cause of delight. The denial of ordinary humanity leads to a humorless form of religion, heavily weighted toward duty and public morality and having little emphasis on spiritual delight. For Saint Augustine, on the other hand, delight was the principal engine of the spiritual life. It is by tasting the goodness of the Lord that we are drawn to invest more energy in the spiritual pursuit. Benedict too is of this school. He speaks about the monk who has made much progress having delight in the virtues (*delectatio virtutum*; RB 7.69), and at the end of the Prologue, he speaks of the "indescribable sweetness of love" (RB Prol 50).

In this matter the moderation of Benedict shines forth. He is aware that it is easy for the monk to be seduced by pleasure and to be led into sin. More important, he understands that to base choices on their potential for pleasure is to subvert the desire he had before him when he entered monastic life. Let him enjoy whatever simple pleasures life affords, but let him not cling to them or make his happiness depend on them. As we have all experienced, these moments of delight are passing. They come and go. What matters is that in all this vicissitude our will remains stable and our commitments unaltered.

13. To love fasting.

There are only two items in Saint Benedict's list where he speaks of *loving* a desirable action or quality. There are another three items where the monk is admonished *not to love*: these concern much speaking, laughter, and contention (RB 4.52, 54, 68). Here, it is fasting that must be loved; later, it is chastity (RB 4.64). In other words, he is telling us not only to practice virtue in matters concerning food and sex but to love doing so. It is my understanding that law cannot make provision for internal acts or attitudes. It moderates external behavior. That Benedict here goes deeper than outward actions seems like a clear indication that he is doing more than laying down the law. As will appear throughout his Rule, but especially in chapter 72, he is concerned with the subjective dispositions from which the good actions stem. In other words, he has in mind the purified heart that is attracted by virtue, practices it, and, as we have said above, finds a certain satisfaction or delight in so doing.

There is a scientific hypothesis that intermittent fasting has more beneficial effects than a more generalized program of reducing energy intake. It is thought to slow aging, safeguard mental ability through neuro-regeneration, and have a good effect on such illnesses as Alzheimer's disease and Parkinson's disease.[11] Perhaps observing the austere dietary regime recommended in the Rule might lead to a longer life!

Fasting in a cenobitic community today is fundamentally a matter of accepting the eating arrangements of the local community, without making excessive demands or engaging in campaigns of complaint and crusades for improvement. This acceptance will necessarily entail a certain amount of self-denial, since we all have different preferences and, as Saint Benedict notes, the possibilities of a particular community may be limited by its economy and the skill of its personnel. What Benedict prescribes regarding food in his chapter on the measure of food is plentiful enough: the fact that he warns his monks against overeating is an indication that what was provided was more than the bare minimum (RB 39.7-9). Since in most monasteries nowadays there is an element of self-service in the refectory, much remains within the choice of each person. It is always possible to take more or less or none at all. This would probably meet with Benedict's approval since he remarks that he is reluctant to specify how much others should eat, since everyone has particular needs determined by both nature and grace (RB 41.1-2). His own preference is for abstemiousness, as he states this later: "Not to drink wine in excess. Not to be a great eater" (RB 4.35-36).

There is a curious chapter in the Rule that concerns the mealtimes of old men and infants (RB 37.1-3), although it is not clear how infants came to be living under a monastic rule. Perhaps the term is used loosely for boys or youths; perhaps it is an ironic reference to the immature. For infants, eating is an absolute imperative: necessary for their well-being and growth. For the old, there is an observable regression; comfort foods are perhaps the only pleasure left and eating tends to become a very important exercise in the daily round, sometimes surrounded by a certain amount of repetitive ritual. Benedict agrees that the old and the young may be exempted from the common rule in this matter. This means that he expects the mature and adult members of the community will take pains to exercise a firm control over their appetite for food, keeping within the bounds fixed by custom both regarding the time of eating and the amount consumed. Any tendency to compulsive eating behavior must be considered an indicator of immaturity—if not of something more serious.

Fasting is understood as a remedy for a tendency to gluttony. Among the vices gluttony often seems to us relatively harmless; it is no more than trivial self-indulgence with long-term effects only when it is extreme. No one else is hurt by it. Mostly, we are too polite to mention it, notwithstanding widespread evidence—if you will pardon the pun. Maybe spirituality needs to take overeating more seriously, and not only for its impact on bodily and emotional health. At the same time, it would be wrong to think that gluttony is the only eating disorder to afflict people. "Immoderate restraint causes a more pernicious fall than easygoing satiety."[12]

Gluttony has been described as a "gateway sin" in that it often leads to more serious aberrations. It is, at it were, the thin edge of the wedge. It is not that it leads necessarily to dramatic infidelities or eventually to apostasy; it more likely induces a cycle of stagnation in which spiritual progress is halted, and as a result, compensation for this is more eagerly sought in food. The desert fathers, for example, certainly believed that there was a connection between gluttony and sexual temptation. Following that tradition, Saint Aelred of Rievaulx writes:

> Our first conflict is against Amalek, that is, against the spirit of gluttony since, it seems to me, that the virtue of abstinence is the beginning and foundation of all the virtues. For no other reason, I believe, is virtue so rare than this: nearly everyone has abandoned that which nurtures all the virtues and without which no approach to the other virtues is possible. I am speaking of the virtue of abstinence.[13]

Gluttony takes different forms; it is not merely the ingestion of vast amounts of food. A disordered appetite for food can also express itself through fastidiousness in the choice of dishes or by an inappropriate eagerness that cannot wait to be satisfied. In a sense, dieting, especially when it is a matter of lifestyle rather than a medical necessity, can be a form of gluttony when it consists of making a disproportionate fuss about food. Listen to what Abba Sarapion has to say, as reported by John Cassian:

> There are three kinds of gluttony. The first urges a monk to hurry to a meal before the hour which has been decided and prescribed. The second ravenously rejoices in a full stomach, irrespective of the kinds of food. The third desires more carefully prepared and finer foods.[14]

Fasting should not be given more importance than is its due. It is probably better to arrive at a state of relative indifference about what is eaten rather than using a lot of energy in trying to keep to a strict regime—especially if this makes demands on others. Fasting can operate at the level of symbol. Persons with a good level of self-knowledge may choose to fast because they believe that the discomfort occasioned by the limitation or deprivation of food is an accurate representation of their interior state, of their utter neediness, of their spiritual hunger. Of course, they will practice this asceticism in deep humility and in the spirit of the Gospel, so that no one knows that they are fasting and no effect is visible to the observer. And, if the practice continues, they will certainly need to take counsel on the matter, as Saint Benedict recommends (RB 48.8-10).

14. To improve the lot of poor people.

Almsgiving was traditionally associated with fasting in the early church. The idea was that we make available to others what we have denied ourselves. This is an important complementary principle. Saying no to oneself is an essential practice in spiritual living, because it restricts the ego and allows the deeper energies of the personality to exercise control. Saying yes to others is, at least, equally important. We all know people who, for a time, are so concerned with their own spiritual lives that they seem insensitive to the needs of others. It may be very virtuous to throw the television set out the window, but perhaps it would have been better to check that other people are not adversely affected by our action. Even if no one else in the house watched it or wanted it, we could, perhaps, have given it away to someone who might have enjoyed it more. Growth in spiritual vigor is normally signaled by a greater and more proactive concern for the welfare of other people.

Benedict follows the Rule of the Master in using the verb *recreare*, which means literally to re-create or, perhaps, to restore to good condition. It seems to imply an effect more ample than material assistance. The *Passio Iuliani et Basilissae*, generally cited as a source for this section, does not have this verb; it reads, "Above all let them act solicitously in their care for the poor,"[15] placing the emphasis on the disposition of the carer rather than on the outcome. *Recreare* is a very generous word. People who, through illness or unemployment or plain bad luck, descend into poverty are often afflicted by a steady erosion of self-esteem. It is as though their personality is being demolished. They need handouts, but they need more than handouts. As Mother Teresa of Calcutta seems to have recognized, they also need to have their personal dignity reaffirmed, and this can be done only by one who genuinely believes that it is a privilege to help them. It is not merely a matter of having by nature an outgoing and empathetic disposition. To possess such humility and to have such a high level of spiritual perception that one really sees Christ in the neighbor is an indication of a very high level of spiritual growth. Such as these understand why Saint Benedict affirms that Christ is more truly received in the poor than in the rich (RB 53.15).

Unless a monk holds an office which involves him in almsgiving, it is unlikely that he will have much occasion to follow this recommendation, if it is taken literally, at least on a regular basis. The recommendation can, however, be understood in a wider sense. Every community discovers that the poor are always with us: those who seem to have little talent for anything, those with poor social skills, those burdened with mental or emotional disorders, those whose virtue and commitment seem slight. These are the poor who are in our midst. We are called on, not only to tolerate their weaknesses of body and behavior—as it were, to secure our own virtuousness—but even more to do what we can to make their lives happier and more wholesome. Our concern should be to improve their lot, to re-create them, insofar as it lies within the sphere of possibility for our limited abilities. Sometimes it may be a simple exercise in providing a few moments of relief by a shared joke or pastime or by enjoying some recreative activity. Sometimes charity may recommend that we tiptoe around them. At other times we may need to be on the lookout for potential sources of disturbance. This may sometimes require tactics so subtle that the beneficiaries are not aware of them, especially when it is a matter of our interposing ourselves preemptively between them and a possible source of hurt or anxiety.

It is the other-centeredness of this precept that is to be emphasized. Sometimes social workers and other professional carers have to be reminded that it is not about them and how they feel so much as about the person in need of care. Serving the poor, insofar as the opportunity presents itself, can be focus for many virtues, but most of all it is an invitation to self-forgetfulness and a moment of solidarity and communion with those whom many consider to be the less privileged but who, mysteriously, may be spiritually richer than we are.

It is to be noted that Benedict has omitted two items that occur a little later in the list given in the Rule of the Master:

"To make loans. To give to the needy" (RM 3.20-21). The reasoning behind this omission is probably that the monk has nothing to lend or give away, so the injunctions are useless.

15. To clothe a naked person.

Saint Benedict is here recalling the list of good works, performed or omitted, about which there will be inquiry at the time of the Final Judgment (Matt 25). Monastic life does not usually offer the possibility of a high score for most of the items in that particular list, unless symbolic fulfillment of the precepts is considered valid. Clothing the naked is one of the so-called corporal works of mercy. It is more likely to be done by the community as a whole rather than falling to the lot of an individual monk.

On the other hand, in his chapter on what the monks wear, Benedict insists that when new garments are given, the old are to be returned to the clothing store for the sake of the poor (RB 55.9). To be sure, this is to prevent the disorder of hoarding, but it is also an invitation to the monk to release his grip on an object that may be useful, so that it may serve for the benefit of others. Even if monastic garments were not reused whole, the cloth could probably have been usefully recycled. In premodern times pieces of cloth were regularly cut from old garments to serve as patches.

The principle remains constant. The monk is to mortify himself by doing whatever needs to be done to make the lives of others more tolerable. And perhaps Saint Benedict would have hoped that the act of compassion would be completed by a genuine feeling of compassion, a deep sense of solidarity with the sufferer. This was certainly the approach taken by the twelfth-century Cistercian authors who recommended not only the *actus compassionis* but also the *affectus compassionis*.

16. To visit a sick person.

This is a good work that often can be done within the confines of the monastery (RB 66.6-7). Benedict prescribes a special room for the sick (RB 36.7) where their particular needs can be met without causing disruption to the regular life of the community. This parallels the position that he takes with regard to the welcoming of strangers. On the one hand, strangers are to be welcomed warmheartedly as Christ (RB 53.1-15), but on the other they are to have a separate kitchen and sleeping area, and the brothers are not to mingle promiscuously with them (RB 53.16, 22, 23-24). While a special regime is offered to guests and those who dine with them, the community is to maintain its ordinary discipline (RB 56.3). In a similar way, whatever needs to be done to give diligent and loving care to the sick is to be done, while the rest of the community, "the healthy and especially the young" (RB 36.8), is to carry on as normal.

In later centuries the infirmary became almost a parallel monastery built adjacent to the main precinct, housing a variety of different patients: those too old to follow the regular life, the demented, those suffering from chronic illness, those who had accidentally injured themselves, those with fevers of one kind or another, and those who had recently undergone bleeding. A mitigated form of the common life was followed by those who were well enough. The twelfth-century Cistercian customary, the *Ecclesistica Officia*, understood the infirmary as a place of silence, with necessary conversation carried on quietly and in a place apart. To visit the sick required the permission of the infirmarian, sought by sign language (EO 92.1-2).

It is hard to know whether Benedict envisaged applying this recommendation to the monks or to what extent he would have considered a visit from the brethren to have been a source of comfort. Certainly, in the case of the spiritually ill, he makes provision for the spiritual seniors to visit the wavering brother, as it were, secretly, to offer him support and consolation (RB 27.3-4). Most probably the everyday principles of common sense and *humanitas* would have applied here, as elsewhere in Benedict's view of practical everyday life. We learn that Saint Bernard of Clairvaux had the habit of visiting those in the infirmary each day after Compline,[16] and it is not improbable that others with pastoral responsibility would have made time to visit the sick.

The situation today is different. People with serious needs may need to be transferred to hospitals and other care agencies, and in those monasteries large enough to have complete facilities, they are operated under similar professional standards and are almost independent from the daily life of the rest of the community. It is important that illness does not serve as a quasi excommunication, banishing the sick from interaction beyond necessary quarantine and what is needed for their care. It is easy for the healthy to be so concentrated on the doing of their own pressing tasks that they cease to be mindful of those whom illness prevents from taking part in community activities. It has to be remembered by others how much pain isolates—since no one else feels it in the same way—and so can contribute to a deeper sense of loneliness. Sensitivity and experience are important in visiting the sick—and following the advice of their carers. Some people are naturally more sensitive to the effects of isolation than others and find a certain pleasure in dropping in to visit for a few minutes of light conversation. Others are more reserved, not wishing to be intrusive and, in some cases, doubting whether a visit from them would be a source of comfort. And the patients will have different needs according to temperament and the measure of their sickness. Some are happy with voluble sociability; others prefer a quiet presence and a prayer or maybe being read to. I have known seriously ill patients pretending to be asleep to avoid having to deal with visitors' effervescent spirits that they knew they could not match. The bottom line in visiting the sick is a sensitivity to their needs, expressed or unexpressed.

Some communities make provision for interaction between the permanent residents of the infirmary and the healthy by scheduling different people to perform small services such as taking meals, delivering mail, or pushing wheelchairs, so that every day there is some contact with those outside the confines of the infirmary. In other places the infirmary is located close by the main traffic routes of the monastery so that it is relatively easy for casual contact to come about in the course of the day.

17. To bury one who is dead.

In the Old Testament book named after him, one of the principal good works that Tobit did was to bury the dead in observance of the Law of God: a final act of solidarity. Treating the dead with honor is as disinterested an act of kindness as it is possible to have. In every other kind act, the recipient is able to repay the good deed in some way: by gratitude, by a word, by esteem, by assuming a future obligation to reciprocate. The dead cannot repay a kindness. There is no repayment expected in burying the dead.

Many monasteries have their own cemeteries in which monks of previous generations lie awaiting their resurrection. Death in a monastery has traditionally been surrounded by solemn ceremony and, in a stable community, is something of a regular occurrence in which many have a part to play. When Benedict speaks of burying the dead, he is probably not thinking of monastic funerals. He probably includes this item as part of a preexisting list. In the Middle Ages, when plagues of various kinds were a quasi-regular scourge, cemeteries attached to the monasteries became the final resting place of many victims. In some ancient monastic sites can be seen a place where the laity could deposit corpses for burial.

Maybe modern equivalents of this good work may include offering hospitality in a monastic cemetery or columbarium for those desiring burial in a sacred ambience. Although not a corporal work of mercy, monasteries have traditionally followed the church's tradition of praying for the faithful departed. The knowledge that the monastic community is praying for the deceased loved ones can be a source of comfort to the survivors.

18. To come to help in trouble.

Here, Saint Benedict uses the verb *subvenire*, which usually meant coming to the aid of somebody in some kind of difficulty or embarrassment. It is, of course, the verb *venire* with a prefix attached.[17] This gives a proactive note to the recommendation; we move ourselves in order to provide help to somebody else.

Trouble comes in many different forms, internal and external, and it has an uncanny knack for catching us wrong-footed. Things that we can handle without perturbation one day may, on the next, become the straw that breaks the camel's back. There is a strong subjective component in trouble; not everybody is affected by a particular event to the same degree. This means that it is easy for us to lack sympathy or even become angry with a person who, it seems to us, is disproportionately upset by some small matter. The most obvious source of disturbance may gain its power to upset only because there is a confluence of several other less obvious factors. More often than not, we do not know a great deal about the extent to which others are interiorly oppressed and so may be too ready to think ill of them when they fail to cope with what seems to us a slight reversal. Helping others is an invitation to self-forgetfulness, and sometimes it involves suspending our own perceptions and judgments. In trying to help someone else, I have to keep saying to myself, "It is not about me, the helper; all the emphasis must be on the person who needs help."

We will often be aware that somebody near to us is going through a difficult patch but will not know the reason for it, and we may be unsure how we may help. Sometimes trouble skews peoples' reactions; in contrast to their normal affability, they may react negatively to a friendly joke or distantly to an invitation meant to demonstrate solidarity. Understanding and empathy are of prime importance here: to be willing to let go of our own way of looking at things and to try to experience matters as the other person does. Saint Bernard used the word "compassion" to describe this quality—the spontaneous and yet cultivated ability to feel what another person is feeling. He taught that compassion comes about only as a result of deep self-knowledge which, in turn, is the effect of having gone through hard times oneself. A collateral benefit of having passed through various kinds of trouble is that we are usually rendered more sympathetic to others who are having similar experiences. This is the kind of situation envisaged in the title of one of Henri Nouwen's early books, *The Wounded Healer*.

The Epistle to the Hebrews states that Jesus, "because he himself suffered when he was tempted, can help those who are being tempted" (Heb 2:18). In the same way, our own troubles will often provide us with the experience and the capacity to be sympathetic to others in their difficulties, but we have to take their unique story seriously. This means more than superimposing a chapter from my own autobiography and quickly coming up with equivalent solutions. It means, above all, uninterrupted listening, holding up a sympathetic mirror while other persons find within themselves the power to verbalize what they are feeling. Sometimes all they need is a listening ear, especially in those situations where the objective troubles at the heart of the upset are themselves insoluble.

Of course, not all troubles sear the soul. Some ways of helping are merely practical, helping to clean up a spilled can of paint, pushing a stalled car off the road, or chasing a goat out of the garden. These simply demand a willing expenditure of energies. But this external help can be given in different ways: it can be done scoldingly, as if suggesting that the person needing help is incompetent, or help can be given humbly while communicating a fuller solidarity, as if saying, "I have made, or could have made, the same mistake myself." The precept to remember here is the one given earlier by Benedict: "Let him not do to another what he does not wish to be done to himself," and its correlate: Let him treat others as he would like to be treated in similar circumstances.

It is also possible to come to another's help preemptively. This is done by foreseeing a situation that is likely to land another person in difficulty or cause distress and stepping into to forestall the hurtful outcome. This is a very pure-intentioned sort of kindness, because the beneficiary is unlikely to be aware of what has been done on his or her behalf. It corresponds to what Jesus recommended in the Sermon on the Mount: "As for you, when you perform an act of mercy, let your left hand not know what you right hand is doing. Thus your act of mercy will be in secret, and your Father who sees in secret will repay you" (Matt 6:3-5).

Saint Leo the Great speaks about the spirit with which these acts of kindness should be performed. They are to be undertaken not as a matter of routine or duty but as a source of joy for the one who has been given the opportunity to be generous.

> Let acts of kindness be our delight and let us be filled with those foods that will nourish us for eternity. Let us be happy in giving food to the poor whose hunger is satisfied by our

gift. Let us be joyful in clothing those whose nakedness we cover with necessary garments. Let our humanity be experienced by those who are sick in bed, the weak who are feeble, exiles in their hardship, orphans who are without resources, and lonely widows in their grief. There is no one who cannot be generous in doing some small thing to help such people. Income is never too small when the heart is large; the measure of kindness and mercy is not dependent on great wealth.[18]

19. To console one who is feeling pain.

The needy person is here described by Saint Benedict as *dolentem*. The noun *dolor* and its cognates have a wide variety of meanings; they encompass both bodily pain and various kinds of mental and emotional perturbation. In daily life we will certainly meet those who are suffering. The root cause of this suffering, and its expression, may be physical or psychological or both. In every case it is the whole person who suffers. A toothache is not something that is isolated in the mouth; it invades and dominates the whole of a person's existence. Pain colors every other experience; if it is severe enough, it banishes everything else from consideration. Visible pain nearly always has an invisible companion and, sometimes, what is less apparent is the stronger source of suffering.

After medical options have been exhausted, there are various nonmedical ways of easing bodily pain and helping people to live with it. The growth in palliative care in our own time is a positive and humane step that helps many people pull back from the cliff of hopelessness. In a normal monastery where death is a regular visitor, there may be many occasions for using simple means to make the final period of a person's life not only more tolerable but even beautiful. The monastic custom of gathering around a dying monk and surrounding him with prayer is not only a gesture of solidarity but sometimes also a necessary support against temptation. Saint Aelred remarks, "Even in the case of those who are very perfect, the devil often stands ready at their departure from this life."[19] Care of the dying is one way that we can console those who are suffering pain.

There are other forms of pain which are not terminal but can cast a veil of misery over the sufferer. These burdens we are called to lift a little, if we can. Such times can also be periods of scarifying temptation against faith, hope, and charity. We do well never to underestimate what another person is suffering, whether the source is bodily, emotional, or mental, visible or invisible. Nor must we allow ourselves to feel under-resourced to help anyone else in such a situation. Like King Jehoram when confronted with Naaman's leprosy, we may feel like exclaiming, "Am I God? Can I kill and bring back to life?" (2 Kgs 5:7). It is true we cannot work miracles, but what we have is our own humanity; all we need to do is forget ourselves, reach out to the other, and do what we are able.

Today we are more able to recognize psychological suffering, even if we do not know its precise cause. As people live longer, there seems to be a greater incidence of dementia and senile confusion. Apart from the professional care such people need, we are called upon to play a supporting role through how we relate to them, in what we do and in what we omit to do. "Let them tolerate most patiently their infirmities of body and behavior" (RB 72.5). To begin to treat well those who are suffering from emotional or psychological disturbance, two preliminary steps are necessary. The first consists in controlling our own speech so that we do not give way to the thoughtless venting of our own frustration or annoyance. There is no need for us to draw attention to defective behavior; it is obvious to everybody. The habit of criticism and mockery hardens our stance toward the disturbed person and does us no good. Then, second, if we strictly control our speech, we begin to find it easier to think less badly of those involved, to be a little more understanding. In an inner ambience of charitable thought we are more likely to act kindly in their regard and, by our attitude, to be a small source of consolation to them.

Fear is a common source of suffering. It shrivels our natural optimism and makes us view the future with apprehension and anxiety. There are circumstances in which fear is appropriate, and it can lead to prudence in our choice of practical options. Some fears are circumstantial. We may be in a war zone with bullets whizzing round our head, so we duck. We may be afraid to cross a busy highway when visibility is low, so we walk to a safer crossing point. More abstractly, appropriate fears can be generated by statistics: We calculate our chances of developing cancer or dementia and initiate suitable preventive measures. We all know, however, that not all fears are reasonable and proportionate. Because of this unreality, such fears can create serious disturbance in our inner and outer lives, sometimes without our being able to determine the precise origin of our distress. For example, fear of failure or of displeasing some parental figure can cripple the spark of originality that each of us has. We may feel disinclined to act, but we do not recognize the reason for our reluctance. Our fears may be more global: fear for our own salvation or for the future of the planet. The rule of thumb is: if such fear leads to appropriate action then it is energizing and good. If fear paralyzes and numbs, it is probably unreasonable.

Helping others to verbalize their fears and to sort through the various elements that give them their force is another means of consoling one who is feeling pain. As in so many other situations, listening responsively to others with an open and caring heart is one of the best means of helping them. Fears can be assuaged by creating community in which fearlessness is encouraged. The Acts of the Apostles frequently uses the notion of boldness or freedom of speech (*parresia*) to characterize those whom the Holy Spirit empowered. A healthy community does not want its members to bottle up their thoughts and feelings within them and so provides channels for their healthy expression. The fundamental philosophy underlying community life is also important. In the twelfth century, when an unhealthy level of fear of the final judgment and eternal damnation prevailed, the Cistercian writers and preachers insistently proclaimed a gospel of confidence in God's mercy and were unafraid to set forth the steps by which we can most fully avail ourselves of this divine generosity. We can create an ambience that reduces unnecessary fears. When a group of people are confident about the ultimate meaningfulness of human existence, they exude a therapeutic optimism which is both attractive and sustaining for those who, otherwise, might spend their lives in unnamable dread.

Fears are often associated with low self-esteem, whether this is the result of life experiences or the tireless efforts of others who take it upon themselves to humiliate and belittle. Helping those scarred by their past to be more creative for the future is a noble endeavor. Each time we help remove a brick from the protective wall they have built around their inner self, we are aiding the ongoing work of liberation, bringing freedom to those who were captive and releasing their creative energies for the benefit of many.

Some people around us may be going through a vocational or midlife crisis which results in inner confusion and isolation and sometimes in fearsome levels of anxiety. In these cases the support we offer must affirm their basic goodness while respecting their freedom to make or reverse a choice in order to take a path that will ultimately be more life-giving. And it will often mean turning a blind eye to transient behavioral expressions of their inner turmoil.

Likewise, we may need to examine our relationship with those who suffer shame and marginalization due to public failures such as substance abuse, sexual misconduct, money mismanagement, culpable driving, or simply by being a nuisance in community. This is a sure test of the genuineness of our charity. Saint Benedict devotes two chapters of his Rule to this question. He offers a threefold pastoral strategy. The abbot is to be solicitous that his measures provide a remedy rather than merely punish offenders, and so, like a wise physician, he is to keep increasing the strength of his cures, if they have proved hitherto ineffective, in the hope of bringing about an improvement (RB 28.1-7). Meanwhile, he is to make use of "spiritual seniors," who are to encourage the delinquent to change his ways, and "to comfort him lest he be sucked into an overwhelming sadness" (RB 27.2-4). Third, the abbot is to rely on the power of prayer to effect some change in the heart of the sinner (RB 28.4). "Let love for him be strengthened, and let there be prayer for him by all" (RB 27.4). In such circumstances, it is important to remember one's own fragility and to be somewhat reluctant to cast the first stone. And it is good to remember that situations are often more complex than a black-and-white bottom line indicates. In addition, it is not unknown that accusations have been made against those who are innocent, and even when allegations are proved false, a residue of suspicion clings to the person accused that may unfairly change the way we relate to him and render us somewhat distant and unsympathetic. In the spirit of the Gospel, Benedict places no restrictions on those who are appropriate targets for our loving concern: we are to offer consolation to any who are suffering pain—physical, mental, or emotional.

We will also encounter people who are grieving. Grief is what we feel when we experience an unrecoverable loss. The special mental component of grief is that the loss is final and cannot be reversed. Grief is what we feel at the death of a loved one, but there are many occasions when it strikes us. Other examples beyond bereavement include the total rupture of a relationship, the loss of a position with which we had identified, an irreversible decline in health and in the possibilities that good health brings, and the restrictions imposed on our life as youth gives way to age. These losses are so total, within their own sphere, that we find difficulty in accepting that a door has closed in front of us definitively. Without knowing it, we pass into a phase of semi-denial, in which the absoluteness of our loss is mitigated. In our experience of the death of someone dear to us, it takes time to accept the finality of what has happened. We find ourselves imagining future conversations; we dream about dead persons as if they were still alive. After the amputation of a limb, the brain seems unwilling to concede what has occurred, and the lost limb seems to be still there. And in our grief for lost youth, we sometimes make fools of ourselves by pretending that we are decades younger than our birth certificate indicates. The ultimate futility of denial intensifies what we suffer at such a time. The truth is too horrible to embrace, and our resistance to it clouds our inner space and so makes matters worse. But life goes on, and in the best of outcomes, the truth must be accepted, and a new way forward devised. With each door that closes, another doorway opens. Meanwhile we will appreciate whatever comfort and understanding others can bring us.

The word that twelfth-century Cistercians used to describe the negative aspect of human life was *miseria*. It meant much more for them than "misery" does for us. It was the sum total of all that undermines the happiness and fulfillment we desire in life, all that the human race lost in being expelled from paradise. The experience of suffering is common to every human being, and those who follow Christ will certainly be called, in some way, to fill up in their flesh what was lacking to Christ's passion (Col 1:24). "Each of the faithful has his or her own struggles."[20] Saint Aelred of Rievaulx lists some of the elements in a throwaway line: "Pertaining to unhappiness are all the miseries of this life: labors, pains, weariness, poverty, bereavement, all types of illness, trouble. O my brothers, who can number them all?"[21] We may not feel so disheartened all the time, but sometimes we do feel that way, and that is when we hope there would be someone nearby who is ready to offer us consolation.

"Consolation" must be one of the most beautiful words in our language; even its sound bespeaks a sustained softness that soothes and comforts. It is the kindness of human solidarity gratuitously given to those who need it most. Pain comes in many forms. That means that the consolation offered must be correspondingly pluriform. We know from Elisabeth Kübler-Ross's work *On Death and Dying* that grief goes through different stages: denial, anger, bargaining, depression, acceptance. As we try to help, we need to be conscious that each stage requires a different response. The same is true in many other situations of human suffering. As people go through different phases of coping with suffering, they are consoled by different means. The most fundamental of these is empathy, matching our mood with theirs: "Rejoicing with those who rejoice, weeping with those who weep" (Rom 12:15). And the paramount expression of empathy is, as I have said before, an attitude of attentive listening that pervades our whole being, offering the hospitality of our heart to the other person.

The Holy Spirit is the prime source of consolation for all believers. Addressed in the New Testament as *parakletos*, the Holy Spirit is called to stand at our side as our advocate, mediator, friend, intercessor, and helper. The Paraclete brings us comfort and strength from the spiritual world when the world around us rises up against us. The work of the Spirit is to offset the discouragement and loss of morale that are the result of living in an environment that undermines the confidence that comes from the heartfelt acceptance of the Good News. The liturgical sequence *Veni Sancte Spiritus* speaks thus of the Holy Spirit:

Consolator optime,	O excellent Consoler,
dulcis hospes animae,	Pleasant guest of the soul,
dulcis refrigerium.	Pleasant refreshment.
In labore requies,	Rest in [times of] labor,
in aestu temperies,	Relief in [times of] extreme heat,
in fletu solatium.	Comfort in [times of] weeping.

Presence, refreshment, rest, relief, comfort: these are the Holy Spirit's gifts. How do we offer consolation to others? By following this example. We stay with the person who is suffering, not allowing their pain to drive us away; physically, emotionally, or mentally we remain present. We offer them a moment of refreshment to compensate for all they are undergoing, leaving aside our own concerns and problems to bring a little joy. We give assistance in what has to be done so that they may rest awhile. As best we can, we provide relief from the severe storms that ravage their equanimity. And, weeping with those who weep, we offer our tears as a slight balm to alleviate their pain.

20. To make himself a stranger to the actions of the world.

Benedictine asceticism is, fundamentally, the practical implementation of Gospel ideals. The best way of denying oneself in order to follow Christ is simply to strive effectively to live by his teaching. If I base my everyday choices on the Gospel, then I certainly will become a stranger to the ways of the world.[22] If I invest all my energies in living a life characterized by humility, altruism, nonviolence, chastity, forgiveness, truthfulness, indifference, and detachment, it is unlikely that I will become powerful, rich, and famous. An evangelical way of life is not a road to this-worldly greatness. Seekers of eternal life have to be prepared to put aside ambitions for success in the temporal sphere.

Even from New Testament times, there has always been some ambiguity in texts commenting on the relationship of the world to the Christian, the church, and the monastery. The difficulty was felt particularly in the immediate aftermath of Vatican II as the council fathers tried to redress the balance.[23] If it is true that "God so loved the world as to give the only-begotten Son" (John 3:16), then why does Saint Paul advise Christians, "Do not be conformed to this world" (Rom 12:2)? Why does Saint James say, "Do you not know that friendship with the world is enmity with God?" and "The one who wishes to be a friend of the world makes himself God's enemy" (Jas 4:4)? Why does Saint John say, "Do not love the world or anything in the world. If anyone loves the world then the love of the Father is not in him" (1 John 2:15)?

Withdrawal (*anachoresis*) was one of the features of the kind of monasticism that Saint Benedict envisaged. Other forms, such as those that developed around Saint Basil or Saint Augustine, were more urban and, thereby, inevitably were somewhat involved in the life of the city. Saint Benedict chose a different path. Pope Gregory the Great describes thus the process of vocation in Saint Benedict's own life:

> He despised the study of literature and left behind his father's house and wealth and, desiring to please God alone [*soli Deo placere desiderans*], he sought the habit of the holy way of life. He withdrew, knowingly unknowing and wisely unlearned.[24]

Later on, Gregory describes the process as "seeking the desert places," "preferring to suffer the evils of the world than [enjoy] its praises," and "seeking seclusion in a desert place."[25]

In Benedict's case it was not only a matter of resisting the allure of worldly values but of geographical displacement away from population centers into areas where the pressure to conform would be less urgent. By the time he was writing his Rule for Monasteries he would insist that the monastery must, as far as possible, be self-sufficient, "so that there is no necessity for monks to go wandering around outside, because that is not good for their souls" (RB 66.7).

Fuga mundi (flight from the world) and the stronger *contemptus mundi* (contempt for the world) became part of the lexical armory of monasticism, and the terms were also used metaphorically in the wider church.[26] The physical separation and the looming enclosure walls should not, however, distract us from the purpose of disengagement. It is from the *actions* of the world that Saint Benedict wishes the monk to keep his distance. The separation is more behavioral than geographical. Monks withdraw to seek and to find God. They are looking for a life in which they can live mindfully in God's presence, apart from the distractedness that follows multiple concerns, and able to spend their days in an environment that is conducive to recollection and prayer. This is a simple life: a life with clearly defined objectives, one that enables the monk to achieve the integration of his psychic energies and focus them single-pointedly on one overriding goal. Monastic life is defined not by that from which it separates itself but by that toward which all its efforts are directed.

No matter how isolated the monastery is, or how high its walls, "worldly" news, beliefs, and values are going to arrive in the cloister, and the monks will not be immune from them. This means that leaving the world behind is not a single step taken at the beginning of the monastic journey but a battle that has to be waged throughout many decades. There is no other way of maintaining the evangelical distinctiveness that is at the heart of the monastic way. "There should be a wall between us and the world . . . so that we do not run back to

the things we have renounced."[27] Even in the most observant
of communities, the values of "the world" infiltrate. They are
carried in the hearts of those who join the community. Sometimes these ingrained tendencies enter into immediate conflict with the monastic way; sometimes they lie dormant for
a period and then suddenly burst into life. This is the reason
why, after a fervent beginning, a newcomer begins to relax,
and old behavioral patterns emerge. Selfishness, competitiveness, ambition, envy, and the like may begin to animate conduct—as well as other tendencies, lying beneath the surface
of consciousness. The reversion to normal "worldliness" after
a relatively brief period of remission often catches persons
by surprise. They may cave in immediately. They may lose
heart and become discouraged when they discover that the
transition into monastic living is not as smooth as they had
thought and hoped. Or they may enter into denial and resist
any efforts on the part of those charged with their pastoral
care to help them to own, confront, and reduce the power
of such tendencies. We may hope, however, that with a little
wise guidance they may gird their loins and prepare for many
years of spiritual warfare. Their experience may be like trying
to hold a small boat on course while the current continually
causes it to veer in another direction. The effort is wearying,
but it is necessary if progress toward the destination is to be
achieved.

This undesirable reversion to attitudes formed as a person was growing up is greatly facilitated by contact with the
various means of social communication. Many think of the
mass media simply as sources of information and entertainment that are part—and often a considerable part—of daily
life. What is often overlooked is that these seemingly harmless
pursuits are not only filling empty time but also forming the
mentalities and attitudes of those who open themselves to
them. It is often a simple question of mathematics. A person
who spends two hours a day with the mass media and one

hour with the Scriptures is surely more likely to be formed by that at which he spends more time. The fact that the influence is subtle and goes undetected in no way diminishes its potency. When this exposure continues day after day for a period of years, then the formation of the mind of Christ in the person will have to battle serious opposition.

In monasteries today many older people whose lives were previously filled by work of one kind or another now find themselves with a great deal of time on their hands and nothing much to do. This can often lead to quite a considerable time being spent mindlessly and with a consequent erosion of personal morale. What Benedict says about Sundays may often apply in such cases: "If there is someone who is so negligent or slack that he does not wish or is not able to meditate or read, let him be given a work to do so that he may not be disengaged" (RB 48.23). This assignment is not simply for the sake of increasing the amount of work done in the community, it is to prevent the person who is unoccupied from becoming a prey to infestation by contrary influences because "idleness is the enemy of the soul" (RB 48.1). This is not to suggest that there is no value in relaxing activities or in slowing down as the years pass. It is, rather, to wonder whether means can be found whereby retirement may more effectively become a time of fulfillment, contentment, and mellow wisdom.

The fact is that the mass media, and especially the internet, offers the means for hitherto thoughtful "people to slip comfortably into the permanent state of distractedness that defines the online life."[28] But there is more. Spending hours surfing the web not only consumes the day and induces a state of mental acedia but also opens the doors to influences that may profoundly weaken commitment to the values that undergird monastic or Christian life. In terms of the Platonic distinction between "knowledge" and "opinion," it has to be said that we live in an age in which opinion reigns supreme. The internet has spawned thousands of websites in which opinions are vented with great assurance but with little attention to science, logic, or alternative possibilities. Our online activity can easily degenerate into a smash-and-grab raid for unsourced information rather than engaging in a reasoned review of available evidence. Wild ideas can be expressed with fearsome certitude and little prospect of correction. Take the foolishness that surrounded the rampant assertion that, according to the Mayan calendar, the world was to end in 2012. It didn't, as far as I know. But the idea spread like wildfire.

In the early days of computers, specialists used to emphasize the importance of the careful inputting of data with the maxim GIGO: "Garbage In, Garbage Out." The same applies to our own minds. If we fill our minds with garbage, then, when it comes time for serious thought or prayer, we are liable to reap what we have interiorly sown.[29] Our spiritual sensitivity can easily become degraded by frivolous pursuits. Instead of being reflective persons of some depth, we can easily become preoccupied with things of little or no importance and weaken our capability for sustained reasoning. When asked what he considered to be the most serious problem of our time, the General of the Jesuits, Father Adolfo Nicolás, replied, "the globalization of superficiality."[30] By this he probably meant that all over the world we are becoming more content with questions and answers that touch only the surface of our complex human existence. We are losing the knack of going deeper. We are permitting ourselves to be brainwashed by "hidden persuaders" so that we are becoming less adept in thinking for ourselves, and in the process we are in danger of creating a dystopia for the future. If there is anywhere on earth where one would reasonably hope for a more profound experience of reality, surely a fervent monastery would be a prime candidate. That is a significant aspect of *fuga mundi*. It is flight from "the world" in order to maintain personal integrity and, in the process, be in a state whereby good can be done for the world.

We live in a world in which relentless self-promotion is rampant. Every newspaper and every news bulletin loudly proclaims the cosmic importance of whatever story it has confected to fill the daily space. Advertisers hawk their products with absolute assurance. Politicians proclaim their unswerving adherence to whatever noble principles the opinion polls suggest. Nobody seems to want us to think; they simply ask for our assent. We are assailed on every side by people trying to sell us something. It is this loud and intrusive boastfulness (termed *alazoneia* in1 John 2:16) that one would hope to escape in a monastic setting. It can be secured only when those who live there deliberately, prudently, and with due measure make themselves strangers to the actions and attitudes of ambient society by limiting their exposure to these clamorous voices.

21

To put nothing before the love of Christ.

It is precisely by giving nothing priority over Christ's love
that we are set on the road to becoming strangers to the actions of the world. "To put nothing before the love of Christ"
is one of the most frequently cited verses in the Rule, along
with RB 72.11: "Let them prefer nothing at all to Christ."
For many readers this maxim is a clear statement of the all-
pervasive Christocentric character of Benedictine spirituality.
Monastic life is all about personal devotion to Christ, living
in union with him through imitation, opening oneself to his
teaching, seeking to live mindfully in his presence, serving him
in the needy, seeking union with him in prayer, and reposing
all one's hope for future blessedness in his mercy. This aspect
of Benedictine life is well highlighted by the titles of the principal books written by Blessed Columba Marmion, abbot of
Maredsous: *Christ, the Life of the Soul, Christ the Ideal of the
Monk,* and *Christ in his Mysteries.*

Some commentators remark that the expression "the
love of Christ" could refer either to Christ's love for us or
to our love for him. It is probable that Benedict is thinking of Christ's love for us. This is confirmed by a passage in
Saint Cyprian's treatise on the Lord's Prayer, which is a likely
source for this section:

> The will of God is what Christ did and taught. Humility in
> lifestyle, stability in faith, reserve in words, justice in deeds,

mercy in works, discipline in behavior, not to know how to
do [another] injury, but when injured to be able to bear
with it, to maintain peace with false brothers; to love God
with the whole heart, loving God as a Father and fearing
God as God; *to put nothing at all before Christ* because he
put nothing before us, to adhere inseparably to him and to
cling bravely and confidently to his cross.[1]

Some degree of reciprocity is indicated here. We love
Christ because Christ first loved us (1 John 4:19). This is the
theme developed by Saint Augustine in connection with the
verb *redamare,* to love in return. Our love for God and for
Christ is a spontaneous response to the experience of receiving love from God or from Christ. The call to a more intense
Christian life or to monasticism is fundamentally an experience of the attractiveness of God's love. We are drawn toward
God, desiring to respond to that outpouring of love not only in
word or deed but also to say yes with every fiber of our being,
"from the whole heart, the whole soul, the whole strength."

Monasticism is not merely a career or lifestyle choice. It is
not professional religion, like priests engaged in official temple
worship. It is not some species of social welfare work, having
as its prime purpose the service of the underprivileged. Even
less is it some form of institutionalized narcissism in which
individuals can work on their own perfection without reference to anything outside themselves. To think in such terms
is, in every case, to miss the point. There is at the heart of the
monastic impulse something profoundly mystical without
which nothing else that happens in a monastery makes any
sense. The monastery is the School of Christ (*schola Christi*)
in which disciples learn by experience to put on the mind of
Christ and so acquire what the medieval monks termed "the
philosophy of Christ" (*philosophia Christi*).

To become Christlike, living in a monastery is not enough.
We have to engage in the spiritual craft for which monastic

life was instituted, using all the tools that Saint Benedict lists in this chapter. But there is more. These good works must be infused by a good zeal that separates from vices and leads to God and to eternal life (RB 72.2). "Good zeal" is another way of describing love. Our deeds are done in the love that flows from the conscious presence of Christ in our life "so that our whole life may find its support in Christ, so that in all our judgments, from beginning to end, we may imitate Christ the Judge and think of Christ as present and closely watching our deeds."[2] By giving priority to Christ's love, we allow that love to inform our thoughts and choices, to govern our dealings with others, and to support and sustain us when we encounter situations that are hard, unfair, and unjust.

If we allow our spiritual sensitivity to develop at its own pace, Christ becomes our companion in life, constantly at our side, "a dear friend, a wise counsellor, a strong helper."[3] At the beginning, our sense of solidarity with him requires of us a great deal of active effort to keep returning to his presence, leaving aside the many potential sources of distraction that bestrew our daily path. We need, as it were, to keep filling our heads and hearts with spiritual thoughts to prevent their being drawn in other directions. Progressively, however, the work requires less energy. These intermittent contacts have begun to create in us the sense of an abiding relationship. Christ is always near to us, through many different meeting points, and we slowly learn how to turn to him not only in times of difficulty but, eventually, more often. This I-Thou relationship slowly evolves into something like a double consciousness; we are fully and actively aware of what is going on around us and the work in which we are engaged, but permeating this activity is another awareness that seasons what we do with a spiritual salt. We begin to understand what Saint John meant when he spoke about our remaining in Christ and Christ remaining in us. This stage of being spiritually awake may endure for a long time.

With God's grace we may be called even deeper into the mystery for rare moments or sometimes for longer periods. We experience such a deep union with Christ that we no longer have any sense of a separate existence: "It is no longer I that lives, but Christ lives in me" (Gal 2:20). When we pray, it is the voice of Christ that prays within us. It is through the eyes of Christ that we look toward the Father and cry, "Abba," just as it is through his eyes that we look upon the multitude and feel compassion. Our relationship is no longer between subject and object, nor is it an intersubjective I-Thou relationship. We have been invited to enter into the subjectivity of Christ in such a way that self-consciousness and self-will have been set aside. Alas! This ontological freedom from the limits of temporal existence is itself only temporary.

The progression through these stages is by no means smooth. It is punctuated by serious crises, the outcome of which is by no means certain—at least, so it seems to the person who experiences them. In even the best of us, there is much selfishness and stupidity that needs to be subverted before grace is able to produce that simplicity and singleness of heart in which contemplative experience is possible. These painful transitions are exquisitely tailored to the individual. To the one passing through them, they do not seem like common crises that can be identified in a textbook. They may well involve deconstruction of much of what the person holds dear. Nothing is exempt from these refining fires: lifestyle, career, relationships, personal philosophy, spirituality, prayer, reputation. In this connection we may recall Saint Mary McKillop, a true daughter of the church, who kept the faith through a period of formal excommunication. Our faith may not be tested to that degree, but tested it will be.

This persevering devotion to Christ is not the same as the sentimental attachment to an imagined Jesus that may have characterized the early stages of our spiritual journey. This may have been a good point of departure, but there was much in it that needed to be left behind. Saint Bernard, in his treatise *De diligendo Deo* (*On the God Who Is to Be Loved*), speaks about the necessity of infusing into this piety a substantial self-knowledge so that our spiritual life is grounded on truth rather than delusion. To this self-honesty must be added compassion for the neighbor. Only when this selfless love begins to permeate deep into the human spirit and begin its work of interior transformation is authentic contemplation born. By this time the heart has moved a long way from sentiment and pious images; its intensity derives from the firmness of a will fixed on God. This is why Saint Bernard and other Cistercians of his time were fond of quoting 2 Corinthians 5:16: "Though we once knew Christ according to the flesh, we know him thus no longer." The public face of Christ fades from view, as it were, and the person is introduced into a mysterious intimacy with the incarnate Word, often described in terms of spiritual marriage.

This is where the Christocentric practice of the Rule leads and was probably intended to lead, although Saint Benedict himself never explicitly developed its mystical dimensions as much as later authors. Giving nothing priority over an openness to receive Christ's love will, under grace and over a lifetime, lead to profound contemplative experience and the simultaneous transformation of the whole person, "from glory to glory into his own likeness" (2 Cor 3:18).

22-26

Not to go all the way with anger. Not to prolong a time of rage. Not to hold deceit in the heart. Not to give a false peace. Not to abandon charity.

Saint Benedict has reworked the text of the Rule of the Master at this point. The earlier rule is a little longer. The reason for the changes is not clear, but the result certainly gives a tighter focus to the paragraph. This is what the Master writes:

> Not to go all the way with anger. Not to hold onto a time of bad temper. Not to hold deceit in the heart. Not *knowingly* to give a false peace. *To keep faith with a brother. Not to love detraction. To fulfill promises without deception.* Not to abandon charity. (RM 3.24-31)

This series of sayings concerns the inner face of community life. In any highly regulated group of people, especially in some cultures, there is strong social pressure to avoid anything that might disturb social harmony. Confrontations are avoided. Bad temper and tantrum behavior are considered unacceptable, and, as a result, relationships may not always be what they seem to a casual observer. Some members may be seething with long-standing resentments. Others may engage in passive-aggressive tactics. There may be those who avoid potential conflict by effectively withdrawing to the margins of community life. Underneath the placid surface of the community there may be little love. People may go about their own tasks efficiently and effectively, cooperating where necessary but otherwise leading independent lives. Intimacy and affection are more likely to be experienced outside the community to which they have pledged their lives.

This is not the kind of community that Saint Benedict desires, as is clear from chapter 72 of the Rule. The school of the Lord's service is a school of love, and unless it clears away the obstacles to love in the hearts of the monks, it is failing in its purpose. It is not enough to produce a community regimen governed by good order and courtesy. The test of its quality is the love that the brothers have for one another, a love expressed effectively through mutual service but also experienced affectively through patience, tolerance, and mutual enjoyment.

22. Not to go all the way with anger.

Anger is what we normally feel when things go against us. We do not manufacture anger. It is a passion. It is something that is produced in us by adverse circumstances, independently of the will. Some of the saints have been famously short-tempered. It is important, therefore, that we make a distinction between the spontaneous surge of anger and what we do with that anger, between the feeling of anger and its expression. The moral character of anger is determined by the extent to which we allow it to determine our choices and, hence, by what those choices are. Evagrius of Pontus writes: "Whether all these [thoughts] upset the soul or not is not up to us. But whether they remain or not remain and whether they [are allowed] to move the passions or not is up to us."[1] Anger will arise in certain situations, but it is up to us whether we go all the way with it.

Aelred of Rievaulx was aware that the feeling of anger quickly imprinted itself on the body and so became visible to others. Primitively this was probably a defense mechanism such as we see in the animal kingdom, threatening the supposed enemy with imminent violence:

> Look at the angry person agitated by the goads of wrath and plunged into a kind of madness. The eyes shine, the lips tremble, the shoulders pump up and down [*ludunt*], the head seems scarcely attached to the neck or the arms to the shoulders. "They grind their teeth and stiffen" (Mark 9:18).[2]

The only creative response to an angry impulse is to recognize the feeling and, as far as possible, to build a wall around it so that it does not influence the choices that we are to make or the actions we adopt as a result of these choices. At a later time, when the arousal has weakened, we may wish to explore the matter further and to try to arrive at some understanding of how a particular person or incident has triggered this response. Then, if we have a good degree of self-knowledge, we may wish to initiate a more extensive trackdown, seeking to understand why we are vulnerable in certain areas and then to try to elaborate possible ways of attenuating this sensitivity.

Less creative ways of dealing with anger arise spontaneously. Because something or someone has made us feel bad, we want to reciprocate and inflict our pain on another, in the hope that trouble shared is trouble halved. And so the passion of anger is translated into the action of aggression, whether this be by violence of word or deed. Anger is a passion that disturbs our equanimity and makes us feel bad; aggression is an action by which we hope to make someone else feel bad. Anger arises independently of the will, aggression comes about only with the will's consent given at the moment or prepared in advance by a habit or history of violent responses.

We go all the way with anger when our response to negative stimulation is aggression.

Instead of concentrating on the initial incident, we may begin to intensify our angry feelings by drawing on the catalogue of historic grievances that we always have with us. The present offense is then compounded by adding memories of previous injuries. It does not matter whether the memories are true or false or the injuries real or imagined; they serve to reinforce our feelings of victimhood and so provide sufficient justification for any retaliatory action we may take. Whatever hurt we inflict on another cannot equal our sense of being wronged. This is why sometimes a small irritation can sometimes explode into a firestorm of rage, causing all who witness it to draw back in horror. This also is going all the way with anger.

Sometimes a person seems to deal well with a negative situation, but this is only on the surface. The energy that could have been directed in an all-out assault on the triggering person is instead directed inward. Under an outwardly placid exterior a sea of resentment is roiling. Whether consciously or not, revenge will be taken. This may take the form of passive aggression, a withdrawal from those perceived as causing the pain, a refusal to acknowledge them or cooperate with them. It can give rise to a subtle determination to undermine any authority or activity associated with them. Or, it may express itself in mockery and detraction, exposing and magnifying their faults, and seeking to lower the esteem in which they may be held. This underground guerilla warfare can sometimes continue for years. Less visible and less dramatic, to indulge oneself in such tactics is also to go all the way with anger.

From this we are led to conclude that in many angry outbursts the energy is derived not from the triggering incident but has been long stored from many past incidents. The present event merely offers the occasion for the release of these seething resentments. That is why it is sometimes impossible for those who participate in the scene to calm the outflow of wrath, and if they are not careful, they may easily find themselves enveloped by it.

It is normal to feel angry in certain situations, but it is helpful to remember that this anger occurs on a spectrum that goes all the way from minor irritation to overwhelming wrath. Anger must be proportionate to the offense. It may not be grossly inappropriate to feel a moment's annoyance if one's favorite seat has been occupied by someone else, but to respond to that situation with a huge temper tantrum goes beyond all rationality. There are situations in which anger provides us with the energy to act appropriately, but where the response is disproportionate, it is likely that the triggering event is merely symbolic.

There is much wisdom in Saint Benedict's formulation. He does not say, "Do not be angry." That would be a useless admonition. Instead he advises us "not to go all the way with anger." We need to learn a degree of restraint so that our response is measured, reasonable, and appropriate. Too often violence is precipitated by a too-rapid interpretation of events that if considered in a calmer light would have generated a different response.

23. Not to prolong a time of rage.

Outbursts of bad temper are bad enough; cherishing and nourishing anger is far more serious, because a more deliberate act of the will is involved. The verb I have translated as "prolong" is *reservare*; it means "to store up" or "to keep for future use." Saint Benedict's use of the phrase "a time of rage" indicates that he views such outbursts as essentially temporary and transient. They will pass unless there is an active effort to maintain the rage. The person in such a state is unwilling to let go of grievances, and these progressively become a second skin in which they live constantly. This radical unforgiveness is, of course, the opposite of what the Gospel teaches, and it goes against what is presupposed in monastic community, where community members are in constant contact, and daily reconciliation becomes not only an ideal but a necessity (RB 4.73).

It is hard for others in the community when someone lives on the brink of anger. It is even harder for angry persons, because this unprovoked inner disturbance becomes the underlying motif of daily existence. It becomes like a cancer that steadily degrades whatever virtues they have, interfering with their relationships and diminishing their *joie de vivre*. More than this, angry thoughts will begin to invade the time set aside for prayer, leading the person into a dense grove of recrimination and self-pity that blocks out any sense of contact with the spiritual world. Astute guides are aware that chronic desolation in prayer can sometimes be the symptom of a deep-seated lack of forgiveness. In this connection it is good to remember the words of Jesus, "When you stand praying, if you have anything against anyone, let go of it" (Mark 11:25).

Evagrius of Pontus was one of the great masters of contemplative life and a man of profound psychological insight. He is one of the comparatively few people who has written a great deal about the interaction between anger and prayer. Some of his wise sayings are usefully recalled at this point.

The first point he makes is that if we wish to pray well we first need to settle disputes amicably so that they do not intrude into our time of quiet. We need to be dedicated to harmony in our social relations. "Whatever you might do by way of avenging yourself on a brother who has done you some injustice will turn into a stumbling block for you at the time of prayer."[3] And: "When you are praying such matters will come to mind as would seem clearly to justify your getting angry. But anger is completely unjustifiable against your neighbor. If you really try, you will find some way to arrange the matter without showing anger. So then, employ every device to avoid a display of anger."[4]

The second point he notes is the danger of cultivating the memory of the injuries that have been done to us, of indulging ourselves with thoughts of victimhood. This is the point that Saint Benedict is making when he writes, "Not to prolong a time of rage." Evagrius writes: "The one who binds to his soul the memory of evil done is like one who hides fire in chaff."[5] And: "A strong wind drives away clouds: memory of evil done drives the mind from knowledge [*gnosis*]."[6] And: "The man who stores up injuries and resentments and yet fancies that he prays might as well draw water from a well and pour it into a cask that is full of holes."[7]

The third observation Evagrius makes concerns the frequent experience that an anger which is dormant during daily activities has a tendency to rise to the surface of consciousness when the mind is attempting to be disengaged during the time of prayer. "You opened the door to thoughts of evil done, and you troubled the mind at the time of prayer by constantly imagining the face of your enemy."[8] Stored anger, whether fully conscious or not, does more than disturb our prayer, it progressively erodes our quality of life. In Evagrius's view it leads to a serious decline in both mental and physical health.

> The most fierce passion is anger. In fact it is defined as a boiling and stirring up of wrath against one who has given injury—or is thought to have done so. It constantly irritates the soul and, above all, at the time of prayer it seizes the mind and flashes the picture of the offensive person before one's eyes. Then there comes a time when it persists longer, is transformed into indignation, stirs up alarming experiences at night. This is succeeded by a general debility of body, malnutrition with its attendant pallor and the illusion of being attacked by wild beasts.[9]

His conclusion is that "no one who loves true prayer and yet gives way to anger or resentment can be absolved from the imputation of madness."[10]

It is always tragic when a community is beset by criss-crossing currents of secret angers. Factions form, break up, and re-form. Discussion is deadlocked, without the cause of the obstruction becoming evident. There is a high level of irritability and resentment. Issues are never quite what they appear. Some people in monasteries have capacious memories, they can easily recall what was done to them or refused to them thirty or forty years later, no matter how minor the initial problem. They are never free of the burden of past hurts; they themselves are incapacitated, and if they are in a majority, the community easily becomes dysfunctional.

Not prolonging the time of rage involves the positive effort to put aside the memory of wrongs done and to live each day as it comes, without every choice being dictated by the past. This is to be free of the past. The key word is "free"; without such freedom we are living in a kind of slavery, bound by habitual reactions and forever reinforcing the animosity we feel toward others. Here, we are speaking of everyday grievance. Some wounds caused by traumatic events in the past cannot be so readily shrugged off. They need ongoing professional assistance, and it is the duty of those with the responsibility of pastoral care to make sure that such help is available.

For everyday hurts, Saint Benedict's advice is worth following: To accept that sometimes we will feel anger and sometimes, according to our temperament, that anger will be expressed outwardly. But whether we are the givers or receivers of an angry outburst, we should resolve to let the storm pass and then do our best to restore the relationship to its previous state, even if it means not insisting on our due rights.

24. Not to hold deceit in the heart.

Some years ago Paul Ekman wrote a book on lies, in which he detailed nine motives for lying.[11] Those he described were usually the result of circumstances in which people found themselves unwilling to speak the whole truth, and so they lied. There is, however, another situation that Ekman did not envisage. A person whose attitudes are dominated by self-love and who habitually regards others with cool indifference will not be living in a truth-filled relationship. Lies are woven into the very fabric of life. Uncharity is falsehood at the level of being; it is being untrue to our nature. It is the denial of our status as social animals and, in a community context, the denial that we are all members of a single body, with a single linked destiny. Falsehood at the level of being inevitably gives rise to falsehood at the level of thought and speech. These are not occasional or situational untruths but the normal expression of a broken relationship. This brokenness will often be manifested not only in issuing false press releases about ourselves but in negative comments about others, in backbiting, and detraction. That is probably why the Rule of the Master included an item against detraction in this group of sayings.

No doubt this is why Saint Benedict includes in his list of matters dealing with the interior dynamics of community relations this recommendation that we do not hold deceit in the heart. The verb "hold" (*tenere*) is an important indicator that he is thinking in terms of a long-lasting state, more or less consciously prolonged. A deceitful person is one whose interior reality does not correspond to what is publicly on display. This makes life very complicated. On the one hand, steps must be taken to ensure that what is concealed remains so. But then a substitute image must be projected to ensure that curiosity is not aroused and further questions asked. What often happens next is that this false self-presentation is modified according to the different persons at which it is aimed. So there are several different and sometimes incompatible narratives put into circulation. The deceiver then has to remember which parts of the whole belong to each story. He has to ensure that those who are familiar with one set of deceptions do not communicate with those familiar with something completely different. And this process has to continue for a lifetime. Meanwhile others are wondering which of the many self-presentations is real. The film *The Talented Mr. Ripley* illustrated well the spiraling complications that can follow on a single thoughtless untruth.

It is to be hoped that the deceit practiced in monasteries does not attain this magnitude, but the expectations of community life often serve to motivate people to want to appear better than they are. Benedict will speak about this tendency later in this chapter (RB 4.62). This is particularly strong in shame-based cultures, where "keeping face" is of the utmost importance to a person's self-esteem. To the extent that the inner reality does not correspond with what others see, there is a note of dissonance injected into all relationships and communications, even when no actual untruths are uttered. The transparency often noted in the lives of the saints is absent.

In shame-based cultures and wherever social harmony is a prime concern, difficulties are driven underground and issues are not faced. A conflict whose existence is denied cannot be resolved, and so it can continue unabated: it continues for a long time secretly influencing choices, subverting common initiatives, and undermining mutual trust. It is true that in a lifelong and intentional community not every outbreak of dissension needs to be immediately confronted and adjudicated, but long-lasting animosities hidden beneath surface politeness should be a point of concern. If the situation can somehow be addressed with due respect given to all parties, and delicately, so much the better.

In both social and individual deceit, there is a problem of language. Language is intended for communication. In a situation of deceit, however, language becomes a tool for mis-communication. Sentences can be crafted with words that may not be demonstrably false but yet are intended, if believed, to lead the hearer into an erroneous conclusion. More than that, language can become an instrument of concealment, so abstruse and obscure is it that the hearer is left bamboozled.

Simplicity in self-presentation makes for the possibility of community life where misunderstandings are minimized and where those conflicts which occur can be dealt with directly. Most deceitfulness is the product of a lack of humility; we try to protect ourselves from the consequences of what we are and what we have done. As men and women grow in self-honesty and openness to others, they will feel less need to hide behind a respectable façade and more comfortable in being seen as they are: what you see is what you get. This is part of the ideal that Saint Benedict places before us.

25. Not to give a false peace.

In a monastic community there are many symbolic gestures of unity and harmony, not the least of which is the regular celebration of the Eucharist. Saint Benedict speaks of this as a routine and orderly communal ritual (RB 63.4), and it is clear from the passage where he refers to giving the kiss of peace to guests that this is meant to be more than an empty gesture (RB 53.5). The words of Jesus in the Sermon on the Mount can often be a challenge in the context of difficult relationships: "And if you are offering your gift on the altar and you there remember that your brother [or sister] has something against you, leave your gift there, in front of the altar, and go away and first be reconciled to your brother [or sister] and then come and offer your gift" (Matt 5:23-24).

Instant reconciliation is certainly the ideal, but the evangelical admonition is challenging because not all interpersonal ruptures can be quickly healed by a single, unilateral gesture. This is especially true in the light of Saint Benedict's injunction "not to give a false peace." Are we to wait until death or dementia intervenes to break down the dividing walls?

Perhaps, as a preliminary, we can begin to put into practice some of the other recommendations of the Sermon on the Mount. For example: "Love your enemies and pray for those who persecute you" (Matt 5:44-45). Love here means less a feeling of affection than a benevolent act of the will that avoids wanting disaster to fall on enemies but wishes them well. As an expression of this chosen path of benevolence, we pray for those who give us a hard time. Thus Jesus himself prayed for his executioners (Luke 23:34), as did Stephen the protomartyr (Acts 7:60). It is perhaps worth remarking that it sometimes happens in monasteries that molehills quickly become mountains. We need to be on our guard against too easily labeling others whose activities are an impediment to our self-will as "enemies" and "persecutors." In a culture such as ours, claiming too eagerly the cachet of "victim" often masks our own complicity in the misfortunes that beset us. Praying for our "enemies," thinking well of them, and trying to see matters from their perspective may help us reduce our interior defensive rhetoric and be at peace.

Very often interpersonal estrangement comes from the inability of one or the other or both parties to accept the reality of the other person as different but not necessarily threatening. This means that we have to be sufficiently secure in ourselves that we do not feel constrained to keep weighing others in some subjective balance and finding them wanting. We cannot afford to be angry with anybody (Matt 5:22). If we want to work toward reconciliation, we must be prepared to leave aside the harsh condemnation of the other person that certainly contributes to the distance that has grown up between us. Here again there is good advice in the Sermon on the Mount:

> Do not judge so that you will not be judged. You yourself
> will be judged as you judge [others]. The measure you use to
> measure [others] will be the measure used for you. Why do
> you look at the speck in the eye of your brother [or sister]
> and not perceive the plank in your own eye? How can you
> say to your brother [or sister], "Let me remove the speck
> from your eye," when, behold, there is a plank in your own
> eye. Hypocrite! First take the plank from your own eye and
> then you will see clearly to remove the speck from the eye
> of your brother [or sister]. (Matt 7:1-5)

Even when we pray for those who trouble us and try to
understand them, there may still remain some blockage to the
restoration of good relationships and, probably, some residual
resentment on our part because of the suffering we have endured. And so humility and patience are needed, as Saint Benedict teaches in the fourth step of humility (RB 7.35-43): "[The
monk] who is genuinely humble is patient, judging himself to
be worthy of whatever he suffers, despising no one, judging no
one, condemning no one."[12] The practice of endurance is, as the
New Testament often reminds us, essential for the building of
character (Rom 5:3-4; Jas 1:2-3; 1 Pet 1:5-7). Nonresistance
to evil and the redemptive role of pain are somehow at the
heart of the Christian message. "But I say to you, do not resist
an evil person. When someone slaps you on the right cheek,
turn the other [cheek] also" (Matt 5:39). We will not have to
suffer continually, but like everyone else, the Christian will
experience times of mental, emotional, and physical suffering.
With the right attitude, these trials can be purifying, and so
they intensify our spiritual life, though at considerable cost.
The point of the Gospel message is that we consent to bear this
suffering, to absorb its venom, as it were, without reciprocating
or compensating. As Saint Paul says, we make up in our flesh
what is lacking in the sufferings of Christ (Col 1:24).

We all live under the prospect of God's ultimate judgment, even though this is a truth that we ponder only reluc-

tantly. We may be able to deceive ourselves and others about the rights and wrongs of a particular situation, but before the judgment seat everything will be naked and exposed (Heb 4:13): no equivocation, no obfuscation, no playing to presumed prejudice. In view of this, we need to live always with a healthy dose of skepticism concerning our total blamelessness and so to be prepared to take some responsibility when interpersonal conflicts arise and, as far as possible, be willing to settle our differences before things go beyond repair (Matt 6:25). At least in our own minds, we need to stop blaming the other person and focus more on ourselves and the things that we can do to improve the situation. Even though we cannot achieve perfect peace, we may be able to work toward a cease-fire—at least from our side of the trenches.

To avoid giving a false greeting of peace, we need to use the ritual as an invitation to examine our conscience. Jesus did not refer to the obstacle as a grievance that we have against someone but as a grievance that somebody else has against us. This means that we need to go beyond our own feelings of inner tranquility to see whether by our actions or omissions we have been the cause of another's harm or hurt. If our conscience reveals something, we need to make haste to correct it. The greeting of peace is potentially a moment of conversion and new life, if we are alert to its implications—without necessarily interrupting the celebration of the Eucharist.

26. Not to abandon charity.

The language in this admonition is striking. There are many facile injunctions in Christian tradition encouraging us to practice love. This one is different. It seems to me that there is a note of desperation in it, as though continuing in charity were under threat. I can think of several examples where this might be the case: a superior confronted with a sociopathic member of the community, a cantor having to cope with a recalcitrant choir, formators squirming under the dire projections and rejections of those in their care. How is it possible to continue loving those whose every effort seems directed to making one's life as miserable as possible?

Perhaps we do a disservice in hinting that love is always delightful. Sometimes, certainly, love is a joy and a consolation. At other times a heroic struggle is required to ensure that we do not abandon charity either by giving way to a storm of anger or by withdrawing into an arctic silence. In such situations we hold on to charity by our fingernails, as it were. Consider another example. Love can be so intense that it produces an overwhelming sadness when the loved one is absent or estranged; the illness and death of one whom we love afflict us as though it were our own. When one who is dear engages in destructive behavior, we are strongly conflicted. In all these cases when our love for one person is troubled, it becomes a little harder to continue going out to others in love. We tend to remain within ourselves, cradling our woundedness. Concentrating exclusively on ourselves becomes one avenue by which we abandon love.

The fact that maintaining love sometimes requires considerable effort tells us something about the nature of love. It is, first and foremost, an act of the will. Impaired as our human nature is, it is not guaranteed that every act of the will is accompanied by a corresponding feeling of warmth and affection. Nor is it always certain that the actions that love dictates will always be pleasant to perform and welcome to the recipient. There is such a reality as "tough love," a love which countenances short-term hostility in order to achieve long-term and enduring benefits. If this were not so, none of us would ever have been brought to the dentist! Love is an act of the faculty of will. It goes beyond the sensory data provided by present experience and draws on other sources in forming its judgment. Because of this, a loving act can sometimes seem hostile if it is not considered in the context of past and future.

When we are commanded to love, we are commanded to be concerned and active in bringing about the total welfare of another person. We are not told to become slaves to their whims or their unreasonable demands.[13] This is obvious in the case of rearing children, but the situation sometimes arises with adults as well. We are to give them honor and respect, as has been discussed earlier; we are to help them as we can when they are in difficulty; we are to be proactive in seeking reconciliation. We are not to become complicit in their self-destruction. Our efforts may or may not lead quickly to the warmth of friendship, but they are expressions of love. We are restraining our impulses or diminishing our exercise of self-will to give them room to breathe and grow. This is love of a very disinterested kind. And because it is gratuitous and there is no immediate reward for us, it is not surprising that when our efforts are rejected or not appreciated we are hurt. We are tempted to abandon love. Here as elsewhere the Benedictine virtue of stability comes into play. Love that is subject to vicissitude is a very weak form of love. Real love is "as strong as death . . . many waters cannot extinguish it, nor floods sweep it away" (Song 8:6-7).

The RSV translation of the Bible rendered the Hebrew term *hesed* as "steadfast love," and our pale imitation of God's covenant fidelity to his people seems to be what is intended here. We remain committed to the welfare and the salvation of brothers and sisters even when they are against us and want to accept nothing from us. This is perhaps indicated by the sentence in the Rule of the Master that Saint Benedict omitted: "To keep faith with the brother" (RM 3.28). Genuine love is always tested; it is only through many difficulties and reversals of fortune that it attains to profound communion—if it ever does in this life.

Saint Aelred of Rievaulx spoke about an *affectus officialis*.[14] This is the kind of attachment that grows up between the giver and receiver of good offices. A person appointed as superior may notice a surge in pastoral solicitude toward people previously outside the scope of affection. Those who care for the sick sometimes develop a great love for those in their care. Often, but not always, this warmth is reciprocated. This is an example of how practical love leads to a real interior affection for the other person. In other words, effective charity lays the foundation for affective charity. We cannot always generate feelings of love for another person at the snap of a finger, but by consistently being courteous, cooperative, and kind, our own prejudices are slowly neutralized, and it becomes possible for a fuller expression of love to emerge.

It is crucial that love is always grounded in truth; it cannot be a pretense. Love must be sincere. Saint Paul claims that his love for the Corinthians possessed this quality (2 Cor 6:6). Genuine love cannot be manufactured, and it cannot be effectively counterfeited. Love comes from a certain integrity of disposition on the part of the lover who is spontaneously drawn to the good qualities perceived in the beloved. It is a common experience that these good qualities are not necessarily noticed at a first meeting: sometimes there is a delay while prejudices and contrary impressions are neutralized. We love because we recognize the good in another person. If there is no love, it is because of a failure or blockage in us; our lack of love says something about us and nothing about the other person. All that exists has been created by God and is good. In the words of the Scholastic philosophers, goodness and being are coextensive. If the goodness of another is not apparent to us the problem is ours, not theirs.

Christian love transcends the sphere of the sentimental. Its roots are sunk deep in the soil of our inmost being. It flourishes when the heart is pure and the eye is simple. It languishes to the extent that we suffer from inward division and our lives are buffeted by the movements of self-will and private angers. For many of us, the result is that our love is selective and exclusive. We do love, but that love is confined to those who love us and who tolerate our imperfection. We abandon love when we exclude from our affection those who are different and those who seem not to love us. In this case, because love is indivisible, even our love for others is in danger of becoming a form of self-love, a behavior that prevents rather than promotes personal growth. We abandon love when we begin placing limits on it by building boundary walls that include some people and banish others from our concern.

The simple precept of not abandoning love is a lifelong program that requires a progressive suppression of the movements of self-will and calls us to the practice of a charity without frontiers, such as Jesus taught and practiced.

27-28

Not to take an oath in case one breaks it. To bring forth truth from the heart and from the mouth.

These two admonitions concern the truthfulness of relationships between persons. Saint Benedict recommends that mutual openness is such that, on the one hand, strong asseveration is not required and, on the other, communication has a direct route from the heart to the mouth and thence to the other person.

27. Not to take an oath in case one breaks it.

This precept simply echoes the words of Jesus: "I say to you, take no oath whatsoever. . . . But let your word be 'Yes. Yes.' and 'No. No.'; anything beyond this is from the Evil One" (Matt 5:34-37; see Jas 5:12). The Rule of the Master has "not to love to take an oath" (RM 3.32), which seems to indicate a degree of flippancy in being ready to take an oath too readily; Saint Benedict omits this word. The inclusion of the adverb *forte* in the formulation of this sentence suggests that there is something unintended or accidental about the perjury. It is not that the person taking the oath deliberately swears to falsehood but, rather, a case in which what has been affirmed under oath turns out not to have been the whole truth. In this case Saint Benedict thinks it inappropriate that God has been called as witness to even a partial falsehood. He would say that it is better not to take an oath at all than to risk jeopardizing the honor of God.

More generally, this recommendation could be seen as advice to avoid the kind of strong statement that has the potential to intimidate others. The common life of those who form a monastic community lasts for a lifetime. Remaining fully participatory in community life over such a long period calls for a certain sensitivity in mutual relationships, leaving room for others to be different, to hold different opinions, and to do things differently. This often involves softening the focus of personal views and learning to be tactful and respectful in their expression. Opinionated bombast is not unknown in monasteries, but it rarely serves a useful purpose. In this context it is worth recalling Saint Benedict's teaching in his chapter about humility: "If a monk speaks, let him speak gently and without laughter, with gravity, and using few and reasonable words. And let his voice be not loud" (RB 7.60).

"An oath confirms [what has been said] and puts an end to all contrary argument" (Heb 6:16). The taking of an oath and other boisterous means intended to support and add emphasis to a statement are admissions that a simple recital is insufficient and its truth not self-evident. As external buttresses, they tend to weaken the internal credibility of what is said, especially when "the lady doth protest too much, methinks." A community held together by strong bonds of mutual trust is able to communicate with a directness in which all who speak feel that they are heard with respect. Strong and overbearing language undermines the common confidence that, because all persons are held in honor, their views are to be heard respectfully.

Richard Sennett believes that we ought to learn or re-learn the art of conversation in the subjunctive mood. By this he means interacting less assertively, offering our views in a way that leaves listeners at liberty, and not demanding their instant compliance. Subjunctive statements are peppered with such words as "possibly," "probably," "maybe," and "perhaps." They prepare a soft landing for whatever views we are expressing:

> When I became a social researcher, the subjunctive mood loomed larger for me in thinking about human relations. . . . The social engine is oiled when people do not behave too emphatically. . . . The subjunctive mood is most at home in the dialogical domain, the world of talk which makes an open social space, where discussion can take an unforeseen direction. . . . By practising indirection, speaking to one another in the subjunctive mood, we can experience a certain kind of sociable pleasure: being with other people, focusing on and learning about them, without forcing ourselves into the mould of being like them.[1]

Another aspect of declining to swear oaths comes to mind. In speaking about antisocial behavior in monastic communities, one of the verbs Saint Aelred uses is *litigare*: to litigate, to make an issue of something. This is more than complaining or murmuring. "Litigation" (in this informal sense) implies a process of building a case for or against a particular course of action, combining incidents and securing witness in order to advocate a contrary policy. Such a campaign does not, of course, involve the swearing of oaths but it certainly goes beyond ordinary grumbling.

The prohibition of taking oaths has a possible source in the writings of Saint Ambrose.[2] Monks will not often be called upon to take oaths so, in one sense, this item seems irrelevant in the context of monastic life. If we try to go deeper, however, we may well find that the concerns underlying this recommendation are real and are worth considering as we examine our lives to ensure that they conform as fully as possible to the teaching of the Gospel.

28. To bring forth truth from the heart and from the mouth.

It is possible to see in this admonition no more than a warning against lying, such as we find in Ephesians 4:25: "Therefore, put aside all falsehood and let everyone speak truth to their neighbor." There is, however, much more than that to be found in it. This recommendation is not negative but positive. Saint Benedict is telling us not to allow the truth that is implanted in the soil of the heart to remain hidden but actively to allow it to come to the surface whereby it may become accessible to others. Paul Claudel wrote somewhere that the role of faith was to evangelize all our faculties. Faith is a gift that is sown in the depths of our being, but it is meant to grow and expand. It touches our feelings so that we have an experience of faith, without there being much in the way of exterior stimulus. It floods our intellect, bringing with it convictions about unseen realities, as the author of the Epistle to the Hebrews writes (Heb 11:1). Faith animates our will and so governs our choices both in the things that we do and in what we endure. A history of faith-inspired choices forms our character and produces an outward radiance of holiness that is perceptible to those with eyes to see. Faith is transformative not only of ourselves but also of those around us, just as the Virgin Mary's faith bore fruit not only for herself but also for all our human race. This is the vista conjured up by the hymn for the office of Terce: our whole humanity unites in giving expression to inward charity; by our faith-filled way of living we not only sing praise to God but also stir our neighbor to greater fervor.

Os, lingua, mens, sensus, vigor	Mouth, tongue, mind, sense, strength
Confessionem personent,	Let them sound forth praise;
Flamescat igne charitas,	Let Charity burst into fire and flame
Accendat ardor proximos.	Its heat setting neighbors alight.

In the context of the Second Vatican Council, when a defense of the contemplative life was being sought, appeal was made to the role of contemplatives as corroborating witnesses to the more visible forms of evangelization. Many felt uneasy about this approach, which seemed to place them on a self-conscious pedestal, crying out, "Look at me." The giving of Christian witness is not an easy concept to understand or to practice, especially in the light of the Sermon on the Mount's injunction to perform our good works in secret (Matt 6:1-18). But, in the same sermon, Jesus also said:

> You are the salt of the earth. If salt loses its savor, how can it be seasoned? It is good for nothing but to be thrown out and walked over by people. You are the light of the world. A city built on top of a mountain cannot be hidden. People do not light a lamp and then put it under a measure, but they put it on a lampstand and it shines forth for all who are in the house. So, let your light shine before people so that they may see your fine works and glorify your Father in heaven. (Matt 5:13-16)

We are all obliged to use the graces that we have been given, as the parable of the talents (Matt 25:14-30) reminds us. The spiritual gifts that we have received are bestowed not for our private enjoyment but for the enrichment of all.

"What is prohibited is not the visibility of [good] works, but a vain intention in doing them."[3] Doing obvious good need not involve trumpeting our virtue. Sometimes it means sacrificing our humility in order to provide a benefit for a neighbor. It is, furthermore, a matter of becoming and being what God has intended us to be, driven more by inner imperatives than by the desire to accomplish the particular external outcome of gaining public esteem. The work of asceticism is designed to produce over the years a transparency by which our inner qualities become perceptible to others, while often remaining invisible to ourselves. It becomes increasingly obvious as the years pass that one of our prime responsibilities to the other members of our community is the giving of good example. It is a case not of flashing our virtues around but simply of maintaining our steady fidelity to conscience and to the ordinary exercises by which the common life is sustained: liturgy, prayer, common work, sociability, and the other staples of cenobitic existence.

The obligation to let our particular light shine goes against a common but erroneous interpretation of humility. True humility involves recognizing our gifts as gifts and not as self-generated assets. To deny our giftedness is to cast doubt on the bounty of its giver. Powered by the truth that genuine humility embodies, we may be drawn into projects and activities that rely more on the grace of God than on any sense of native ability. Maybe, like some of the prophets of the Old Testament, we squirm under the burdens which God's gifts bring and try to evade them. But the obligation of fidelity to God's creative plan, embedded in our being, remains. A gift is not only an endowment; it is also a summons, a call to action. It may well be that the salvation or well-being of others depends on our using the talents that have been given to us. Unfortunately, unless the task is of our own choosing, often we prefer to remain inert. We resist the call and find something else to do instead. This is not humility; it is sloth.

The outshining of our light often has an element of the paradoxical about it. Sometimes the things we do badly and are a source of unease to our ego are precisely the channels by which God chooses to bring others to a more abundant life. How many times have I been delighted when people tell me they were greatly moved by a sermon and, then, how dismayed when they explain why they were graced, and I realize that what they heard was not what I said or what I intended to say but what they needed to hear. "God writes straight on crooked lines." Even though I did not generate the inspiration, if I had not offered my clunky considerations, the Holy Spirit would have had nothing on which to build the moment of grace and the other person would have been left impoverished.

A famous quotation, often wrongly attributed to Nelson Mandela, speaks to this point. It was first published by Marianne Williamson two years before Mandela's inauguration as president of South Africa:

> Our deepest fear is not that we are inadequate. Our deepest fear is that we are powerful beyond measure. It is our light, not our darkness that most frightens us. We ask ourselves, Who am I to be brilliant, gorgeous, talented, fabulous? Actually, who are you *not* to be? You are a child of God. Your playing small does not serve the world. There is nothing enlightened about shrinking so that other people won't feel insecure around you. We are all meant to shine, as children do. We were born to make manifest the glory of God that is within us. It's not just in some of us; it's in everyone. And as we let our own light shine, we unconsciously give other people permission to do the same. As we are liberated from our own fear, our presence automatically liberates others.[4]

It takes only a moment's reflection to reveal that letting our light shine forth requires a large measure of humility. It means ignoring the inner voice that tells us we are not good enough. We have to be willing to act upon the Spirit's gift of *parresia*, or freedom and boldness in speech, about which the New Testament often speaks. By God's gift we are free to be ourselves. It is to everyone's benefit that we are perceived as what we are, not more, not less. And that is why it is good to bring forth truth from the heart and from the mouth and, bashful though we be, to let our life speak.

29-33

Not to return evil for evil. To do no injury, but
to endure patiently injury done to oneself. To
love enemies. Not to return curses to those who
curse but rather to bless. To endure persecution
for righteousness.

These verses concern our dealing with the malevolent behavior of others. This is more than a question of chronic animosity or silent opposition. It is active hostility. Anyone who
thinks we can sail through forty years or so of monastic life
without encountering such antagonism seems not to have read
Saint Benedict's seventh chapter. In his discussion of the fourth
step of humility, Benedict recommends patience in difficult
situations such as the following: hard things (35), unfavorable
things (35, 38), undeserved injuries (35, 42), suffering (38),
testing (40), examination by fire (40), being led into a trap
(40), tribulations (40), having people over one's head (41),
adversity (42), being struck on the cheek (42), having one's
coat stolen (42), forced to walk a mile (42), false brethren (43),
persecution (43), and being cursed (43). There is no need to
be unedified or disheartened by this list: misunderstandings
and conflicts can occur between good people, as happened in
New Testament times between Peter and Paul. If we live long
enough, we can be sure that we will experience this.

In such situations Saint Benedict is recommending patient
endurance of the negativity, not allowing ourselves to be trig-

gered into reciprocating the injuries done, maintaining our inner peace, being prepared to absorb some of the malice directed at us in the hope of neutralizing its poison—though at considerable cost to ourselves. This is no more than Gospel teaching put into practice (see 1 Pet 3:8-9). We do not want bad things to happen to us, but when they do, they can be the occasion of great spiritual profit. They can also be occasions for growth in self-knowledge; we are forced to admit into consciousness those unwelcome truths about ourselves which good times keep at bay. As Saint Aelred says: "Adversity demonstrates whether we are what we appear to be."[1]

In our achievement-oriented society, we tend to assess the character of persons by what they do successfully. Such a judgment can be very shallow, since we do not know their motivations and intentions; indeed, they themselves may not be fully aware of them. Interior dispositions determine the moral quality of behavior; external outcomes may be irrelevant in certain circumstances. A far better way of judging character is to note how people operate in difficult times. When we are suffering, the pain we experience seizes much of our attention. It becomes difficult to give our full attention to our work, to other people, to anything beyond our immediate hurt. The ability to go beyond or beneath the suffering, to remain faithful to our commitments and dedicated to the goal we have set before us takes courage and determination, but it also is indicative of character. The choices we make in less-than-optimal situations are far more significant than those into which we slip without much effort.

29. Not to return evil for evil.

In our own minds, we rarely admit to being the initiator of a quarrel or the cause of the souring of a relationship. Many currents of thought in contemporary society encourage us to see ourselves as victims of forces outside ourselves and, particularly, of the actions of other people. We find in our victimhood a near-universal source of exculpation. It becomes easy for me to believe that because I have suffered at the hands of others, nothing I do can outweigh the wrongs that have been inflicted on me. In this manner, conscience is disabled and moral considerations cease to be a component in the making of choices. To be a victim is to have a lifelong "Get Out of Jail Free" card. Even the most blatant act of bitter zeal is justified, in my own mind, by what I have suffered. All that I am doing is redressing the balance. As a victim, any attack I make, even a preemptive attack, is always deemed by me to be an act either of self-defense or of just retribution. If I find myself in this space, I need to stop and review the situation more objectively, perhaps with the help of a true friend. The fact that life has been hard and unfair to me is no excuse for my sense that I am obliged to make it equally hard and unfair for others.

Returning evil for evil may not always be as simple as "an eye for an eye and a tooth for a tooth." Aggression is often directed at substitute targets. For example, if I have been wounded in some way by parents in the process of growing up, I may transfer the resentment I feel onto any others who, years later, have a quasi-parental role in my life. Religious superiors and formators know all about this phenomenon. When I feel bad without cause, it is easier to find culprits in my immediate neighborhood than to retrieve authentic memories of the real origins of my distress, which long ago were driven underground, or to find some resolution through negotiation with persons who are long dead.

To live in such a way that everyday actions are determined by everyday situations and not by unknown events of the past, I need to prime my conscience to exercise its functions in the choices I make, operating rationally by weighing the elements of the situation and not being impelled toward a particular option by the way I feel. This means that I often have to let go of resentments and learn to act in the kind of freedom about which Jesus spoke and the martyrs practiced.

30. To do no injury, but to endure patiently injury done to oneself.

The monk is meant to be a gentle, nonviolent person who lives peaceably with his brethren in an environment separated from the various forms of violence which afflict ambient society. It is true that there have been warrior monks in history, but these are the exceptions. In general, especially when they have kept themselves at a distance from the worst features of the clerical caste, authentic monks are perceived as sympathetic men, gentle in their dealings with others and sobered in their judgment by their depth of self-knowledge. Ideally, monasteries are experienced as safe places, where no harm will befall those who enter their gates.

To be a nonviolent person it is essential to be able to bear injuries done to oneself without the desire for retaliation. Saint Benedict thus returns to the theme of patient endurance which he saw as our principal means of identifying with Christ—now in his suffering but in the future in his glory (RB Prol 50). Unless we are able to bear equably the rough-and-tumble of human community, we will never find peace within ourselves and we will be constantly driven to find cause for complaint in the conduct of others.

Buddhists extend the principle of nonviolence beyond the human sphere to include all sentient beings, and we may be aware also of stories of Christian saints who developed good relations with animals and birds. In some cases there is a kind of mystic experience of identification with all that exists. This sense of solidarity with the whole of God's creation is a good context in which to develop the kind of attitude to life that would rather endure injuries than inflict them on others. One who approaches life with this attitude is content to bear hardship as part of the price of being human. Such a person is far less likely to repay others for the pain of which they are perceived to be the cause. Patient endurance is not the denial of the presence of evil in our world but the willingness to absorb part of that evil as a means of reducing the total level of toxicity.

31. To love enemies.

The question of loving enemies is one that haunts many fervent Christians. How can I love someone who has hurt me in the past and still regards me with a malevolent eye? The answer is simple: with great difficulty. There are, however, several lines of thought which can help me to live less conditioned by wounded feelings and more open to the eventual possibility of reconciliation. The Rule of the Master has an additional phrase that Saint Benedict dropped: "To love enemies more than friends" (RM 3.36). This is to go beyond even the teaching of the Sermon on the Mount and demands a degree of heroism that few are likely to attain.

In the first instance, it is worth recalling that to hate enemies or to be coldly indifferent to them usually does not do them much harm: if the common courtesies are observed, they may be unaware of the resentment roiling within me. But any withholding of love is damaging to myself. Love is indivisible. A single, long-term antipathy can seriously impair any other love that I experience, crippling its natural tendency to go beyond self and rendering it less effective in countering its innate egocentric tendencies. It may well be that I feel my life is more interesting if I am obsessed with a few, frequently vented animosities, but this is not so. My friends are bored by my unending tirades, and to others I am likely to become a laughingstock. The real damage, however, is to myself. I need to move on and get on with my life. There is no point in conducting a lifelong courtroom drama in my own imagination, seeking vindication and revenge. I need to draw a line under the past, learn from it what I can, and seek to build a better future. Love is often a matter of letting go.

Love is also letting be. In a positive sense, this means doing all we can so that other persons may become everything of which they are innately capable. But there is a complementary aspect which involves allowing them to be what they are without desiring or hoping that they might change into something that meets with our approval. If a relationship is bad, it is unrealistic to hope that it may be improved by the other person doing something about it. To love my enemies means accepting that coexistence with them is inevitable and that nothing is going to change soon or without effort. If I want things to get better, I have to try to see what I can do, how I can change my behavior and my thinking to eliminate whatever I contribute to the unhappy situation. Ongoing and unilateral benevolence is the only way things are going to get better.

Love sometimes calls us to accept a measure of wholesome self-doubt. Indeed, for many people it is worthwhile to pray earnestly for the grace of self-doubt. Too often we are far too sure of ourselves, and we grant to our slightest opinions a measure of certainty they do not merit. Frequently voiced complaints have a tendency to become more firmly entrenched with each repetition. Every time I tell my story, it comes packaged in an interpretive framework crafted according to the particular meaning I wish the narrative to convey today. I cast it in terms that I believe will convince my hearers. Very soon the interpretation begins to color the details, and whatever residue of truth the story contains becomes enmeshed with later nuances and additions. I may not necessarily be aware of what is happening. The human memory is not simply an inert storehouse of experiences that can be recalled with objective accuracy at a later date. It is subject to a constructive function in the process of recall. As far back as 1932 Frederic Bartlett argued that "we make sense of past and present reality by selectively picking up the most salient features of available information which we then fill out with plausible interpretive additions which best fit our interests and schemas."[2] If my relationship with another person is determined by memories I have of wrongs done to me, it is prudent to verify whether these are substantially true memories or whether they have become predominantly subjective constructs. If I have a care for the healing of the relationship, I need to seek counsel. This means I have to be prepared to open my memories to alternative interpretations and perhaps to allow myself to be led to the point of uttering those rarely spoken words, "I was wrong." It is obvious that the role of the person with whom I take counsel is not to reinforce my version of events but to help me to see its limitations and perhaps its distortions. If I really want to love those whom I perceive to be my enemies, then I have to verify that my perceptions are not skewed by other elements in my personal history.

The most potent medicine of all for bad situations is, as Saint Benedict teaches, the prayer of intercession (RB 28.4). This is more than a quick glance heavenward in the hope of an instant resolution. Often what is involved is a long and sometimes grueling contest with God—if we may use this image. The Gospel precept of love of enemies contradicts both our natural instincts and the way we have been formed by society. To enter into such an elevated sphere requires a radical change in our perceptual horizons. If I am to love my enemies and sincerely pray for their welfare, I need to undergo a personal conversion. Such a transition does not usually occur without a great deal of resistance. Previously, I was thinking that what had to change was the relationship.

Now I discover that I am the one who must change, and that this change will involve corners of my life that I never thought were connected to the present difficulty. The focus has shifted from the enemy to me, and very soon I find myself praying predominantly for the grace of my own conversion.

32. Not to return curses to those who curse but rather to bless.

Now Saint Benedict turns his attention to curses, a practice not common in contemporary Western society. A curse is the solemn expression of a wish that bad things might happen to another person. Because we undervalue the potency of words, being cursed may seem to be the least of our troubles. In the ancient world, however, cursing was a much more serious business. To put the evil eye on people was to set a blight over their entire life, depending on the potency of the one uttering the curse. For this to happen, the recipient of the curse had to believe in its efficacy. Even today, in those cultures where witch doctors still hold sway, a person who is cursed may well sink into irreversible decline.

Our mode of operation may be milder and less ritualized than what we see in primitive cultures, but it is equally malicious. In the monastic microcosm, we can curse people through whispered calumny, detraction, and mockery; by blacklisting them; by seeking to isolate them; by frustrating their initiatives; and through many other tactics deliberately designed to make others think badly of them and to reduce their vitality and *joie de vivre*. Persons thus cursed may not know who is the origin of their social exclusion but find themselves forced to live in an atmosphere of unarticulated social disgrace that inexorably erodes their self-esteem. I do not know why this happens or why those with pastoral responsibility do not intervene. Nor do I know how persons caught in such a situation can call down blessings on those that have cursed them, since responsibility for this sad state is collective rather than assignable to a particular person. Perhaps all they can do is to "bless God and not murmur" (RB 40.8).

This present precept reflects Luke 6:28, Romans 12:14, and 1 Peter 3:9 where we are taught to meet a curse with a blessing. It is more than advice to endure being cursed, allowing abuse to rain down upon us like a stone drenched by a storm; we are called to act positively and to respond to the curse with a blessing. This injunction continues Saint Benedict's insistence that, if we are taking our Christian discipleship seriously, we are to see the impossible commandments of the Sermon on the Mount as livable, not by our own efforts, of course, but as fruits of God's grace by which all things become possible.

33. To endure persecution for righteousness.

Five times, in different ways, Saint Benedict repeats the New Testament message of endurance and nonretaliation. This should quickly dispel any notion that monastic life leads to eternal life by any other way but one that is hard, rough, and narrow. It is a lesson that most of us do not want to learn. We would prefer to go to God by pleasant pathways, and we are shocked when we discover that this is not possible. When we begin to experience difficulties and have to struggle to stay afloat, there is a real danger that we will lose our nerve and run away, looking for some easier route. The grim truth is that hard times are often, if not the sign of progress being made, at least the opportunity for some solid progress to occur.

But are there persecutions to be endured in a monastery? To answer this question we need look no further than monastic history. Monasteries, like any other institutions that have lasted many centuries, pass through periods of decline, especially when ambient society and the church itself are in periods of transition. Often enough this diminishment in monastic observance is not dramatic; it is simply a gradual loss of focus and an unchallenged enthusiasm to mitigate the Rule. The latent vigor of tradition reasserts itself, however, to prompt certain individuals to seek a change in direction. It is at least arguable that the best moments in monastic history have been periods of reform, marked simultaneously by a zeal for the original sources of inspiration and a close attention to "the signs of the times."

In most cases reform does not come easily, even when it is promoted by wise and charismatic persons. There is always resistance. Any who propose a tightening of observance will quickly experience a reactive backlash from those who want things to continue comfortably as they are. This reluctance has often resulted in harsh treatment of would-be reformers not only by the local communities but also by higher ecclesiastical authorities. The prevailing notion has often been that the highest good of a corporate body is for it to continue exactly as it is; there seems to be an inbuilt institutional immunity to any call to a higher level of fidelity.

Of course, not all self-styled reformers embody the essential charism of a particular group, but even so, they need to be taken seriously. Their call for change is the result of a perception that something is wrong with the corporate body. Their way of dealing with this perception is advocacy. Others who are conscious of the same malaise may choose to respond to this feeling in different and less obvious ways. A maverick can play a prophetic role in making visible the need for change, even when the particular solutions are not feasible. A community that welcomes such prophets is less likely to have blind spots that can lead to decline in the quality of the common life. We need to listen to people even when we do not want to hear what they have to say, because sometimes there is a layer of truth beneath the surface.

The beatitude promised to the persecuted was reserved for those who suffer persecution for the sake of righteousness (Matt 5:10). In Mark's gospel, in the same breath that he promises his disciples a hundredfold reward, Jesus warns that it will come along with persecutions (Mark 10:30). Ordinary common sense warns us to be careful about believing that all persecution is because of righteousness or wholehearted dedication to discipleship. Often it is the result of our own stupidity, insensitivity, and imprudence. In such cases we deserve the opprobrium that is heaped upon us. Saint Benedict is aware of this. To qualify for the happiness Jesus promised, it has to be that we are treated harshly precisely because of our fidelity to grace, to our vows, to the monastic tradition, and not because of some stubborn pigheaded plans of our own.

This same distinction with regard to carrying Christ's cross was made by Dietrich Bonhoeffer. We should not trivialize the cross by applying its name and function to every minor reversal of everyday life. The cross is not a minor inconvenience; it sears the soul. Because Christian discipleship is inherently cross-oriented, it will lead us inexorably to rejection and shame as it draws us into closer communion with Christ. There is no byway which we can take to avoid arriving at this point, though the intensity of the experience will not be the same for everyone.

> To endure the cross is not a tragedy; it is the suffering which is the fruit of an exclusive allegiance to Jesus Christ. When it comes it is not an accident, but a necessity. It is not the sort of suffering which is inseparable from this mortal life, but the suffering which is an essential part of the specifically Christian life. It is not suffering *per se* but suffering-and-rejection, and not rejection for any cause or conviction of our own, but rejection for the sake of Christ. If our Christianity has ceased to be serious about discipleship, if we have watered down the gospel into emotional uplift which makes

no costly demands and which fails to distinguish between natural and Christian existence, then we cannot help regarding the cross as an ordinary everyday calamity, as one of the trials and tribulations of life. We have then forgotten that the cross means rejection and shame as well as suffering. . . . The cross means sharing the suffering of Christ to the last and to the fullest. Only a man thus totally committed in discipleship can experience the meaning of the cross. . . . Each must endure his allotted share of suffering and rejection. But each has a different share: some God deems worthy of the highest form of suffering, and gives them the grace of martyrdom, while others he does not allow to be tempted above that [which] they are able to bear. But it is one and the same cross in every case.[3]

In such a situation, there is a great sense of loneliness; the temptation is to feel that God has abandoned us and that there is no hope for the future. The pain that is experienced narrows one's horizons, and it becomes difficult to judge matters in perspective or within a broader context. This concentration on self intensifies the pain. In the little book written in the final stages of his life, after enduring a false and public accusation of sexual misconduct and two bouts of cancer, Cardinal Joseph Bernardin describes this aspect of carrying Christ's cross:

The essential mystery of the cross is that it gives rise to a certain kind of loneliness, an inability to see clearly how things are unfolding, an inability to see that, ultimately, all things will work for our good, and that we are, indeed, not alone.[4]

This is a standard of discipleship from which most of us fall short and for which, to be honest, we have little desire. The inclusion of this item in Saint Benedict's list illustrates the idea that the monastic vocation is similar to that of the martyrs, even when it does not involve the shedding of blood.

The point about carrying Christ's cross or being the victim of persecution for righteousness is that this fate is not a self-chosen option. Christ himself instructed us, "If they persecute you in this city, flee to another one" (Matt 10:23). "To flee persecution is not the fault of the one who flees, but of the one who persecutes."[5] Enduring persecution, whether it be minor or massive, is something to which we are called by circumstances—even in a monastery—with the permission of our all-loving Father. "Everything which is brought upon us by God, whether in the present it seems sad or joyful, is designed by a most loving Father and the most kind Physician for our welfare."[6] We do not seek trouble, we invest reasonable efforts in minimizing its power to harm us, but we cannot escape what is unavoidable. Since we cannot evade trouble by fleeing externally, we must consider the possibility of moving to an inner space: going deeper into our own hearts and trying to find there a place of refuge and peace. But we must be forewarned. In times of crisis, prayer is not always found easily. It is true that our own expressions of pain readily pour forth, but often we do not have the consolation of feeling that our prayer has been heard or that God is coming to our aid. Often enough there is considerable delay. The immediacy of God's response to the prayer of the afflicted, about which the psalms so often wax lyrical, is concealed from us. Thus, to the external troubles is added an interior crisis of faith and hope. And much distress.

34

Not to be proud.

The injunction to avoid pride seems lost in its present location, all alone between those recommendations that deal with patient endurance and those touching on fairly trivial biological failings. Given the importance placed on pride by the great masters of monastic spirituality, one would have thought that it would have been given more emphasis and perhaps more development. Maybe Saint Benedict is simply thinking of the social forms of pride—haughtiness, arrogance, and pomposity—rather than its more serious manifestation as rebellion and rejection of God. Some support for this interpretation can be found in the chapter on the cellarer, where he lists the vices the officeholder should avoid. Among other things, he says that such a person should be "sober, not a big eater, and not haughty [*elatus*]" (RB 31.1). It may well be that behavioral expressions of pride are indicative of a serious inner problem, but they could also be simply a learned pattern of action that is no more than a sign that some progress is yet to be made before perfection is attained.

Pride was regarded as the sin of the fallen angels and the most serious of all human crimes. In its fullest expression, pride was understood as an act of rebellion against God, a rejection of God, which not only creates a fundamental dissonance between the human being and the Creator but also infiltrates everyday behavior and poisons it. Pride makes the monk desire to be, and believe that he already is, autonomous and can live his life independent of God. According to Evagrius of Pontus, it "induces the monk to deny that God is his helper and to consider that he himself is the cause of virtuous actions."[1]

Although pride may well be the most fundamental of all the vices and operate secretly behind their more visible facades, its most dramatic manifestations appear only at the end of a long period of decline. The youthful Bernard of Clairvaux gave a humorous but serious exposition of the downward steps of pride to complement Saint Benedict's upward steps of humility. After a long decline, the person arrives at the lowest point. "The twelfth step [downward] may be called the habit of sinning whereby the fear of God is lost and contempt for God is gained."[2] The point is not so much to elaborate on the misery of this ultimate fall from grace but to indicate that this is the direction in which all the other failures in humility, slight though they seem, are heading.

In his fifth discourse given for the feast of Saint Benedict, Aelred of Rievaulx has a long treatment of the vices a monk is likely to encounter in his monastic journey.[3] He is clearly following and expanding the teaching of John Cassian on the same topic. When he arrives at the point of speaking about pride, he also sees its supreme manifestations as occurring only at the end of a long downward progression. He then nominates five stages which lead to this unhappy conclusion.

1. Vanity: We Delight in Being Praised by Others.

This is a common enough trait in human behavior. From infancy our conduct has been governed by a desire to win the approval of significant persons and to avoid disapproval and punishment. As a result, even in adult years we tend to behave before others in a way that will win acceptance and praise. We put a spin on the truth of our being, so that the other person does not see us as we are, but as we would wish them to see us. Even in Western societies, saving face is important. In hiding behind a false self-presentation, untruth has been introduced into the relationship. "All pride is falsehood."[4] Everyday examples of this are trivial and apparently harmless, except that any untruth has a tendency to expand. This is why Aelred goes on to affirm, "What are human words but bits of wind?" and "It is a great thing for a person to despise human praise and to be content with the testimony of conscience." A high level of maturity is envisaged here; we make our choices on the basis of an enlightened conscience, and we bear the consequences. To base our actions wholly on human approval is a way of acting that is empty of substance; that is why we name it "vanity."

2. Ambition: Self-Exaltation in Order to Be over Others.

Contemporary Western society is achievement-oriented, and the signs of success in this sphere are rank and status, often indicated by material possessions. As a result, it is not unknown for people to bring into the monastery with them an ambition for the highest offices and the most visible marks of status. Perhaps the structures of seniority in the community and the fact that abbots wear crosses, rings, and miters provide an incentive for some to desire to advance to the higher echelons of the monastery. Some disguise their ambition as a pursuit of excellence or efficiency, but the real reason behind their striving is the desire to be at the top of the field. Others are possessed by a darker yearning to exercise power, animated by the delusional hope of having the whole community dance to the tune they are playing. When the hope of advancement governs our choices, it introduces into our lives a further element of falsehood:

> In addition, if we seek after honors though they are worthless and slight, that is, if someone desires to be prior or abbot or cellarer or something like this, and makes choices and acts, as far as possible, to bring this about, if he envies those who [have these offices] and engages in detraction about them, then he, without doubt, is still rendered unclean by worldly desires.[5]

To such as these Aelred exclaims:

> As for you whose ambition is for the heights, what cheek [you show] when you desire to give orders to those who are better than you or disdain to be put on a level with your equals and presume that you are better [than they].[6]

Those who are prone to this form of pride should look around their community. They will find that those who are held in the most affectionate esteem are usually the humble, the old, the young, and, generally, the powerless, whereas middle-aged mavericks and manipulators are barely tolerated. Ambition may seem like a fast track to secure the love and affection of others, but each mile traveled on this path takes us further from that goal.

3. Boasting: We Publish Unduly Any Good We Have Done.

We tend to think of persons who boast as loud-mouthed braggarts; people like this rarely gain the approval they desire. We soon discover that there are far more subtle ways of boosting our own value in the sight of others. In this, as in the previous two steps, truth is a casualty. We magnify our own achievements and minimize our failures; we ignore whatever others may have contributed to the success of the undertaking. Boasting of our virtuous deeds runs completely contrary to Jesus' teaching that the good that we accomplish is to be done in secret (Matt 6:2-16). As Aelred says: "My purse is a purse with a hole in it, letting out through the opening of its mouth whatever it receives and losing what it has acquired."[7] The danger is that I become so concentrated on proclaiming to all the good that I have done that I lose sight of what others have done well, and, as a result, I begin to believe my own press releases and become convinced that I am superior in virtue to everyone around me. As politicians quickly discover to their own dismay, those who believe their own propaganda are setting themselves up for a serious fall.

4. *Contempt: We Believe Everyone Is Inferior to Us.*

Because we believe ourselves to be superior to those around us, we lose any sense that we have obligations in their regard. Progressively, we become estranged from the support and guidance of others and through an unconstrained desire for false autonomy become determined to be masters of our own destiny.[8] "From [this vice] arise blasphemies, rebellion, contradiction, disobedience, and a thousand other pestilences."[9]

5. *Self-Love: We Put aside the Judgment of Others.*

"One who despises the judgment both of God and of human beings glories in being self-sufficient in himself, imagining that he is what he is not, that he knows what he does not know and that he can do what he cannot."[10] Pride leads to such a complete state of falsehood that we are condemned to a delusional narcissism, insulated from any authentic self-knowledge, and unable to enter into truthful relationships with others. Our whole life becomes a sham. Saint Bernard of Clairvaux taught that genuine humility is a matter of affirming the truth about ourselves, about our neighbor, and about God.[11] This ultimate stage of pride is the diametric opposite, establishing us in a state of falsehood and delusion about ourselves, about others, and also about God. In such an extreme condition, it is no wonder that no crime against God or neighbor becomes unthinkable.

These portrayals are pedagogical tools rather than descriptions of real people. What Aelred is saying is that even the tiniest manifestations of pride have within them the potential to carry us far beyond where we want to be, into a state of estrangement from God and others and into a life based on falsehood. We can take some comfort in the fact that we are still some way off from the worst manifestations of pride, but perhaps we can also develop a degree of caution about going further down this path on which perhaps we have taken a few unthinking steps.

35-38

Not to drink much wine. Not to eat much. Not [to be] sleepy. Not [to be] lazy.

This group of maxims is about how we deal with biological imperatives.[1] Even the most ascetic of us is obliged to eat, drink, sleep, and rest sometimes. Saint Benedict is suggesting not that we cease from these necessary animal activities but that we observe a measure in them. Moderation is easiest to maintain when we adopt a rule of daily life and live by it. So, in Benedict's Rule, we find chapters on eating (RB 39), on drinking (RB 40), on sleeping (RB 22), and on the interchange between work and leisure (RB 48). Yet the Rule is notable for its discretion and its acceptance that different individuals have different needs (RB 40.1-2; 37), and so it leaves room for individual variation. Within the limits fixed for the community, the individual is free to choose; the quality of the choice will be determined by whether it is made on the basis of need or of uncontrolled want. And so arises the subjective possibility of overeating, overdrinking, and oversleeping, even though the individual keeps within the limits fixed for the community.

35. Not to drink much wine.

Saint Benedict seemed to accept the tradition that "wine is no drink for monks" (RB 40.6). It is hard to know what else might have served as a standard beverage during the sixth century in Mediterranean countries. Drinking wine was often safer than drinking water. It is perhaps noteworthy that when the rebellious monks of Vicovaro decided to rid themselves of Saint Benedict, it was into his cup of wine that they introduced the poison, perhaps animated by the sure and certain hope that it would not go undrunk.[2]

At the very least, monks needed wine for the celebration of the Eucharist. It was perhaps inevitable that they would engage in viticulture in those regions where this was possible. And so, wine-making activities developed in the monasteries. Perhaps this is why, even today, monks are often associated with alcoholic beverages, especially those of a superior standard. When enemies of monasticism wished to revile monks, the standard charges were that they were fat and lazy and heavy drinkers. Ignaz von Born, the grand master of a Masonic lodge in Vienna at the time of Mozart, defined a monk as "an anthropoid, cassock-wearing, thirsty animal that howls at night."[3]

Today, a person with a drinking problem is usually supposed to have some underlying issues that need to be resolved in order that the power of the addiction may be reduced. It may well have been the case that the ancient monastic masters who condemned overdrinking suspected that there was more to the situation than a gigantic thirst, but they probably had less means of investigating this than we have. Saint Benedict understood that deprivation of the allowance of wine was a serious punishment (RB 43.16). Perhaps he was not aware that daily consumption of alcohol builds up a physical dependence that may be disguised if the daily *hemina* is provided (RB 49.3), but he certainly knew that the absence of wine was likely to be unpleasant enough to provoke murmuring (RB 49.8). On the other hand, it is clear from hagiographic literature that abstinence from wine was considered a virtuous and even heroic choice. William of St.

Thierry writes of Saint Bernard that "he takes wine rarely and only in small quantities since, he says, water is more suitable both for his illness and his appetite."[4]

36. Not to eat much.

It seems that eating disorders are increasing, at least in visibility. The old monks, however, had no notion that eating too little might be a problem; to them it seemed like virtue. So they concentrated their exhortations on the vice of eating too much. We have already considered the question of gluttony when we were speaking about fasting (RB 4.13); here, there seems to be more of an emphasis on moderation and abstemiousness—eating what we need or a little less. Some experts say that if most people in affluent countries ate a little less they would be healthier. No doubt Saint Benedict would agree.

Moderation is not determined according to a mathematical measure. It is worthwhile because it is deliberate, the expression of personally held beliefs and values. Persons who eat a little less are in control of their appetite for food. How much they eat is determined by personal values which place some restraint on what, when, and how they consume food. The moral value of their abstinence is determined according to their intention in practicing it, not by the amount they did not eat. Control in eating boosts morale and self-esteem, just as its lack lowers a person's sense of self-worth, especially when they feel that others disapprove of them.

Moderation is also a factor in long-term viability. Monastic masters often quote the Latin tag, *ne quid nimis*, nothing excessive. The marathon of lifelong fidelity is won not by a short burst of energy but by a slow release, monitored to ensure that there are sufficient reserves to complete the journey.[5] Alternating bouts of feasting and fasting are, most likely, not acts of free choice but a matter of being compelled now by one impulse and now by another. On the contrary, a steady rhythm of life in matters concerning bodily appetites is a good basis for spiritual living.

A final note about the question of overeating. It is important that we imitate Benedict's respect for the fact that people are different. All of us have different interacting needs that determine our behavior at table. Unless we have a particular responsibility for others, it is better for us to concentrate on our own eating habits rather than on those of our neighbors.

37. Not [to be] sleepy.

Since the hours of sleep were highly regulated in Saint Benedict's day, and there was a common dormitory, it seems that this injunction is referring less to long hours spent in bed than to willful drowsiness at other times. Many important activities of the monastic day demand attentiveness but do not involve much physical activity. Listening to the readings at Vigils, *lectio divina*, and periods of personal prayer—not to mention homilies—are some of the moments of the day when a monk may be assailed by a strong tendency to fall asleep.

Evagrius of Pontus noticed a tendency to start yawning as soon as we begin to engage with sacred reading or turn to prayer. His explanation is that this is the work of demons who try to undermine our vigilance at these special moments so that we do not reap the benefit of our spiritual activities.

> There are some filthy demons that are permanently stationed at the side of those who read. They try to influence their minds, many times even using the text of the divine Scriptures as triggers of evil thoughts. It also happens that the demons make [the readers] yawn more frequently than usual and cast them into a heavy sleep that is quite different from normal.[6]

Whether we accept Evagrius's explanation, the fact remains that external quiet, bodily stillness, and a lack of interior stimulation are ideal conditions for taking a nap. Especially if we are already tired. Saint Benedict recognized that the absence of work on Sundays would be difficult for some and so asks that some chores be found for them to keep them busy (RB 48.23). And during the extra time provided for reading during Lent, he has a couple of monks designated to go around the monastery and ensure that nobody is wasting time (RB 48.17-18).[7] The twelfth-century Cistercian customary prescribes that if monks have the hoods up when they are reading, they should arrange them so that it can be seen whether they are sleeping or not.[8] In my early days of monastic life, when the Office of Vigils seemed very long, in Latin, and was celebrated in minimal illumination, it was not unusual to drop off to sleep, the spirit being willing but the flesh weak. Since, at that period, *lectio divina* was done in common, the same phenomenon could be observed there.

Human nature is inclined to be indulgent in the face of such inherent weakness, but a case of a chronic inability to stay awake during prayer or reading is not a slight matter. It means that the person is deprived of regular contact with God's word and is not establishing a closer relationship with God in the context of daily experience. It will not be long before the effects of this starvation will be noticed in daily experience and behavior. A person in this situation is likely to have a reduced sense of spiritual values and, as a result, will often react disproportionately to events perceived as negative.

Falling asleep during prayer needs to be investigated if it is a regular occurrence. The cause may simply be insufficient sleep—most often the result of not developing good personal habits of going punctually to bed. As Cardinal John Henry Newman wrote, "Go to bed in good time, and you are already perfect."[9] Sleepiness can also be the result of insufficient attention to bodily factors: time, place, posture, and weather. In such cases, the remedy is relatively simple; experiment until arriving at a more favorable set of circumstances. Sometimes it is the technique of prayer that needs to be changed; there are advantages to having a fixed pattern of prayer into which we can enter with a minimum of fuss, but every so often these patterns need to be changed to facilitate greater transparency of our life before God. If we are attempting to pray in a way that is not yielding results and degenerates into sleepiness, we may need to take counsel about modifying our approach. There are times in the life of prayer in which major transitions occur, and these are often marked by an apparent incapacity to pray in a way that is meaningful. These also are best resolved with wise counsel. In all these cases, we need to be dissatisfied when our time for prayer or reading is consumed by sleep, and in most cases, the remedy is close at hand.

There is another reason why people habitually fall asleep at such times—in order to escape from God. This is what we might call the "Jonah Syndrome." We do not wish to have anything more to do with God because we are afraid of what might be asked of us. Perhaps we are burdened by a disturbed conscience that we do not wish to examine further. Perhaps we are unwilling to submit areas of our habitual conduct to closer examination. Perhaps we are happy enough in our comfortable rut and do not wish to be summoned to a more adventurous and demanding mode of discipleship. Perhaps we do not wish to abandon our cherished way of prayer for something purer and simpler. In all these cases, there is evidence of resistance to God and perhaps even a trace of rebellion against God. If there is a suspicion that such is the case, there is reason for some soul searching to be followed by taking counsel from someone who understands what we are experiencing.

I suppose there is some possibility that what we are experiencing as sleep is really some exalted form of mystical experience. About that, I have nothing to say beyond the words of our Lord: "By their fruits shall you know them" (Matt 7:16).

38. Not [to be] lazy.

The term used here by Saint Benedict is *piger*, an ugly word that denotes dullness, sluggishness, and any lack of enthusiasm or generosity. It is the characteristic of the monk who expects to be served rather than to serve. Such a person is one who is content to leave things undone, to be so locked into private zones of activity that anything outside those areas is necessarily the responsibility of someone else. Such a person suffers an incapacity to be moved by everyday emergencies, preferring to pass by on the other side of the road rather than to lend a helping hand. This is more than mere inactivity, which is signaled by the word *otium* and its cognates; it is a subjective unwillingness even to think about acting, a deadness to the needs of others or to community concerns.

There is always a danger that the leisure necessary for the contemplative life degenerates into that idleness, which is "the enemy of the soul" (RB 48.1). It is sometimes hard to tell the difference between these opposites, both covered by the same term, *otium*,[10] because physical inactivity must be seen as ambiguous—its moral value is to be determined from the quality of the nonphysical activity for which it provides the occasion. The use of the word *piger* indicates that Saint Benedict is referring to a person prone to doing as little as possible, where nothing is happening that would justify the inactivity. When this state becomes habitual, it is regarded as the vice of acedia:

> [Acedia] instills in the heart of the monk a hatred for the place, a hatred for his very life itself, a hatred for manual labor. . . . It depicts life stretching out for a long period

of time and brings to the mind's eye the toil of the ascetic struggle . . . leaving no leaf unturned to induce the monk to forsake his cell and drop out of the fight.[11]

This listlessness is a special danger in the contemplative life where ample space is given for prayer and reading. These spiritual works produce little in the way of external results or immediate gratification, and perseverance in them can be demanding. It is relatively easy for someone to become lax in these essential elements of the monastic lifestyle and so begin to fill the time available with trivial pursuits of one kind or another: looking out the window, wandering around, consuming endless cups of coffee, reading newspapers from front to back, browsing the internet, playing solitaire, doing Sudoku puzzles, engaging in long meaningless conversations.

The problem with these apparently harmless, time-filling activities is not only that they consume the hours that could have been devoted to useful occupations but also that they leave the listless mind open to unprofitable and harmful thoughts which render the uncommitted heart prey to unwholesome desires:

> "Idleness is the enemy of the soul" (RB 48.1). Every idle person is [caught] in desires. Let them hear this, those who are seeking opportunities to wander about, for whom the common work is a burden and who, while the brothers are intent on necessary tasks, give themselves to idleness and conversation.[12]

Acedia is the opposite of stability; it prevents the monk from staying where he is and continuing to do what he is doing, and sends him off searching for something less boring and more gratifying to fill in time.

> Bodily wandering is a certain lack of quiet that does not allow a monk to be in one place but forces him now to go

> outside and now to come inside so that he can scarcely keep
> to one task or stay in one place for a single hour. For example,
> if he begins to sing he can scarcely endure to sing to the end
> of one verse or two. If he begins to read then, before he has
> finished one page, he rises and, if he cannot go out from the
> cloister, at least he departs for another part of the cloister.[13]

The bodily mobility is paralleled by an equal lack of interior stability. The emotions pass through many upheavals which translate into inconsistent behavior. Even spirituality can be continually in flux with constant changes from one practice or emphasis to another, so that little progress is made anywhere. The *gravitas* that Saint Benedict hoped his monks would acquire is out of the question. Those possessed by the demon of acedia remain light-headed and their spiritual lives never pass beyond the insubstantial vagaries of whatever entertains them from moment to moment:

> Those [monks] are [like the] sea, tossed about by various
> disturbances of the passions and the vices. They are always
> in motion, always moving and never stable, never remaining
> in the same state. Now they are puffed up with pride, now
> they burn with anger, now they are sad, now they are giddy,
> now weighed down by silence, now dissolving in laughter.
> They transgress the instructions of seniors. They disturb the
> peace of the brothers.[14]

Sluggishness is the opposite of vitality; it is a heaviness of being which translates readily into positive unhappiness and the pursuit of anything that could serve to relieve the mortal monotony of daily existence. In this item Saint Benedict is not so much concerned about the absence of productive work but the crippling effect that such deadness of spirit has on the whole person.

39

Not [to be] a murmurer.

It is commonly said that grumbling or murmuring loomed large in Saint Benedict's list of behaviors unacceptable in a monastery. There can be many reasons for an outbreak of murmuring, not all of them equally heinous, as I have tried to demonstrate elsewhere.[1] Even Saint Benedict himself grants that sometimes there may be just cause for giving vent to a grievance (RB 41.5). The best way to prevent this particular source of grumbling is to remove its cause. Other kinds of murmuring require different remedies.

In its present context, this admonition seems to regard murmuring as supported by sluggish inactivity on the one hand and a desire to blame others and bring them into disrepute on the other. Everyday experience probably confirms this. Those with plenty to do roll up their sleeves and do it. They deal with difficulties in a practical way and probably feel some degree of satisfaction in overcoming whatever obstacles they encounter. Those who are less involved in working have much more time to observe and criticize. They seek an external cause of their own interior deadness and lack of enthusiasm and readily find it. Once having located a target for blame, they hasten to have their diagnosis confirmed by speaking to others about how they perceive the situation, hoping to kindle in them the same emotions that they themselves experience. And so sluggishness leads to murmuring, and murmuring leads to detraction. And all the while, those who allow themselves to succumb to this downward dynamic are, more often than not, completely unaware of what is happening. As result, their words and actions rarely come under the scrutiny of conscience.

Many of us live in what has been termed "a culture of complaint," in which "the expansion of rights goes on without the other half of citizenship—attachment to duties and obligations."[2] If things are not going well with us, we quickly assume that the cause of our misfortune can be found in the actions and omissions of others. So many of our contemporaries have grown up with a strong sense of narcissistic entitlement. Other people have a duty to make my life as smooth and happy as possible. If I am unhappy, it is because others have done something to make me miserable. Alternatively, they have failed to do whatever was needed to make me happy. The underlying assumption is that happiness is the default state of every human being. This attitude is especially visible in advertising for consumer products. This seems to assume that happiness is to be sought in the acquisition and enjoyment of goods external to ourselves. It is implied that without these goods we cannot be happy. Happy-face culture, however, is a surefire source of the sort of disillusionment that makes us strive all the harder for goods which promise a contentment they cannot yield.

Eastern European philosophers, like the Romanian E. M. Cioran, have been less sanguine in their understanding of human reality. Leszek Kolakowski from Poland, for example, writes that the word "happiness" is not applicable to human beings:

> This not just because we experience suffering. It is also because, even if we are not suffering at a given moment, even if we are able to experience physical and spiritual pleasure

and moments beyond time, in the "eternal present" of love, we can never forget the existence of evil and the misery of the human condition. We participate in the suffering of others; we cannot eliminate the anticipation of death or the sorrows of life.[3]

This seems like a grim approach to life, but it is an approach that enables us to deal more adequately with its bad moments without sinking into mental confusion and losing our nerve. Like the other twelfth-century Cistercians, Aelred of Rievaulx was in no doubt that since the Fall human life was wracked by many miseries: "Pertaining to this unhappiness are all the miseries of this life: labours, pains, weariness, poverty, bereavement, all types of illness, trouble. O my brothers, who can number them all?"[4]

We live in a valley of tears. A person who understands this truth not only has greater endurance in supporting the troubles that life often lays at our doorstep but also is animated by a more lively hope for the world beyond: "Here we have no abiding city, but we seek the one that is to come" (Heb 13:14). A few items later, Saint Benedict will speak about the importance of eschatological desire in helping the monk support the hard and rough things encountered on the journey to God. Here it is sufficient to say that those who murmur have lost sight of the goal of their monastic journey. They are locked into their present discomfort and shortsightedly seek to find culprits for their existential misery. To live like this is to live a falsehood. Its only effect will be to generate more pain, not only for ourselves, but also for those around us who are foolish enough to take our complaints seriously.

40

Not [to be] a detractor.

Inactivity makes room for idle chatter and gossip which, in turn, frequently lead to uncharitable words and detraction. In the context of a monastic community, detraction and calumny are both double sins. On the one hand, they are sins against the person who is the object of negative speech and, often, they are acts of injustice which require some form of compensation or restitution for the wrong done to the other person. Here we have to be clear in our own minds. Detraction is not only a sin against charity. It is a sin against justice and, to be forgiven, restitution is required as well as repentance. To the extent that we have attempted to damage or destroy the reputation of another, we must make practical amends. We have stolen something from another, and we must give it back. Calumny and detraction are also sins against the unity of the community, attacking one of its members in the hope of diminishing that person's value in the eyes of others. When one member suffers, all are affected and the well-being of the whole body is undermined. Saint Aelred of Rievaulx frequently returns to the topic of detraction in his discourses to his monks, calling it "a huge sin" and insisting that a monk should never indulge in it, even to save his own life.

> Since it is not right for the servant of God to enter into liti-
> gation even with heretics (2 Tim 2:24), it is manifest that

133

murmuring and detraction are huge sins. If a Christian is not allowed to lie [to preserve] his life or his or another's flesh, so a monk should not engage in detraction or murmuring in order to preserve his own or another's flesh.[1]

Detraction is the most cowardly mode of aggression. We do not confront the other person; nor do we offer them any opportunity of self-defense. We do not need witnesses or evidence. We simply make an unsupported negative statement and call on our hearers to accept it without qualification. We not only narrate a particular unflattering incident, whether it is factual or fabricated, but also extrapolate from it to arrive at generalized conclusions, larding our recital of external events with generous helpings of our own interpretations. And we go further; we proceed to give a reading of the person's intentions and motivations, even though we have no means of knowing what these were. The guilty verdict is inevitable, and we feel no compunction at all for our part in it. Mostly we walk away feeling blameless, but an injustice has been done. Our sense of righteous innocence is no more than an indication of an inoperative conscience.

Of course, there are degrees of calumny and detraction. Not every slander does equal harm to our neighbor. But there are grounds for serious concern about the person constantly given to detraction, one who, in the words of the Rule of the Master, loves detraction (RM 3.29). Why is this person constantly harping on the faults and imperfections of others? Why is it not possible to have an ordinary conversation about ordinary things without continually veering in the direction of unkindness and untruth? Is it simply a lack of self-discipline? Perhaps. In some persons there never has been a deliberate effort to limit criticism or rash judgment, and, as a result, negative comments readily pour forth whenever the speaker feels bad about something and wants to spread the feeling wider.

Saint Bernard of Clairvaux was often called on to intervene in the affairs of the wider church. He had a large part to play in the resolution of the schism of the antipope Anacletus II (Peter Leone), finally succeeding in having Innocent II recognized. He returned to his own monastery in 1138 and apparently, found himself or others targets for detraction and so immediately launched into a vigorous denunciation of this vice. We can do no better than to listen to what he says. He frames his tirade in terms of the verse of the Song of Songs on which he comments: "The upright love you."

> I think this is the meaning of the addition "The upright love you." This is not an absurd [interpretation]. I find in every group of young attendants that there are some who closely observe the actions of the bride for the purpose of disparagement, not for imitation. They are tortured by the good deeds of their seniors and so they feed upon what they do wrong. You will see them walking privately, coming together, sitting side-by-side. Soon their wanton tongues are loosed in hateful whispering. One is conjoined to another [so closely] that there is no breathing space between them, so great is their desire to engage in detraction or to listen to it. They enter into close relationship in order to speak ill [of others]. They are in concord to create discord. They agree to form highly hostile friendships and, by common agreement, with malicious intent, they find pleasure in hateful discourse.[2]

Bernard supports his case by calling a number of scriptural witnesses, including Romans 1:30—"Detractors are hateful to God"—and then continues:

> It is no wonder that this vice is recognized as the principal enemy and persecutor of charity (which God is), one more bitter than the other vices. You can notice this yourselves. Whoever engages in detraction first betrays the fact that he himself is empty of charity. Then, what else does he intend

in engaging in detraction, except to bring the one he is slandering into odium and contempt among those to whom he speaks? The slandering tongue strikes a blow against charity in all who listen to it and, as far as possible, wounds and destroys [charity] utterly. Not only that, but it strikes even those who are absent, to whom the word comes, flying forth from those who were present. You see how easily and in a brief period of time the swiftly running word is able to infect a huge multitude with its pestilential malice.[3]

Again, Bernard summons appropriate texts from the Bible, this time from Psalms 13:3 ("Their mouth is full of cursing and bitterness; their feet are swift to shed blood") and Luke 6:45 ("The mouth speaks out of the fullness of the heart"). Then he proceeds to show how not all detraction is straightforward. Sometimes it uses artifice to make itself more acceptable to those who hear it:

This pestilence assumes different appearances. Some vomit out the virus of detraction nakedly and irreverently—whatever enters their mouths. Others hide the malice they have conceived under a cloak of pretended reluctance which they are not able to maintain. You will see them begin with sighs and then, heavily and slowly, with a sad face and downcast eyes, in a mournful voice, they will allow their evil speech to escape. This is so much the more persuasive, and easily believed by those who listen because they bring forth [their detraction] with an unwilling heart, feeling more sorrowful than malicious. They say, "I am sorry, because I love him greatly, but I have never been able to set him right in this matter." Another [kind of detractor] says, "I knew all about this, but it would never have been revealed by me. Since it has been made known by another I cannot deny the truth. It pains me to say this, but this is really the case." And he adds: "What a great loss! Otherwise he is capable of so many things. But, to speak the truth, he cannot be excused in this matter."[4]

We may well wonder what was happening at Clairvaux to bring forth such a fierce denunciation and whether it was Bernard himself who was the victim of such malicious slanders. Certainly, we are left in no doubt that he regarded this vice as serious and pernicious. Perhaps we would do well to examine our conscience on this topic, especially in the light of what Saint James teaches in his epistle. He seems to consider that good people, who are often intent on avoiding evil actions, are often too indulgent to themselves when it comes to being blameless in their speech: "If any think themselves to be religious and do not put a restraint on their tongue, they deceive themselves and their religious practice is empty" (Jas 1:26). And he returns to the point with a longer exposition in a later chapter (Jas 3:1-12) and concludes, "Do not speak against one another" (Jas 4:11).

41

To commit his hope to God.

Hope is a theological virtue, a divine gift that allows us to live in union with God while still living in the world of space and time. Hope is commonly associated with a positive expectation to be realized in the future, but in the New Testament real hope often comes to the fore in hard times. "Trouble brings about patience, patience a tested character, a tested character hope" (Rom 5:3). To some extent it seems that theological hope is most exquisitely realized when everything is hopeless. Saint Paul gives us the example of Abraham who believed with a hope in God that transcended human hope; he hoped against hope (Rom 4:18). "A hope that sees is not hope" (Rom 8:24), and so theological hope means going beyond, and maybe against, the evidence of our senses and our intellect. Hope is not a calculated optimism but an abounding trust in God.

This trust in God is not based on our present experience of God, or even on the memory of what God has done for us in the past. Theological hope grows out of our firm faith in the all-powerful and all-loving God, unrestricted by space and time and working always for our good. As Saint Thomas Aquinas wrote:

> To the second objection it is to be said that hope does not lean principally on grace already possessed but on the divine mercy and omnipotence, through which even one who has not had grace can receive it, and so come to eternal life.[1]

Theological hope is therefore limited only by the infinitude of God. It is not intrinsically threatened by desperate circumstances occurring within space and time but rests on the solid and eternal rock of the divine nature. This means that, strictly speaking, theological hope is not directed toward desirable outcomes in this present life, but its energy lifts up the heart of the believer toward eternal life.[2] As Saint Paul writes, "If for this life only we have hope in Christ Jesus, then of all people are we the most to be pitied" (1 Cor 15:19). Theological hope is the effect of Christ's indwelling at the level of spirit; it is the ground of our fervent belief and desire to share in the eternal happiness of heaven: "Christ in you: the hope of glory" (Col 1:27).

It must be added, however, that while eternal life is the principal object of theological hope, we do not always have to wait until after death to experience some of its reality. In a certain sense, from time to time we may have the experience of a foretaste of what has been promised us—an example of experiencing that the last things are already in the process of realization. By God's mercy, our hope for ultimate beatitude may be supported and sustained by moments of grace which are symbols and pointers to the future reality. Jesus told his disciples to pray without hesitation or calculation for whatever they desired (Mark 11:22-24). When our prayers for things that do not matter much are heard, our confidence in the generous mercy of God is increased. At the end of a long apprenticeship in trust, we are much more likely to commit our hopes and our self to God with all our heart, with all our soul, and with all our strength.

Committing one's hope to God implies a deliberate action; it is more than living in a vague state of hope that is mostly latent. It means having eternal life as our one principal and motivating goal and reducing all other hopes to a lower plane. It is the choice of God over more tangible sources of security. This commitment of life and hope to God is at the heart of the ritual of monastic profession. The one who is being professed sings the *Suscipe* three times: "Receive me, O God, according to your promise, and I shall live. Do not disappoint me of my hope" (RB 58.21). This triple affirmation is not only a strong moment in the ritual; the theme will also be played out again and again as life proceeds. In the years that follow profession, the monk will learn by experience that it is on God alone that he must depend. While he is learning this, he will have to endure much disappointment and bitterness for as long as his hopes reside in his own abilities or in the actions and attitudes of others. "Put no trust in princes," says the psalmist, "in humans who cannot save; when the breath leaves them they return to the ground and all their plans come to nothing" (Ps 146:3-4). And: "It is better to take refuge in the Lord than to trust in a human; it is better to take refuge in the Lord than to trust in princes" (Ps 118:9).

Of course, putting all our hope in God is not a denial that, for much of our life, we may expect to receive permanent benefits and many graces through the hands of others. This is part of God's provident gift to us. This is the sacrament of the church, both local and universal. As time goes by, however, we begin to perceive that God is the ultimate giver of all good gifts. While it is true that "the gifts and calling of God are irrevocable" (Rom 11:29), sometimes the channels by which these gifts are given change, and we may be caught wrong-footed. When one or other temporal support of our hope falls away, the clarity and serenity of our mind is clouded. We have, as it were, to recalculate hope—to return to fundamental truths in order to regain our balance. Every wound to hope strikes also at faith. "I said: 'This is the cause of my grief: the right hand of the Lord has changed' " (Ps 77:10).

It should not be concluded from this that hope is a grim reality. Hope, as a source of certainty, is also a source of encouragement (Rom 15:14) and joy (Rom 12:11). "We have this hope as a safe and strong anchor for our soul" (Heb 6:19);

it is something that keeps us from drifting off into that abyss of despair that quickly swallows up all our energies. But let us insist. It is a hope based on what God is and not on what we are. And that is, no doubt, why Saint Benedict chose to conclude his long list of good works with the one that needs to infuse them all: "Never to despair of the mercy of God" (RB 4.74).

42-43

When he sees something good in himself, to attribute it to God and not to himself. But let him know that evil done is always from himself, and let him attribute it to himself.

Saint Benedict has introduced several small changes into the underlying text of the Rule of the Master, indicating that he was prepared to nuance his source so that the end product would reflect his thinking more closely. This is what the Master wrote:

> When he sees something good in himself, let him think that it has been done by God rather than by himself. Let him judge evil as done by himself and impute it to himself and to the devil. (RM 3.46-47)

The role of the devil has been reduced for the purpose of placing the whole onus for evil actions on the perpetrator. The change in the first of the two verses is also significant. Whereas the Master thinks of good in terms of what has been done, good works, Saint Benedict does not limit the idea of inherent goodness to actions, leaving the way open to include in the "something good" personal gifts, talents, and attributes. This might be stretching the interpretation a bit, but there must have been some reason for the change.

The first of these two items takes up a theme which had already been mentioned in the Prologue. Perhaps against the backdrop of the Semi-Pelagian controversy, Saint Benedict is insisting on the primacy of grace in the work of sanctification as also in the accomplishment of that transformation that comes about through fidelity to the ordinary activities of the monastic regimen:

> Those who fear the Lord are not elated by their good observance, but consider that the good things in them cannot have come from themselves but are from the Lord. And so they magnify the Lord working in them, saying with the prophet: "Not to us, Lord, not to us, but to your name give the glory." In the same way the Apostle Paul did not attribute anything of his preaching to himself but said, "It is by God's grace that I am what I am." And again he says, "Let the one who boasts, boast in the Lord."[1]

One of the traps of monastic life is to end up believing that, because so much effort is required, we are the ones responsible for any slight progress that we make. We may say to ourselves, "I have worked hard, and now I have acquired this particular virtue." Or: "I have worked hard and have eliminated or reduced this particular vice." We say it cheerfully and proudly as though it was by our own strength that these good results have accrued. When stumbling a few steps forward costs me so much blood, sweat, and tears, it is hard to resist the temptation to claim the bulk of the credit for myself.

It is important to return to some basic ideas about the spiritual life. Fundamentally, whatever good I do, whatever suffering I endure, has meaning only to the extent that it is the effect of God's grace and God's spirit active within my life. There is some merit in being actively virtuous and in building up a strong carapace against the vicissitudes of life, but it makes sense only in the context of working in us to transform us into people who are more Christlike. The vocation I received in baptism is not merely to be good but to become divine. This comes about when I respond to God's invitation to allow my life to be configured to the life of Christ. I am called to be a presence of Christ in my small part of the world. For this to happen, vices need to be subdued and virtues allowed to flourish. I have to cooperate in the processes of purification and sanctification, but I am not their initiator or even their principal agent. They are God's work. As the verse often repeated during the various stages of monastic initiation says, "May God, who has begun this work in you, bring it to completion on the day of Christ Jesus." The work is God's; my struggles are simply the result of having to overcome my inertia and reduce my resistance to what God is achieving.

And what about the evil that I have done? Saint Benedict has inserted the word "always" into the Master's text. Is it true that whatever is bad in my actions is always my fault and mine alone? Is it not often the case that sinners are so because they themselves have been sinned against? Maybe they have been abused in some way that has interfered with their basic human freedom so that their later choices are skewed. Here, we are entering the sphere of what has been termed more recently "social sin." One explanation of this concept is given in the 1984 post-synodal exhortation of Pope John Paul II, *Reconciliatio et paenitentia*:

> Sin, in the proper sense, is always a personal act, since it is an act of freedom on the part of an individual person and not properly of a group or community. This individual may be conditioned, incited and influenced by numerous and powerful external factors. He may also be subjected to tendencies, defects and habits linked with his personal condition. In not a few cases such external and internal factors may attenuate, to a greater or lesser degree, the person's freedom and therefore his responsibility and guilt.

The pope continues by insisting that, notwithstanding the effects of social sin, the responsibility ultimately remains with the individual. This is the point that Saint Benedict is making:

> But it is a truth of faith, also confirmed by our experience and reason, that the human person is free. This truth cannot be disregarded in order to place the blame for individuals' sins on external factors such as structures, systems or other people. Above all, this would be to deny the person's dignity and freedom, which are manifested—even though in the negative and disastrous way—also in this responsibility for sin committed. Hence there is nothing so personal and untransferable in each individual as merit for virtue or responsibility for sin.[2]

In 1993 he reiterated this teaching in his magisterial encyclical on moral matters, *Veritatis splendor*:

> Side by side with its exaltation of freedom, yet oddly in contrast with it, modern culture radically questions the very existence of this freedom. A number of disciplines, grouped under the name of the behavioral sciences, have rightly drawn attention to the many kinds of psychological and social conditioning which influence the exercise of human freedom. Knowledge of these conditionings and the study they have received represent important achievements which have found application in various areas, for example in pedagogy or the administration of justice. But some people, going beyond the conclusions which can be legitimately drawn from these observations have come to question or even deny the very reality of human freedom.[3]

The notion of social sin is very important because it explains *how* the human will is deflected from seeking what is objectively and intrinsically good and allows itself to be drawn in other directions. The pope makes the point, however, that even when strongly conditioned and influenced by ambient society there remains the possibility of choice. At some point in the progression from first thought to final completion of the act, it is possible to refuse to be an accomplice in the evil proposed. This may be less apparent when the temptation has passed the point of no return, and so the sinner will often deny complicity. What is happening in such cases is that the habit of sin has taken hold of the person. Not only is the frontier between choice and inevitability blurred, but the crossing of the frontier is less dramatic and, as a result, less noticeable. But at some point a choice has been made, maybe long ago.[4] For example, a person injects heroin for the first time as a free act. Once the addiction takes hold, freedom is diminished, but responsibility remains with the one who, in the past, freely chose to initiate a course of action that gave the addiction its power.

Monastic life is meant to create a sensitive conscience, and it usually does. The self-honesty that develops over the years does not deny good has been done, but it recognizes the fact that many factors contributed to the success, including the contributions of others and a felicitous conjunction of circumstance. Some happy outcomes may have been unintended. A spiritual person will always celebrate the work of grace in what has been achieved: inspiration, guidance, encouragement, support, and consolation. Such a person may feel uncomfortable with praise given, understanding that whatever has been achieved has been accomplished only by God's gratuitous gift.

Likewise, self-honesty demands that we recognize and affirm our complicity in the bad things we have done, even when it is merely a matter of malign thoughts. This is what Saint Benedict enjoins in the fifth step of humility: "The fifth step of humility is that a monk does not conceal from his abbot any evil thoughts entering his heart or any evils secretly committed by him. Instead, he confesses them humbly" (RB 7.44).[5] The admission of faults and, thereby, their nonconcealment is an important component of monastic living. We cannot evade this honesty by seeking to place the blame on circumstances or on other people. Although our actual guilt may be less complete than it seems, we should be prepared to accept, as Benedict teaches, that the evil we have done is our responsibility and so try to repair the damage we have done. The first step is humble admission.

44-46

To fear the Day of Judgment. To be terrified of hell. To desire eternal life with all spiritual yearning.

These verses place monastic life in an eschatological context. We might recall the title of chapter 7 of the Second Vatican Council's decree *Lumen gentium*: "The Eschatological Character of the Pilgrim Church and its Union with the Heavenly Church." The monastery, insofar as it is a local embodiment of the church, is also eschatological in character; its whole meaning is derived from the fact of its being oriented to the future life. The monastic way is a road to eternal life. The quality of a person's journey will be determined by the intensity with which the goal is desired. The reason why Saint Benedict keeps reminding the monk of future judgment is to make sure that choices made in time are made with an eye to their meaning in eternity.

44. To fear the Day of Judgment.

The prospect of Judgment Day appears relatively frequently throughout the Rule, usually in the context of insisting that persons will be held accountable in the next life for the decisions and choices they make in this life. In addition to our present text, there are twelve other texts. You will notice how, with one exception, they all present the Day of Judgment as fearsome, and in each case there is a verb that bids the person to think, to know, and to remember. Except in the case of the perfectly humble monk, the Day of Judgment is absent from our purview, and so we are inclined to forget about it and act as though our deeds will not come to light at that time. This is not acceptable to Benedict who, with his customary gravity, insists that we make positive efforts to keep in mind the reality of the Last Judgment. Every decision and choice we make will be subject to assay; our ultimate destiny will depend on the result.

- Let the abbot always *remember* that a discussion will be held, on the fearsome Day of Judgment, both of his teaching and of the obedience of his disciples. (2.6)

- But let [the abbot] always *think* that he has received a soul to be governed, of whom an account must be rendered. (2.34)

- Let [the abbot] *acknowledge* as certain that, whatever number of brothers he has under his care, he will have to render to the Lord an account of all their souls on the Day of Judgment and, doubtlessly, of his own soul as well. And, thus, always fearing the future discussion of the Shepherd about the sheep entrusted to him, [the abbot] will be careful in the decisions he makes about [the affairs] of others and so will be rendered solicitous about his own. (2.37-38)

- Let the abbot himself do all things with the fear of God and in the observance of the rule, *knowing* that, beyond doubt, he will have to render an account of all his judgments to the most equitable judgment of God. (3.11)

- [The humble monk], at every hour reckoning that he is guilty of his sins, even now *considers* himself as brought before the fearsome judgment of God. (7.64)

- Let [the cellarer] exercise active care, with all solicitude, for the sick, children, guests and the poor, *knowing* without doubt that for all these he must render an account on the Day of Judgment. (31.9)

- In all his judgments let [the abbot] *think* about the retribution of God. (55.22)

- Let [the abbot] always *think* that for all his judgments and his works he must render an account to God. (63.3)

- Let the one ordained abbot always *remember* what a burden he has received and to whom he must render an account of his stewardship. (64.7)

- Let the abbot always *think* that he must render an account of all his judgments to God, so that the flames of envy or jealousy may not sear his soul. (65.22)

In all these instances the Day of Judgment is to be recalled with some degree of dread. At the end of the present chapter on the implements of the spiritual craft, there is another reference to the Day of Judgment. This time Benedict points to the rewards that await the humble workman:

> Behold these are the implements of the spiritual craft. When they are fulfilled by us, unceasingly, night and day, then on the day appointed for judgment we will be paid with the reward from the Lord which he himself promised. "What God has prepared for those who love him, eye has not seen, nor ear heard, nor has it arisen in the human heart." (4.75-77)

For the most part, however, Benedict uses the notion of God's ultimate judgment as a means of instilling in all, but especially those with some position of authority, the reality of accountability before God. To support this emphasis, it is necessary that there be negative sanctions for those who fail to meet the divine standards. And so arises one of the less-mentioned currents in Saint Benedict's teaching: the prospect of hell.

45. To be terrified of hell.

In the New Testament, Gehenna, the word used by Saint Benedict, is the place of eternal punishment, a fiery abyss to which the unrepentant are sent after the Day of Judgment. This is not a theme to which pious souls frequently return in their meditations, and there are many today who find difficulty in reconciling a merciful God with the reality of eternal damnation. In the first place, we need to move beyond the garish images of apocalyptic literature and the vivid imagination of medieval artists to try to grasp the fact that resistance and rejection of God are destructive of all that we humans hold dear. The premise on which the doctrine of hell is based is that this rejection of God has become irreversibly ingrained in the human spirit and thus has rendered the person incapable of enjoying God's presence or responding to God's love. Just as evil is not a separate reality in itself but deprivation of the good, so hell may be seen primarily as the deprivation of God through the incapacity of the person to be touched by God. This is an unpleasant truth but not one we can afford to ignore:

> The great truths of judgment and punishment are firmly retained throughout the NT, and no theological hypothesis can be biblical which reduces the ultimate destiny of righteousness and wickedness to the same thing; the details of the afterlife, however, are not disclosed except in imagery.[1]

Benedict seems to have accepted the commonplace teaching about hell without difficulty, as part of the wider context in which the life of Christian discipleship plays out. Here are the texts where he speaks about Gehenna:

- And if we flee the punishments of Gehenna because we wish to arrive at unending life, then while there is opportunity and we are in this body, and there is opportunity [to complete] these tasks by this light of life, there is a need to run and do now what will profit us in perpetuity. (Prol 42-44)

- This [obedience] is appropriate for those who consider nothing to be dearer to themselves than Christ. Because of the holy service they have professed, or because of the fear of Gehenna, or [because of] the glory of eternal life, as soon as anything is commanded them by a superior they permit no delay in doing it. (5.2-4)

- And let [the monk] be always mindful of everything that God has commanded and let him always ponder in his mind both how for their sins Gehenna will burn those who despise God and the eternal life is prepared for those who fear God. (7.11)

- Through this love, all that [the monk] used to observe somewhat fearfully, he will now begin to fulfill without effort, as though naturally, from habit. [He will act] no longer out of fear of Gehenna but out of love for Christ, from good habit itself and delight in virtue. (7.68-69)

There are two other texts to be considered, which use the term *infernum* (hell) rather than Gehenna.

- We are rightly taught not to do our own will, since we should be aware of what Scripture says: "there are ways which seem humanly right whose end plunges into the depths of hell" [Prov 16:25].[2] (7.21)

- Just as there is an evil zeal of bitterness which separates from God and leads to hell, so there is a good zeal that separates from vices and leads to God and eternal life. (72.1-2)

In most of these instances, hell is conceived as the polar opposite of all that monastic life aims for: goodness, union with God, and eternal life. Hell is the definitive unhappy ending to a life that has been characterized by resistance to grace. The effect of this emphasis is a kind of moral dualism in which the monk is invited to see each of his daily options as a choice between good and evil, what is ultimately life-giving and what is ultimately self-destructive. The concepts of heaven and hell are introduced as incitements to mindful living: the monk is to be fully aware of the seriousness of the choices he makes every day, conscious that they will either help him advance toward his goal or, if they are defective or malign, retard his progress or even cause him to slip further away from the fulfillment of his hopes.

46. To desire eternal life with all spiritual yearning.

The Rule of the Master reads: "To desire eternal life and holy Jerusalem" (RM 3.52). Saint Benedict's omission and addition are both significant. The probable reason he deletes the mention of the heavenly Jerusalem is that he is not in favor of materializing heaven. He has omitted the other two passages where the Master speaks of Jerusalem (RM 3.92; 90.17), and in the chapter on humility, he omits the long exuberant passage detailing heavenly delights (RM 10.92-120). Heaven is the zone of God, about which we have knowledge by revelation and perhaps through an experiential foretaste. Allowing the imagination to run riot in a way that presents eternal life in terms of total wish fulfillment is not helpful. We do not know the source of all these desires of which we are conscious, but we can expect that many of them will fall away as we advance toward a more complete purity of heart.

The omission indicates something of Saint Benedict's sober gravity in his approach to the spiritual life. The addition, on the other hand, has a touch of lyricism about it. The word here translated as "yearning" is *concupiscentia*. Since the time of Saint Augustine, especially as mediated by the Council of Trent's teaching on original sin, concupiscence has had a negative connotation. This is especially clear when the adjective "carnal" is added. The word itself, however, is neutral; its moral quality is determined by its object.[3] The prefix *con-* may be considered an intensifier of the underlying verb (which is related to *cupire*), perhaps signifying a durative element in the notion. Two further qualifiers are added: the desire is specified as "spiritual" and its all-consuming quality by "all." "To desire with all spiritual desire" is not describing a vague, lukewarm inclination but a deep spiritual yearning that involves the whole of one's being and, eventually, compels all one's energies to participate in seeking closer union with the object of desire.

The theme of desire for God as the engine that drives all spiritual progress is constant in the teaching of the fathers of the church. Spiritual desire was seen as an innate, preelective imperative of human nature which makes us lifelong seekers of a reality that cannot be found within the confines of space and time. Whether we are conscious of it or not, we live our lives in pursuit of the Absolute. We often confuse our desires for lesser things with this more fundamental drive. But as the decades pass we come to understand that material advantages can never satisfy our fundamental yearning for God. This happens as time and again we experience the reality that no accumulation of what were objects of desire can satisfy us. We always want something more and something else. Our hearts are restless until they can rest in the enjoyment of God.[4]

The great proponent of spiritual desire in the West was Saint Augustine. He was followed by Saint Gregory the Great with a more particular emphasis on desire for heaven. Through these channels, especially, desire for God became a major component in the monastic spirituality in the Benedictine tradition. This is epitomized in the title of Jean Leclercq's study of the culture of medieval monasteries, *The Love of Learning and the Desire for God.*[5] The search for God begins with a mysteriously implanted desire for God. It is sustained by allowing oneself to become more and more aware of this deep inner yearning so as to allow it more liberty to determine the choices that we make. Because this deep desire is somewhat detached from the concerns and gratifications of daily life, there is always the danger that it will be displaced by more immediate promptings. To make room for the flowering of spiritual desire, we must be prepared to prune back alternative desires which have the capacity to distract us from our fundamental pursuits and to lead us into the delusion of thinking that everything will be wonderful if only these lesser desires are gratified. The asceticism, which every form of monastic living demands, has as its aim the discernment, purification, and reduction of these clamorous urgings so that the silent voice of a more interior yearning can be heard.

There is curious paradox involved in this monastic emphasis on desire for God. The beginning of the monastic journey is, in one form or another, an experience of conversion: a change in the direction of life. This usually comes about through an unexpected and unsought experience of spiritual reality that is strong enough to cause a radical change of outlook in the person. Those who discover a treasure hidden in a field are quite happy to detach themselves from all that they have in order to acquire that treasure. A person who has been gifted with a life-changing taste of the goodness of God wants to go further into this mystery. The search for the unseen God has begun.

For those people who are led to enter a monastery to continue this pursuit, a surprise awaits them. Saint Aelred describes this phenomenon:

> Not long ago a certain brother renounced the world and joined our monastery. He was handed over by the most reverend abbot to my littleness for formation in regular discipline.

> At one time [the novice] was wondering and asking me the
> cause why when he was still living in a worldly way he very
> often experienced compunction, and was possessed by a feel-
> ing of divine love, and enjoyed a great sweetness of spirit,
> whereas now, he said, I am not only unable to retain [this ex-
> perience] for a longer time, but I rarely get even a taste of it.[6]

Spiritual experience is so deeply satisfying that many who
taste it wish to experience it more fully. And so they enter a
monastery. The honeymoon may continue for a time as they
adapt to a new mode of living, but eventually the waves of
consolation cease and the novice is left with the monotony
of daily chores, the ambiguities of community living, and a
persistent dryness in prayer. To fill this emptiness, temptations
of various kinds begin to intrude upon awareness which, even
if they are successfully repelled, cumulatively cause weariness
and discouragement.

So, what does the fervent seeker after God discover in the
monastery? Not the immediate presence of God, but the absence of God. Although the vestiges or footprints of God are
found throughout creation, in the church, in the Scriptures,
in the community, the full face-to-face presence of God is
always beyond present experience. Even the strongest mystical
experience does not satisfy our yearning but rather makes our
desire all the more intense. Desire is fueled by the experience
of absence. A monastery exists to guide us into the realization
that our desire for God will be satisfied only in eternity, and
hence its structures are designed to help us turn aside from
what is present and look with expectation toward the final
goal. Everything that happens in this present life, including our
occasional foretasting of the reality that awaits us, is meant to
keep us walking along the road that leads to eternal life. This
means keeping alive our faith, our hope, and our ardent desire.

47-49

To have death present before one's eyes every day. At every hour to keep guard over the actions of his life. To know for certain that in every place the Lord is watching him.

These three admonitions bring to our attention the importance of living in a state of mindfulness, constantly aware that what we do in this present life will have a bearing on what happens to us after we die. There is a strong connection between these verses and the first step of humility:

> And so the first step of humility is that a monk always keeps the fear of God before his eyes and flees from all forgetfulness. He must *always* remember all God's instructions. The monk is *always* to turn over in his mind how all who despise God will fall into hell for their sins, as well as the everlasting life prepared for those who fear God. Let him guard himself *at every hour* from sins and vices, be they of thought or tongue, of hand or foot, of selfwill or fleshly desire. Let the monk consider that *at every hour* human beings are always seen by God in heaven, and that their actions in every place are in God's sight and are reported by angels *at every hour*. The Prophet demonstrates this to us when he shows that God is *always* present in our thoughts: "God searches hearts and kidneys." Again he says: "The Lord knows the thoughts of human beings." And in the same vein: "You

understand my thoughts from afar." And: "Human thoughts will be open before you." That he may be careful about his perverse thoughts, the good brother should *always* say in his heart: "I shall be blameless before God if I guard myself from my wickedness." . . . Let us believe that God is *always* present to us even in the desires of the flesh for, as the Prophet says to the Lord, "All my desire is before you." We must then beware of evil desire, because death stands near the entrance of delight. For this reason Scripture instructs us: "Do not pursue your lusts." Therefore, because the eyes of the Lord are watching the good and the wicked, and because the Lord is *always* looking down from heaven on human beings to see whether any understand and seek God; and because *every day, day and night*, the angels assigned to us report our doings to the Lord then, brothers, we must beware *every hour* or, as the Prophet says in the Psalm, "God may, at one time, see us falling into evil and become useless." God spares us at this time because he is kind and waits for us to be converted to something better. In the future he may say to us: "You did this, and I was silent." (RB 7.10-30)

What is significant in this passage is the emphasis that Saint Benedict places on the fact that the need for watchfulness is unbroken; we must be mindful: always, every day, and at every hour. We find the same concern in the verses we are now considering.

47. To have death present before one's eyes every day.

A nineteenth-century visitor to the Cistercian monastery of Sept-Fons in France was amazed to see inscribed over the door leading from the church to the cemetery the words: *Hodie mihi, cras tibi.*[1] Put into the mouth of the deceased monks on their way to burial are the words, "Today I die, tomorrow it will be you." The death of those closest to us, especially if they are our contemporaries, nearly always brings with it thoughts of the shortness of life. As one who has recently entered the eighth decade of life, I know that—even if I happen to have inherited the longevity gene from my father's family—I cannot realistically expect to live for very much longer. This adds urgency to Saint Benedict's admonition to do now the things that will profit me for all eternity (RB Prol 44).

The mindfulness of death is not cultivated in our culture, and its reality is disguised when it intrudes on our lives. We sometimes act like foolish people, pretending that life will continue indefinitely. The philosopher who reminded us that the human being is essentially a *Sein zum Tode*, a being in process toward death, had a point. The one thing that we know about every human being born into our world is that he or she will die. We do not know when, we do not know how, and we do not know in what disposition. But all of us will die. And as we used to be reminded in parish missions, "After death comes judgment."

These unwelcome thoughts need not necessarily depress and paralyze us. They can be a source of energy, bidding us to make the most of the opportunities we have while we still have them. *Carpe diem!* Dilatoriness and procrastination are the cause of many uncreative hours, days, and years. When we consider that our time on earth is limited, that the occasions in which we can show our love to those we love will come to an end, then we become possessed of a certain urgency to do now what we would not want undone at the time of our death. "The person who truly imitates Christ ought to be assiduous in meditating on his final days because he does not know when his Lord will come. If he does this he will not go astray."[2]

Many wisdom traditions link the perception of the shortness of life with wisdom and with the capacity to judge events in perspective. Two texts from the psalms come immediately to mind:

> Teach us to number our days aright,
> that we may gain wisdom of heart. (Ps 90:12)
>
> Remember how fleeting is my life
> and how frail you have created all human beings.
> Who can live and not see death?
> Who can save himself from the hand of Sheol? (Ps 89:47-48)

Benedict wants us to remember death every day. In Saint Athanasius's *Life of Antony*, we find a similar piece of advice: "He exhorted them not to relax their efforts, and not to lose courage in their asceticism, but to live every day as if they were about to die."[3] Elsewhere he explains the significance of this practice:

> To avoid a loss of fervour, it is good to meditate on the saying of the Apostle, "I die daily." If we were to live *every day* as if we were about to die we would not sin. This is to say that *every day*, on rising, we should reflect on the fact that we may not last until evening; when we go to rest we should reflect on how we may never get up. By nature our life is uncertain and is measured out to us *every day* by Providence. If we have such an attitude and live *every day* accordingly, we shall not sin. We will desire nothing. We will have no resentments against others. We will not accumulate treasure on earth but, rather, will look ahead *every day*, to our death. In this way we will become detached and we will have nothing against anyone.[4]

This may seem a little extreme, but perhaps that is because we have become culturally conditioned to excluding death from our everyday outlook on life. And perhaps we do not take seriously enough the words that we pray so often in the Hail Mary: "Pray for us sinners, now and at the hour of our death."

48. At every hour to keep guard over the actions of his life.

Our culture values spontaneity, somehow believing that a good action performed spontaneously is of more value than one done routinely or out of a sense of duty. Yet we rarely get the opportunity to act with real spontaneity: either the present situation demands a particular action of us or our past inclines us in a certain direction, whether we are conscious of this or not. And sometimes we are drawn by hopes, aspirations, and ambitions which often seize the agenda without our submitting them to deliberate judgment. It is an impossible burden to be obliged to make cold-blooded choices all day long. We seem to have only a quantum of energy available to choose between options, and part of the way we simplify our life is to decide on some fundamental principles and live by them, without constantly subjecting them to reexamination. As a result, much of our daily life is lived on autopilot. We go about most of our business without too much self-scrutiny and save our pondering and discernment for greater issues and for those that arise unexpectedly.

We are not able to sustain a high level of attention for long periods. Security firms do not expect those they employ to keep watch without a break. They realize that we cannot remain alert continually; the most they can expect is a drowsy inaction that will, however, maintain a capacity to respond quickly to anything strikingly unusual. Our attention span is limited. To keep guard over the actions of our life at every hour would probably mean that we end up doing very little. We would be so anxious to discern every issue and to get everything right that decision making would become the main work of our day, and little else would be done.

Hour-by-hour vigilance is beginning to sound a little like scrupulosity or obsessive compulsive disorder. Many who enter monasteries already have a perfectionist streak in them;

to tell them to submit their every action to such constant scrutiny would seem to make matters worse. They would be so busy examining their motivations that their level of interaction with the world around them would decrease. Such dedication to continual watchfulness would lead to a false interiority that cannot deliver genuine growth. Karl Rahner wrote about this in his essay about good intention:

> We are always doing something as long as we live. This means in most cases some external action: walking, reading, talking, shovelling coal and many other such things. We do, of course, also have thoughts, inner feelings, "experiences" and attitudes. But one thing cannot be denied: our life consists for the most part of actions which are performed *ad extra*, of activities in which man is occupied with something other than himself, actions by which he intervenes, and effects something, in the external world of things and fellow human beings. Without these activities man could not fulfil his life at all. He cannot live in pure inwardness. He cannot make himself a pure spirit. Even the internal is still achieved in the material of his external actions and of things and achievements to which these actions refer. Not only would this be impossible, even if he wanted to withdraw himself into his interiority, but he would soon notice that his inner experience would become thin and unreal, and that he would not be achieving what he wants, viz. the intensification and deepening of his "interior life."[5]

We have to make sure that the watchfulness that Benedict is recommending is not misinterpreted and made into an absolute, so that it becomes a tyranny that renders life miserable. Some years ago I formulated what I termed a "wobble-centric" approach to the spiritual life. According to this philosophy, we do not proceed in a straight, laser-guided line from beginning to end, but throughout our life, we wobble from side to side. For much of the time, we are off the track and going in the wrong direction so that the snapshot of a particular moment may seem to indicate that we are headed for disaster. Yet, as in riding a bicycle, if we lean too far in one direction, we automatically correct the imbalance and lean toward the opposite side. If we fall over, we pick ourselves up, put ourselves back on the bicycle, and head back for the track. At any moment the bystander may judge that we will never reach our goal, but there seems to be an inbuilt gyroscope that repeatedly makes course corrections when we have strayed too far from the ideal and brings us back on course.

I think it is unrealistic to demand too high a standard of consistency from people who are engaging in lifelong dedication to the monastic journey. In God's providence there will be many occasions in which an individual falls short of the ideal, but these are factored into the total equation and can often be the occasion for valuable learnings, either for one's own life or for the sake of others. When we stray from the ideal we have the possibility of acquiring a higher degree of self-knowledge, we learn to be compassionate for the weakness and failings of others, and we learn to depend more fully on the mercy of our loving Father. It is, often enough, a matter of a *felix culpa*. If there were some who never faltered in their pursuit and practice of perfection, I would be fearful that they may be in the process of becoming self-contented and complacent little Pharisees, and I would probably hope that something might happen that would bring them to a more truthful state.

I understand the principle behind NATO's motto, "Vigilance is the price of liberty," but I also understand the difficulty of maintaining an eternal vigilance in our own lives as Benedict, at first, seems to desire. I cannot think that this means that we live in a state of continuous introspection. Keeping guard over one's actions is most easily done, first, by living in a community in which many of one's daily tasks are already defined and, second, by developing good personal habits to take up whatever slack exists in the common regime. Within this wholesome framework, one can live a fairly relaxed life, engaging one's powers of choice only as a particular situation merits it. Such a life is not filled with the drama of busy watchfulness and wrenching decisions. It cruises along in a state of creative monotony which permits the development of a habit of reflectiveness which, over the years, will lead deep into the zone of contemplative living.

This vigilance is best exercised by living monastic *conversatio* in a spirit of simplicity and joy. It is usefully supplemented by what I might term "retrospective vigilance." It is helpful, especially in the transitional phases of life, to review our daily living through an examination of conscience or, as some prefer to name it, an examination of consciousness. This is not so much a matter of counting our faults or engaging in an orgy of self-recrimination but trying to discern the quality of the choices by which our day-to-day life is being shaped. Here, the advice of Winston Churchill, in a different context, is worth following: "Watch the tides and not the eddies." This can be done by setting aside a regular moment for reflection, by keeping some kind of journal, or by regular sessions with a spiritual director or supervisor. When we stand away from the immediate situation and see matters in a wider context, we are able to understand more fully and, perhaps, more sympathetically by what forces we are being driven. In a life lived within normal limits, fine-tuning is all that is necessary, so that deviant tendencies can be corrected before they become too strong and develop the power to take us to places to which we do not want to go.

Keeping guard over actions hour by hour may be more of a challenge if we live alone and do not follow a rule of life in our everyday activities. As with so many of the items in Benedict's present chapter, this recommendation is most easily and most completely followed by living in a wholehearted commitment to a communal way of life and progressively reducing whatever inconsistencies remain in daily behavior. In such a life-giving ambience, minor faults are dealt with without too much overt attention. Over the years they simply fall away. Or they are worn down by interaction with others. Living alone, especially without a personally adopted rule or structure, demands a much higher level of vigilance.

49. To know for certain that in every place the Lord is watching him.

It is easy to assume that the Lord's watchful gaze is mostly concerned with noticing and recording any wrongful actions or thoughts of which we are guilty. This approach to the divine surveillance then becomes a factor in our having a fearful approach to God and our adopting an unnecessarily strict attitude toward ourselves. Yet what Benedict intends is spelled out in the text quoted above from the first step of humility: "The eyes of the Lord are watching the good and the wicked, and the Lord is always looking down from heaven on human beings to see whether any understand and seek God" (RB 7.26-27). Certainly, Saint Benedict intends that we might be inhibited in sinning by the realization that God is watching us, but there is also the other component of God's watchfulness. The Lord is seeking workers among the multitudes (RB Prol 14), searching for those who have some understanding and seek God. God is seeking us in order that we might seek God. And even when we falter in this search and allow ourselves to become distracted by other things, the invitation remains current. As Julian of Norwich says, "Yet in all this the sweet eye of pity never departs from us, and the working of mercy never ceases."[6]

Perhaps we might switch the metaphor from the divine surveillance to the divine accompaniment. Christ is at our side for every moment of our monastic journey. Jesus is our

Emmanuel: God-with-us. Although we may be far from him, he is never far from us, especially in times of trouble. Monastic life is a training in living in the presence of God, at the Work of God, in the oratory, in the monastery, in the garden, on a journey, in the fields, or anywhere else. Whether we sit, walk, or stand, we should know for certain that Christ is with us, comforting and challenging, rendering possible what was otherwise impossible.

Nor should we consider Christ as being a passive presence in our lives, merely an observer. He is constantly active through the energy of his Spirit, calling out to us, inviting us, stirring our conscience, giving us insight and inclination, courage and perseverance. Christ is constantly at work in our lives; it is only the numbness of our faith that mutes his benevolent interventions. It is the desire to see Christ in the events of daily living that opens our eyes to new possibilities of coming close to him. As Elizabeth Barrett Browning wrote in her poem *Aurora Leigh*:

> Earth's crammed with heaven
> and every common bush afire with God.
> But only he who sees takes off his shoes,
> the rest sit around and pick blackberries.

For most of us, our growth in spirituality will be a lifelong lesson in forgetting about blackberries needing to be picked and learning to see what is present but invisible, in learning to exploit the inherent transparency of beings to discover the world that is hidden from unheeding human gaze.

Christianity teaches us to see more than the eyes can perceive. So, every person I meet can serve as an interface between me and Christ, who said, "Whatever you did to one of these little ones, you did to me" (Matt 25:40). Action is important, but seeing is far more fundamental. How different our lives would be if we really could see Christ present in those whom we encounter in our daily living. Imagine if we went through life possessed by the sentiment expressed in the ancient Irish poem *Faed Fiada* ("St Patrick's Breastplate"):

> Christ in the heart of every man who thinks of me.
> Christ in the mouth of every man who speaks to me.
> Christ in every eye that sees me.
> Christ in every ear that hears me.[7]

To live in this way indicates a transformation of consciousness in which mundane events and realities become portals to eternity. We experience it as possible to reach out and make contact with Christ not only through moments of mystical exaltation but also by simply opening our eyes to see reality as it is, by humdrum service of our neighbor, by deliberately and contentedly letting go of self-will.

As Christ's presence in our lives becomes more than an occasional moment of recognition, we begin a process of transformation. The more we give assent to the action of Christ in our souls, the more possible it becomes for us to become vehicles of Christ's redeeming presence to others. Others experience a certain power in our words and deeds that is not attributable to ourselves but goes beyond both our intentions and capacities. This phenomenon is most noticeable in the lives of the saints, but in a smaller and less conspicuous manner, it is also manifest in the life of every Christian who has opened the door to give Christ entry into their lives. It is to be noted, however, that we will become witnesses to the presence of the power of Christ to others only to the extent that we are fully present to them, just as we allow Christ to be fully present to us. The doors must be opened on both sides. If we are unmindful and distracted in our interaction with others, traffic halts. For us to be agents of Christ to people we must be fully attentive to them. And, by a wondrous exchange, just as Christ comes to them through us, so he comes to us through them.

Certainly we would probably sin less if we were convinced that we were in the presence of Christ, but that is only a part of the story. The complementary truth hidden beneath this sober formulation is that Christ's presence and action through grace will change us for the better over the course of a lifetime. The more conscious we are of this hidden reality, the more cooperative we can be and the faster the journey toward our goal.

50

Immediately to crush the evil thoughts coming into his heart on the rock of Christ and to manifest them to a spiritual senior.

In the Prologue to the Rule, Saint Benedict has already mentioned the problem of contrary imaginations arising in the mind of the spiritual seeker. He sees one who is taking the spiritual life seriously as "one who rejects and annihilates the malign devil when he suggests something, [driving him] out of sight of the heart; one who grabs the thoughts born of him and beats them against [the rock that is] Christ" (RB Prol 28). The thoughts are not deliberately generated; they arise spontaneously. Traditional monastic wisdom teaches that the sooner these thoughts are recognized for what they are and put away, the less disturbance they will leave in their wake.

The image that Saint Benedict uses is taken from Psalm 136 (137) about crushing the skulls of Babylonian infants on the rock. Saint Augustine asks:

> Who are these Babylonian infants? They are [evil] desires [*cupiditates*], newly born. There are people who have to struggle with [evil] desires that are old. But when an [evil] desire is born, before it has been strengthened against you by [evil] habit, while [evil] desire is still an infant, smash it! But be afraid lest, once smashed on the rock, it does not die. So smash it on the rock, the rock that is Christ (1 Cor 10:4).[1]

Thoughts are not just thoughts. They are the beginning of a process that eventually leads to action. A good thought is the beginning of a good action. An evil thought or desire is the beginning of sin. The point Augustine is making is that it is easier to staunch an undesirable blaze of desire while it is yet small. If we allow it to grow, it gains momentum and spreads, and efforts to bring it under control will cost us more and will likely be unsuccessful.

C. S. Lewis makes a similar point in his little book on the psalms. We are all far too ready to capitulate in minor matters when we fail to see that they are the beginning of something major. Before we know it, the harmless suggestion has become an irresistible force:

> I know things in the inner world which are like babies; the infantile beginnings of small indulgences, small resentments, which may one day become dipsomania or settled hatred, but which woo us and wheedle us with special pleadings and seem so tiny, so helpless that in resisting them we are being cruel to animals. They begin whispering to us "I don't ask much, but", or "I had at least hoped", or "you owe yourself *some* consideration". Against all such pretty infants (the dears have such winning ways) the advice of the Psalm is best. Knock the little bastards' brains out. And "blessed" he who can, for it's easier said than done.[2]

Although life in a contemporary monastery cannot compare with the kind of quiet and secluded existence favored by desert fathers and mothers, it is relatively low-impact, compared with ambient society. This means that there is less entertainment and excitement and, as a result, more time for allowing the thoughts to freewheel. This can lead to a rich inner world of reflection, but it can equally leave the flanks exposed to attack from unwelcome desires. Leisure that is intended to be available for reading, reflection, and prayer can be swallowed up not only by frivolous fantasy but also by unexpected uprisings of resentment, anger, envy, and greed. Sometimes they are obvious; at other times they are disguised as legitimate concerns. And, of course, lust is always ready to strike when the time is ripe.

The solution proposed long ago in the desert was the manifestation of thoughts to an experienced elder. John Cassian makes the assertion that this practice is a capital means of reducing the power of temptation:

> No matter how inexperienced and ignorant the young man, the cunning enemy cannot deceive him and has no means of leading him astray if [the novice] trusts in the discernment of the elders and will not be persuaded to conceal from the elder the suggestions which [the enemy] has introduced like fiery darts into his heart.[3]

The reason we seek the discernment of someone wiser than ourselves is that most often evil suggestions come disguised as something worthwhile or at least harmless. We do not intend to give consent to what is wrong, but we are tricked into doing so:

> Often we will experience that what the Apostle spoke about takes place: "Satan transforms himself into an angel of light" (2 Cor 11:14). In this way the obscure and terrifying darkness of the senses is fraudulently presented as the true light of knowledge. Unless we have received them with a humble and meek heart, and kept them for examination by a very mature brother or a well-tried elder and accept or reject [these thoughts] according to their judgment, having diligently submitted them to examination, we will, without doubt, receive in our thoughts the angel of darkness with reverence, [thinking him to be] an angel of light and so perish and be seriously ruined.[4]

This teaching is taken up again by Saint Benedict in his chapter on humility: "The fifth step of humility is that a monk does not conceal from his abbot any evil thoughts entering his heart, or any evils secretly committed by him. Instead he confesses them humbly" (RB 7.44-45).[5] We may ask ourselves what is the purpose of this nonconcealment of faults in a cenobitic monastery. It is not a matter of control from above or the maintenance of discipline. In a way, it undermines discipline in the sense that an abbot who listens to the troubles of his monks is far less comfortable in the role of a policeman than he would have been if he had not been made aware of the monk's private struggles. The practice of self-disclosure was an important element in the solitary life of the desert dwellers, and it continued to be encouraged when monks came to live in community because it was found to be helpful. The purpose of this revelation of thoughts is entirely for the benefit of the one revealing them.

Thoughts that are inconsistent with the values we profess come to our mind unbidden. In one sense, the alternative life they present holds some attraction for us, but at the same time the intrusion of these thoughts is unsettling and annoying. Their persistence disturbs our peace of mind and confronts us with our inner dividedness. The power of these thoughts comes from their indetermination. They float around, painting vague pictures of happy outcomes, but never give any indication of how these daydreams are to become reality. A monk may imagine himself happily married, with a beautiful family, a spacious house, a satisfying career, and the esteem of all who know him. But, as we all know, such a future does not come about except through years of hard work and the endurance of many setbacks. It also demands a good measure of self-forgetfulness.

When we translate these fantasies into words, much of their power over us is dissipated. Their unreality is unmasked. This may come about by writing them in a journal, using a stream-of-consciousness method to ensure that the fantasies are not censored or tidied up before finding expression on a page. For some people, and in minor matters, writing can be sufficient. For many, however, revealing these fantasies to another person can serve as a reality check. A trusted elder who knows us well can help us return to our basic orientation in life, so that from there we can judge for ourselves whether what is proposed accords with our fundamental beliefs and values. And then we have to make a choice.

A further stage in the process of giving and receiving counsel is when we explore the fantasies in order to find their hidden meaning. This requires a little more skill and experience. As a rule, fantasies come from some inner zone of which we may not be fully conscious. Fantasies grow in the soil of unmet needs. If I am hungry, thoughts of food will invade my mind. When I am lonely, my daydreams will often carry me into relationships of unclouded intimacy. If I lack affirmation, then I will imagine myself crowned with success, admiration, and affection. If I can uncover the secret wellsprings of invasive thoughts, then I can begin the process of meeting the needs from which they derive. And then these particular thoughts lose their power over me.

Whatever the mechanism by which the revelation of thoughts operates, it has been found to be a valuable means of dealing with them and of maintaining oneself in a state of interior calm and openness to more wholesome inspirations. The humility that this practice requires helps us to dismantle the façade behind which we had been living and to live in great truthfulness with ourselves and with others.

Benedict's advice is sound monastic wisdom that is echoed throughout the centuries. If you want to be rid of troublesome thoughts and temptations, speak them aloud to a trusted elder and you will regain peace of heart, inner freedom, and a more profound sense of spiritual well-being. As Saint Aelred says:

> Whoever, in contrition of heart, thus accuses himself be-
> fore God and God's representative in a true and pure oral

confession, completely extinguishes the suggestions of the demons and the harmful ambushes of thoughts. When this has been done, after the virtues are added, after his judgment and accusation of himself, whatever thought or temptation appears is immediately dissipated, annihilated, and dissolved.[6]

51-56

To guard his mouth from evil and depraved
speech. Not to love much speaking. Not to
speak empty words or those leading to laughter. Not to love much or violent laughter. To
listen willingly to holy readings. To engage in
prayer frequently.

Following on from the verse dealing with evil thoughts,
the next four verses concern undesirable speech. What makes
speech undesirable? When it is evil or in any way inappropriate, when it is excessive in quantity, when it lacks substance
or is aimed at entertainment, when it leads to noisy outbursts
of hilarity. As we know, Saint Benedict was very serious in
the matter of silence: "Therefore, because of the gravity of
silence [*taciturnitas*] permission to speak is to be granted only
rarely [even] to perfect disciples and [even] for good and holy
words of edification" (RB 6.3).

The connection between speech and thought is not always
recognized, especially by those persons whose tongues often
seem not to be connected with their brains. But it is "from
the abundance of the heart that the mouth speaks" (Luke
6:45). Where no effort is made to exercise control over the
thoughts, speech will often be at the behest of forces operating below the level of consciousness. A simple description of
a daily event will become tinged with resentment, envy, or

self-importance. With each repetition and with each hearing by another, this underlying tendency is reinforced, and, often, the narrative is reframed to reflect this hidden agenda. Unguarded speech is a minefield through which the wise walk with the utmost trepidation.

Benedict is concerned that too much talking easily becomes an occasion of sin. Twice he quotes Proverbs 10:19: "In much speaking you will not avoid sin" (RB 6.4; 7.57). It is not hard to see the strictures of the third chapter of Saint James's letter providing a context for this hardline approach. There are other values in restraining speech, such as conservation of interior energies, greater recollection, preparedness for prayer, and avoidance of conflicts. For both the Master and Saint Benedict, living as they did in an oral/aural culture, the primary consideration in silence is that it reduces the likelihood of unprofitable and harmful conversation.

51. To guard his mouth from evil and depraved speech.

The key word in this verse is *custodire*: "guard." Saint Benedict wants his monks to be constantly on their guard in the matter of conversation. Perhaps "evil" and "depraved" represent the very worst kind of speech in which a monk might indulge and not, as a matter of fact, what is usually heard in monasteries. The idea that a monk has to take precautions against falling into evil and depraved conversation seems like an exaggeration. It does, however, take up the theme with which Saint Benedict begins the chapter on restraint of speech. "I have said, I will guard my ways so that I may not go astray through my tongue; I will place a guard over my mouth. I did not speak and I was humbled and I was silent from good things" (Ps 38:2-3). We need to be careful about what goes forth from our mouth.

The Rule of the Master connects the discipline of silence not only with vigilance regarding our conscious thoughts but also with a certain control of the eyes (RM 8.19). An enthusiasm for news and information of various kinds provides us with the content of many frivolous conversations. We call it "small talk" even though it can consume a large amount of time and, beyond that, can lead to the kind of aimless gossip that easily spills over from the merely entertaining to the subtly malicious. Our participation in such sessions is often the result of our inability to concentrate on what we are doing and the consequent tendency to keep our eyes peeled for anything unusual or worthy of further comment. Those who do their own work and mind their own business will have little to contribute to the daily roundup of newsworthy events. For Bernard of Clairvaux, this aimless curiosity is an early stage of a process that develops into serious spiritual decline.[1]

Silence is a perpetual issue in cenobitic monasteries because, due to the practical demands of interaction and cooperation, it can never be absolute. For this reason the boundaries between silence and acceptable speech are always being breached. This happens despite an abundance of legislation and exhortation.

Here, we must reassert the principles of moderation and reasonableness which are so characteristic of the Rule. Although Saint Benedict may have been reluctant to admit it, light conversation has value. It can act as a lubricant in community relations. Although the topic under discussion may have no lasting significance, the fact that it is being discussed amicably builds up a sense of solidarity and friendship in the community. Casual conversation is an important though undramatic means of achieving reconciliation. As Winston Churchill famously said, "Jaw-jaw is better than war-war." The content of the exchange is less important than the fact that those who have previously kept at a distance are coming together. Often enough, it is by laying a foundation of trivial conversation over months or years that it becomes possible for serious and life-enhancing discussions to follow.

Benedict does not seem to be imposing total silence. He has eliminated the phrase *ex toto* (completely) from the text he is following. Later, in the chapter on humility, he describes the monk who has made considerable progress as one who does not initiate conversation but merely responds to it (RB 7.56). A few verses later he gives seven indicators that what is said derives from wisdom. When wise persons speak their words are

1) gentle
2) without laughter
3) humble
4) serious
5) few
6) reasonable
7) not loud (RB 7.60)

It should not be thought that Benedict is prescribing such a way of speaking as something that may be taught, learned, and put into practice, like a physician acquiring the skill of an appropriate bedside manner. In line with the idea that the steps of humility are not programs of self-improvement but indications that progress is being made, these signs of wise discourse come without any self-conscious cultivation on the part of the speaker. They are the consequences of truthful living, of living in an ongoing attitude of truth before God, before the neighbor, and before self.

In a discourse dedicated to keeping watch over the hand, the tongue, and the heart, Saint Bernard of Clairvaux gives evidence of a remarkably balanced approach to speech. He was convinced that "love is acquired through the practice of social encounter."[2] "Love is maintained and increased through a friendly expression, a pleasant word, a cheerful deed."[3] No wonder that, having warned of the dangers of the misuse of speech, he continues:

> Nevertheless there is great utility in talking, and frequently most precious fruit is found on the tongue. This is because the righteous person lives by faith, and faith comes from hearing, and hearing comes from God's word. How can anyone live who does not believe? How can anyone believe who does not hear? How can anyone hear unless a proclamation is made? . . . This is why it is important to give a greater care and concern [to the tongue] since "life and death are in the hands of the tongue" (Prov 18:21 as in RB 6.5). . . . So let a guard be placed over our mouth and a door about our lips (Ps 140:3), so that life-giving edification may not be eternally banished, nor death-dealing destructiveness have freedom to go forth.[4]

By all means, let us banish "evil and depraved speech" from our monasteries, but let us not become so severe that normal banter and pleasantry are excluded as well. Otherwise, in such an austere ambience the building of affective community becomes very difficult, and the help we can expect "from the fraternal battle-line" (RB 1.5) is unlikely to be readily forthcoming.

52. Not to love much speaking.

One of the ways in which we do violence to other persons is by dominating conversations. When we fall in love with the sound of our own voice and are amazed at the wisdom that flows from our mouths, we so fill the available space around us that others are pushed to the margins. As a result, they are forced to become passive listeners to our not-so-thrilling monologues. If we are like this, we may think that we are good company, but we are mistaken. A good conversationalist does not talk much. A good conversationalist is a person who has the ability and the willingness to draw the other out, to listen with empathy to what is being said, to hear also what goes unmentioned, and to have some appreciation of where the other person is coming from. It is a work of great sensitivity, marked by sincere respect for the one who is speaking and great self-restraint in the one who is listening. It seems that such qualities come more easily to introverts than to extroverts, whether real or pretending.

The theme of listening in the Rule has received a fair amount of attention in recent years. As is often said, the first word of the Prologue is "Listen." The monk listens to and obeys his abbot, the abbot listens to the community and others, and all listen to wholesome readings and are assiduous in paying attention when the Scriptures are read. In a verse taken from the Rule of the Master, Saint Benedict makes a direct connection between silence and listening when he writes of the master-disciple relationship: "It is appropriate for a master to speak and teach, and it is right for a disciple to be silent and listen" (RB 6.6 = RM 8.38). And although Saint Benedict did not consider the relations between juniors and seniors to be one of equality, as is indicated later in the present chapter (RB 4.70-71), the notion of mutuality does come to the fore toward the end of the Rule. There is much to be gained by being a community of unrestricted listening, because God often speaks through unexpected mouthpieces (RB 3.3; 61.4). We will hear what is being said only if we stop talking and give ourselves to listening, not only committing ourselves to silence, but also working hard to welcome what others are saying.

As Saint Benedict clearly recognized, appropriate monastic silence and fruitful listening are the effects of profound humility. They do not come about by external regulation or by training in skills. They proceed naturally from a heart that is content to restrain its tendencies to dominate and, so, ready to make respectful room for others. Not to love much speaking but to be open to much listening is an indication that spiritual growth has taken place. As a person is drawn to the self-discipline of listening, many other virtues and good practices will begin to flourish.

53. Not to speak empty words or those leading to laughter.

There is little doubt that Saint Benedict did not want his monastery to be a place of laughter: "We damn to an eternal exclusion in all places scurrilities, idle words, and talk that leads to laughter, and we do not permit a disciple to open his mouth for such kind of talk" (RB 6.8). Such a hard line was perhaps difficult to maintain, even for Saint Benedict; we find in the chapter on Lenten observance that among the things a monk can profitably renounce during Lent are talkativeness and scurrilities (RB 49.7).

As a monk ages, many of the features of Benedictine *gravitas* become easier. A certain maturity of behavior and mellowness of outlook develop, and there is less likelihood of the giddy antics usually associated with youth.[5] One would hope, however, that in addition to this sobriety of behavior there is an increased level of joy that is not merely interior. Cheerfulness is a huge benefit in cenobitic life, and most of us would agree with the well-known saying of Saint Thomas More that "a sad saint is a sorry saint indeed."

Saint Aelred of Rievaulx certainly does not exclude laughter from the life of those who follow the monastic way. Any who sincerely accept the reality of God's promises and live in firm faith and trust are less oppressed by the burdens of life and inevitably experience a high level of contentment that sometimes brims over into merriment—and even laughter.

> "Isaac" is interpreted as "laughter" and signifies that about which the Lord spoke in the gospel, "Blessed are you who mourn now; you shall laugh" (Luke 6:21). This laughter does not mean scurrility and coarse jokes, but a certain unspeakable joy that we will have [when we are] with God. Of the joy we ought to have some part in this life. We ought to rejoice in that hope that we must have in God and in those promises which God has promised us.[6]

Karl Rahner has something to say on the same topic. He writes of a laughter that is the sign of the inexpressible interior joy that necessarily follows our full and perfect assent to God's will. This faith-inspired laughter will reach its perfection in the next life when the saved will utter their Amen to everything that God has done and allowed to happen; but even now, faith penetrates appearance to find a divine reality that is a source of rejoicing:

> But you shall laugh. Thus it is written. And because God's Word also had recourse to human words in order to express what shall one day be when all shall have been—that is why a mystery of eternity also lies deeply hidden, but real, in everyday life; that is why the laughter of daily life announces and shows that one is on good terms with reality, even in advance of that all-powerful and eternal consent in which the saved will one day say their amen to everything that he has done and allowed to happen. Laughter is praise of God because it foretells the eternal praise of God at the end of time, when those who must weep here on earth shall laugh.[7]

This is, of course, not the laughter that Saint Benedict is condemning. Certainly there is no place for the sort of laughter that is unkind and demeaning of others. And buffoonery and salacious conversation are scarcely compatible with the seriousness of the monastic pursuit. But there is a possibility that what Benedict is here seeking to eliminate is the subversive function that is often associated with laughter. Humor is not always funny; sometimes it is deadly serious. Especially in situations where authority is perceived as oppressive, laughter can be used as a defense against the total institution and a rallying call for those who feel resentful. Such political laughter can reinforce factions in a community and eventually lead to paralysis in decision making and a general decline in morale.

54. Not to love much or violent laughter.

Saint Benedict goes on to insist that the laughter that is to be especially avoided is that which is both excessive and boisterous. The meaning of the term *excussus*, which I have translated as "violent," is not easy to assess. It probably refers to uncontrollable laughter which has the person shaking with mirth and which continues for some time. The fact that, having banned speech leading to laughter, he goes on to single out laughter which is excessive and violent seems to indicate that some kinds of laughter are worse than others. Logically, this means also that some kinds of laughter are less reprehensible, though I am not sure that Saint Benedict would be happy to say so.

Since Saint Benedict manifestly is not averse to repetition, may I be permitted to reproduce here what I wrote on this topic a dozen years ago:

> It is probably true that laughter was a symbolic gesture that contradicted the whole tenor of monastic life, as Benedict understood it. Laughter undermines seriousness, mindfulness, diligence, sobriety, moderation, and kindness and acceptance of others. Loud laughter evokes a lifestyle more typical of gyrovagues (RB 1:11) than of the stolid, stable monks that Benedict cherished. Perhaps this [tenth] step of humility needs to be interpreted in the light of the Beatitudes. In

that case, laughter and rejoicing belong to the next life; here below the lot of Christians is that salutary sadness which went by the Greek term *penthos*. Even in that context, a life without laughter is a very lofty ideal and presupposes a level of spiritual intensity that few experience and none can claim as an habitual reality in their lives. We know that the saints laughed, as do many people who have been icons of Christ in our lives. Think of how much good was done by the smiling popes, John XXIII and John Paul I. Apart from patently unwholesome outbursts that stem from some inner frenzy or are associated with mockery, unkindness, or political division, there is probably no harm in postponing a campaign to eliminate laughter until some of our more significant vices have been curtailed.[8]

55. To listen willingly to holy readings.

The verb *audire*, which Saint Benedict uses here, is broader than a single English rendering. It can mean "to hear" or "to listen" or "to listen with approval, to hear favorably." The meaning is made clear by the addition of the adverb *libenter*, meaning "gladly" or "willingly." In an oral/aural culture, the capacity to absorb a message from a text read aloud was greater, but maybe there was also a tendency to turn the reading into a discussion (RB 38.8). Saint Benedict made provision for common public reading during the liturgy, especially at Vigils, at meals (RB 38), and in the interval before Compline (RB 42.3-4). This was the original form of *lectio divina*; the Rule added to this common exercise several hours daily of personal reading.

Communal reading still has an important role to play in forming the beliefs and values of the community. What is read in private sets up a conversation between the reader and the author, so that the one who reads attentively gains a benefit from the practice. Generally, however, it is readers who are in control: they choose the book; they decide on the level of attention given to the reading; they have the liberty to close the volume and never open it again. When something is read for the whole community, the content does not fall in the sphere of the individual's choice. The reading may concern a topic in which one has little interest, and so one is forced to broaden the scope of one's mental outlook. A common fund of information is gathered, like a surrogate memory; I have heard monks chatting about books read in the refectory years after they were finished. All hearing the same book together is an experience different from everyone reading the same book separately.

Readings in the liturgy constitute a special case. They provide not just information but formation in faith. Sometimes we need to jog our attention to remind ourselves that Christ is present in his word, even when that word is carelessly chosen, poorly translated, and badly read. We need to listen with all the avidity of faith in the hope that we will hear something that will carry us through the challenges of the day. How many times in the gospel does Jesus say to those he healed that it was by their faith that the miracle was worked? The same principle applies to the liturgical readings; all hear the words, most listen to them, but only a few reach out in faith to embrace the living and active salvation that they mediate. The Scholastic principle holds true here: "Whatever is received is received according to the measure of the receiver." God gives abundantly; if we receive little, it can only be that our receptivity is small. The reason for this is often inattention due to familiarity and routine. We never allow ourselves to tune in to what is being read. As Abba Nesteros remarked in another context, "It is an evident sign of a lukewarm and proud mind, if it receives distractedly and negligently the medicine of saving words."[9] Often it is only in times of heightened spiritual intensity that accompany great suffering that we really open the ears of our hearts to receive the consolation of the Scriptures.

In the Liturgy of Saint John Chrysostom, there is a beautiful prayer recited before the proclamation of the gospel. What I hear in this prayer is that the gospel reading is more than mere words; it is an event, an event that is meant to change our lives for the better:

> Illumine our hearts, O Master, Lover of people, with the spotless light of your divine knowledge, and open the eyes of our mind to the understanding of your Gospel preaching. Instill in us also the fear of your blessed commandments, that trampling upon all carnal desires, we may enter upon a spiritual life, thinking and doing all that is well-pleasing to you. For you are the enlightenment of our souls and bodies, Christ, O God, and we render glory to you together with your eternal Father and your most holy and good and life-giving Spirit, now and ever unto ages and ages. Amen.

As a rule, we are reasonably attentive during our personal *lectio divina*. It is my impression that we are less so in hearing God's word proclaimed in the liturgy. To effect some improvement, we need to energize our faith so that we listen attentively to holy readings and by so doing allow the strength of the inspired word to fill our minds and hearts and gradually to transform our lives.

56. To engage in prayer frequently.

The verb I have translated as "engage" (*incumbere*) has a number of stronger senses, some with connotations of energy expenditure and enthusiasm. The noun *incumba*, for example, means a weight-bearing pillar. This implies that persistence in prayer can be experienced as burdensome. Prayer is not always immediately gratifying, although we will often find that it is more tolerable at the end than at the beginning. What matters most is our perseverance in prayer, as Jesus insists in his parable about the widow and the unrighteous judge (Luke 18:1-7). He told this parable so that his disciples would keep on praying and not give up. What matters most is the gift we make of ourselves in the gift of our time.

The first challenge in prayer is getting started. This often involves making a definite transition from whatever we have been doing to a state of prayer. In this matter, good habit and regularity can be of considerable assistance. There is a verse in Saint Mark's gospel that describes Jesus' own practice. It reads, "Very early in the morning, when it was still dark, [Jesus] went out and went away into a deserted place and there he prayed" (Mark 1:35). Likewise, we also will probably find suitable for prayer the early morning hours, when the body and mind are rested and the day's work has not begun. But for early rising to become habitual, a certain amount of self-organization is necessary. Even so, our experience of prayer will begin with an exodus—we have to leave behind what would otherwise occupy our attention, postpone catching up with the news, and make our way to a space where nothing happens. A few steps is all it takes to move into the divine sphere. And there we pray.

The simplicity of this geographical notion of prayer is echoed in Saint Benedict's chapter on the oratory: "If it happens that someone wishes to pray, let him simply enter [the oratory] and pray" (RB 52.4). The oratory is a thin place where the presence of God is more insistent; prayer is more readily drawn from our hearts by the simple act of going there and staying there. There are no promises that a particular session of prayer will be dramatic or illuminating; prayer operates at the level of faith. "Follow the judgment of faith and not what you have experienced."[10] It is faith that draws us to the place of prayer; faith sustains us when prayer seems dry, and faith enables us to stay the distance while God's work is secretly accomplished in us.

The monk who comes to the oratory to pray is translating into practice the hope that brought him to the monastery.

Prayer is the concrete expression of his search for God. Why does he still seek God? Surely he came to the monastery to find God. Has he been unsuccessful in his pursuit? Here we come upon a mystery. The more we find God, the more intensely we seek God. On this matter Saint Bernard of Clairvaux is quite explicit:

> No one has the strength to seek you unless he has first already found you. For it is a fact that you will to be found in order that you may be sought, and you will to be sought in order that you may be found. It is possible, therefore, to seek you and find you, but it is not possible to anticipate you.[11]

The more we find God, the more we realize that infinitely more awaits our discovery. The more someone has had experience of the divine goodness, the more that person desires to be filled with it and the stronger the attraction to prayer. The finding of God is evidenced in a greater intensity given to seeking God, in personal prayer certainly, but also in all the other avenues by which God comes to us: in liturgy, in community life, in service, in self-giving, and in coping with hardship. Monastic prayer is fundamentally the time in which we allow ourselves to experience most fully our desire for God. This is why Saint Benedict sees prayer less as the clamorous recitation of oral formulae than as a deep experience of compunction and desire.[12]

Desire for God grows out of an experience of the absence of God. As Saint Augustine says, "What is desire if not a yearning after things absent?"[13] This is not absolute absence but the realization that there is so much more to God than we have hitherto experienced and the consequent desire to penetrate more fully into the divine mystery. The experience of absence is real and disturbing. In his final book, *The Climate of Monastic Prayer*, Thomas Merton based his presentation of prayer on the experience of dread:

The monk who is truly a man of prayer and who seriously faces the challenge of his vocation in all its depth is by that very fact exposed to existential dread. He experiences in himself the emptiness, the lack of authenticity, the quest for fidelity, the "lostness" of modern man, but he experiences all this in an altogether different and deeper way than does man in the modern world. . . . The option of absolute despair is turned to perfect hope by the pure and humble supplication of monastic prayer. The monk faces the worst and discovers in it the hope of the best. From the darkness comes light. From death, life. . . . This is the creative and healing work of the monk, accomplished in silence, in nakedness of spirit, in emptiness, in humility. It is a participation in the saving death and resurrection of Christ.[14]

The seriousness and sobriety of monastic prayer derives from the fact that it involves a prolonged struggle to maintain faith amid darkness and emptiness. The ancient masters of monastic prayer understood this experience in terms of spiritual warfare, in which the person attempting to pray was constantly assailed by demonic temptations. Their solution is reflected in the present verse of the Rule. Pray frequently but briefly. In that way, they thought, the thread of prayer is maintained throughout the day, but the demons do not get an opportunity to disrupt our prayer because it is over before they have time to organize an attack:

So, prayer should be made frequently but briefly lest, if we delay about it, the devil who lies in wait can introduce something into our heart.[15]

And so, [the elders] have taught that prayer be brought to a swift conclusion. . . . For this reason, while it is still fervent it should be quickly snatched from the jaws of the enemy, who though he is always ready to attack us, is especially ready when he sees us willing to offer prayers against him to the Lord. Then, stirring up various thoughts and humors, he tries vigorously to lead our mind away from the intensity of supplication, and thus attempts to change the fervor that had begun into tepidity. For this reason [the elders] think it more useful that prayers be brief, but very numerous, so that by praying to God more often we may attach ourselves to God continually, and so that, by a compact brevity, we may avoid the darts of the attacking devil, which afflict us especially when we pray.[16]

In a monastery that follows Saint Benedict's Rule, a form of frequent prayer is established by the regular round of communal worship. Throughout the day the monk is summoned to leave whatever work he is doing and to lift up his hands and heart to God through participation in the Liturgy of the Hours. That is the minimum. We know by experience that fruitful participation in the Office is dependent on fidelity to personal prayer, to *lectio divina*, and to some effort toward recollection during the day. "Before the time of prayer we should try to be just as we would want to be when we pray. For the mind is necessarily shaped during prayer by what happened beforehand."[17]

The same principle applies on a larger scale. If we develop good habits of frequent prayer, these will be a refuge and strength for us when troubles come. It is true that a crisis will sometimes precipitate flurries of prayer where previously prayer was none—desperate cries for deliverance. Often, however, if we have become strangers to prayer, then we will find ourselves bereft at the very time we need prayer most. When we go through very difficult times, our minds are constantly invaded by intrusive thoughts and our imaginations run wild, conjuring up even more disastrous scenarios. When we try to pray, the very unfamiliarity of the exercise renders our efforts fruitless.

Prayer can desert us, particularly when we are very ill, when the body is in pain, and the mind may be reduced to a confused jumble of unconnected thoughts. John of Forde advises us to get our life in order while we are still capable of doing so because, as the end approaches, we may find ourselves incapable of doing what needs to be done:

> Indeed, excessive pain, like a stormy winter that precedes death, allows us to think of scarcely anything except its own unremitting severity. There is no place for being sorry because pain fully occupies the person's mind and thought. The soul bidding farewell to this life is like someone on the sabbath, not permitted to do any meritorious work, but able only to do nothing. To do nothing, that is, that might be of profit, meanwhile [suffering] from whatever afflicts, upsets, and tortures.[18]

Cardinal Joseph Bernardin writes about this deprivation, which he himself experienced as he was recovering from long hours of surgery for pancreatic cancer:

> I wanted to pray, but the physical discomfort was overwhelming. I remember saying to the friends who visited me, "Pray while you're well, because if you wait until you're sick you might not be able to do it." They looked at me astonished. I said, "I'm in so much discomfort that I can't focus on prayer. My faith is still present. There is nothing wrong with my faith, but in terms of prayer, I'm just too preoccupied with the pain. I'm going to remember that I must pray when I am well!"[19]

To take the trouble to make more room for prayer in our life is always going to be a step forward, not only for the present, but also in preparation for whatever divine providence has in store for us in the future.

57-58

To confess to God daily in prayer with tears and groaning his past evil actions. Also, to avoid these evil actions.

These two verses advise the monk to bring to awareness each day the wrongful things he has committed in the past and the careless omissions that he has allowed to creep into his life. He is to make humble confession of these failings to God, to feel regret and appropriate shame concerning them, and to make resolutions to avoid them in the future.[1] Notice that the word "sin" is not used but rather "evil actions." Since sin can only be imputed when an action is done in full awareness and freedom, it may be inferred that here there is question of more than moral failings. This is the distinction experts in moral theology draw between "ontic evil" and "moral evil."

As a person makes progress in the spiritual life, conscience becomes more sensitive, not only about the present, but also about the past. When we traverse the avenues of memory, we find many actions that we would prefer to have done differently. This regret particularly concerns omissions; we become aware of how our selfishness so completely dictated our actions that we were not conscious of the needs of others for our love, for our help, for our encouragement and support. The years have passed, and we can no longer undo what we have done or supply for what we have failed to do. Regrets are an integral element of a long life.

This is not to be thought of as a maudlin exercise in self-recrimination. Rather, it represents a growth in truthfulness and humility. We stand before God acknowledging not only the present moment but the totality of our life. We take responsibility not only for our present behavior but also for what we have done or failed to do in the past, exactly as we do when we recite the *Confiteor* at the beginning of Mass. We do not doubt the forgiveness granted us by a merciful God but simply affirm that, on the basis of past experience, we have an ongoing need for God to be indulgent in our regard.

57. To confess to God daily in prayer with tears and groaning his past evil actions.

The practice of salutary grief, *penthos*, or compunction is difficult to understand outside the context of a very intense spiritual life. If we look at the picture of the near-perfect monk who has arrived at the summit of humility, we are surprised to find a man who carries with him, everywhere he goes, a consciousness of sin.

> The twelfth step of humility is that a monk in his body as well as in his heart always manifests humility to those who see him. This is, at the Work of God, in the oratory, in the monastery, in the garden, on a journey, in the fields, or anywhere else. Whether he sits, walks or stands, his head is to be always bowed and his eyes fixed on the earth. At every hour, regarding himself as guilty because of his sins, let him consider himself already at the fearful judgment of God. Let him always say in his heart what the publican in the gospel said, his eyes fixed on the earth: "Lord, I am a sinner. I am not worthy to raise my eyes to heaven." And with the Prophet: "I am bent over and humbled in every way." (RB 7.62-66)

Since we have not yet arrived at this high degree of continual mindfulness, Benedict wants us to make a point of bringing something of it into our lives by a daily review of our need for God's mercy. Perhaps this is an indication that he considered the prayer of the publican in the gospel as a typical monastic prayer, embodying as it does humility, sorrow for sin, trust in God, and hope in divine mercy.

In the first step of humility, Saint Benedict recommends fear of the Lord, by which he understands a recognition of our obligations to God and a self-awareness that includes the full catalogue of one's liabilities. I cannot afford to be lax or half-hearted in living a spiritual life because, if I relax my vigilance, I am liable to be swept off my feet and carried to a place to which I do not wish to go. Saint Benedict includes in his description of this step the phrase *oblivionem omnino fugiat*: Let him flee from all forgetfulness. In this case he is speaking about remaining mindful of God's commandments and of the sanctions that accompany them. But humility also involves eschewing all forgetfulness of our own weakness of will and precarious hold on virtue. To lose sight of our fragility is to court disaster. "Forgetfulness is the death of the soul," says Saint Bernard.[2] Especially when we come before God in prayer, we need to keep before our eyes the truth of our complete dependence on the mercy of God. The emergence of a desire to confess our sinfulness is, accordingly, a sign of progress, an effect of grace, and a cause for thanksgiving:

> The Holy Spirit is in the one who confesses. It is already a sign of the gift of the Holy Spirit that what you have done is displeasing to you. Sins please the unclean spirit and displease the Holy Spirit. Although it is pardon for which you are pleading, nevertheless, you and God are one when the evil you have committed displeases you. What displeases you also displeases God. Now there are two of you contending against your fever: you and the physician. The confession and punishment of sin is not possible for a human being unaided. When one is angry with oneself, this does not happen without the gift of the Holy Spirit.[3]

The test of whether we are sincere in our repentance is whether we are willing to take appropriate practical measures to ensure that we are not ensnared by the same vices in the future.

58. Also, to avoid these evil actions.

Many people have a problem with the Act of Contrition when it states, "with the help of your grace I will not sin again." The words are easy to say, and the sentiment they express is fine, but it is frequently untrue. Mostly, we know that we will sin again, and often we will repeat the very acts which we have sincerely regretted and confessed.

In the event that we have fallen into a serious sin because of a unique set of circumstances, it is not so difficult to resolve never to repeat that particular action. But when there is question of everyday sins, with the incentive for these sins coming from deep inside us, common sense tells us that we are likely to have a long struggle to overcome these wayward tendencies and that any success we have will be one step at a time, spread over many years. The most effective way of reducing the hold that our habitual sins have over us is to remain aware of the danger they pose to our integrity and to the tranquillity of our conscience. By remembering our past evil actions on a daily basis, we are taking the first steps toward a greater freedom from their influence.

Saint Aelred of Rievaulx was one who was pastorally very aware of the tyranny exercised by bad habits and their destructive effect on the morale of the person who was compelled to struggle against them without very much success. He describes a five-step program that calls us to hate the habit, to accept responsibility for the actions that stem from it, to use our mind to weaken its grip on us, to listen to the counsel of others, and to pray for relief. These are practical tactics. He does not merely suggest more willpower or self-control. He advises us gradually to weaken the hold that habit has over us until, by God's gift, we reach the point where its tyranny is broken:

> As I have said, the first thing is that we must detest this vice under which we perceive ourselves to labor. Then, as often as its delight takes hold of us, let us accuse ourselves liberally so that sometimes we receive bodily necessities with tears and never without grief. After this let us carefully make a case against this vice and listen to others who point it out and rebuke it. Finally, and this is the most necessary thing of all, let us ask [God] with whom all things are possible that this vice may be extinguished. [Let us do this] with many prayers and deeps sighs, with great contrition of heart and tears. And let us judge those to be happy who have escaped the slavery of the body and ourselves as wretched since we are weighed down by this weakness.[4]

Our attitude to our sinfulness, expressed in evil actions, past and present, should not be formed merely by psychology or ethics. We need to look on our sins with the eye of faith. In God's providence there is such a thing as a "happy fault," a *felix culpa*, as we sing in the *Exsultet* at Easter. Our sins are more often burdens from which God wishes to liberate us than crimes for which we must be punished. Our failings are meant to shock us out of our complacency and bring us to the point of reliance on God and not on self. Our sins teach us humility and humility is the royal road of access to God. This was stated very clearly by Pope John Paul I:

> I run the risk of making a blunder, but I will say it: the Lord loves humility so much that, sometimes, he permits serious sins. Why? In order that those committing these sins may, after repenting, remain humble. One does not feel inclined to think oneself half a saint, half an angel, when one has committed serious faults.[5]

On this point the smiling pontiff, for all his diffidence, is on the same wavelength as many ancient masters of the spiritual life. We cannot hope to be perfectly sinless, but we can believe and hope that our sins will be forgiven. Saint Gregory the Great taught that failures in relatively small matters were permitted by God as the means by which humility was gained so that success in larger matters did not become a source of complacency or pride:

> The dispensation of almighty God is large. It often happens that those to whom he grants the greater goods are denied the lesser, so that their minds might always have something with which to reproach themselves. Hence, although they long to be perfect, it is not possible for them. They work hard in the areas where they have not been given the gift, and their labor achieves no result. In consequence, they are less likely to have a high opinion of themselves in the areas in which they have been gifted. Because they are not able to be victorious over small vices and excesses, they learn that the greater goods do not derive from themselves.[6]

It is important that we avoid evil actions in the future and that we gradually allow ourselves to be liberated from the servitude of bad habits, but it is unrealistic to hope that we will ever be sinless and never soil our consciences with actions of which we are ashamed. Sinlessness is for the next life; for the present our task is "never to despair of God's mercy" (RB 4.74).

59-60

Not to go all the way with the desires of the flesh. To hate self-will.

In these two verses, Saint Benedict sets forth the principle of resisting the two sources of action that are most likely to frustrate the spiritual project: the desires of the flesh and the will that is fixated on self. These are universal tendencies, even though they take a distinctive form in the lives of different individuals. The description of the sarabaites in the first chapter of the Rule gives an image of the kind of life that results from submission to these natural inclinations:

> The third and very offensive kind of monks is that of the sarabaites. They have gone through no probation by rule or by the experience of a master, and they are soft like lead. By their tonsures they are known to live a lie, since in their works they have kept faith with the world. They live in twos and threes or even by themselves without a shepherd, enclosed in their own sheepfolds and not in the Lord's. Their law is the pleasure of desires since whatever they think or choose they call holy, and whatever they do not want they consider unlawful. (RB 1.6-9)

Cenobites live under a rule and an abbot in the context of an intense community life. These are the structures which make it easier to put a check on the desires of the flesh and gradually to weaken the imperatives of self-will.

59. Not to go all the way with the desires of the flesh.

This admonition echoes Galatians 5:16: "Walk by the Spirit and you will not fulfill the desire of the flesh." Saint Paul is speaking here of "the desire of the flesh" in the singular, rendered in the older Latin versions by *concupiscentia*, from which were considered to proceed the various "works" of the flesh that, in turn, Saint Paul opposes to the "fruit" of the Spirit. By changing the phrase to make it refer to desires in the plural, the emphasis has changed from a general reference to the sum total of human appetites to a more particular focus on "carnal desires," among which the vices of gluttony and lust have most prominence.

These "desires of the flesh" are taken as given. They are a constant in our lives and will weaken only as the vigor of the flesh declines: with age, with illness, and, if the ancient ascetics are to be believed, with prolonged mortification. What is recommended here is that we interpose a moratorium between their prompting and our action. The suggestions of carnal desires are always urgent; they demand our immediate obedience (RB 5.12). They are best dealt with by slowing down the process to give ourselves time for reflection and to create the space we need to attain a greater degree of freedom of choice. If we delay matters to the extent of taking counsel with a wise elder, then a great deal of the urgency evaporates. However we do it, we need to make sure that we are not blindly driven into courses of action that will ultimately prove to be self-destructive.

Here, there seems to be a clear distinction between natural tendencies and the choices that a person makes. Carnal desires are an integral element of human nature, and no one is without them. But we are not fully defined by our inherent desires. Our desires help to determine who we are, but we are not identified with them. We have the power to reflect on the potential consequences of our actions and to make decisions about whether we will go ahead with them. What is being recommended here is that we develop a habit of reflection, recognizing that our desires are speaking to us, trying to discern whence they come, and attempting to assay their value: will they lead to long-term contentment or are they merely invitations to transient pleasures that will leave us with a sour aftertaste?

If the sarabaites are the playthings of carnal desires, then cenobites have more resources with which to counter their suggestions: in particular, a rule, an abbot, and a community. Keeping to the common life both in public and private and aiming at consistency between values and action will considerably weaken the plausibility of carnal desires. This will take time and effort, but once fundamental monastic values have been internalized and strengthened by long practice, then, with God's grace, we may hope for some degree of freedom from intrusive suggestions. The secret lies in the willing acceptance of a disciplined life. As Saint Aelred of Rievaulx says:

> Again we see that we cannot overcome temptations of the flesh by playing and soft living. Whoever is in the filth of the flesh through evil habit cannot be healed except through great contrition of heart, great destruction of the flesh, and assiduous prayer. The one who wishes [simultaneously] to live pleasantly and to overcome the passions of the flesh is treating himself too delicately and deceiving himself. By divine help [Saint Benedict] so manfully resisted this first temptation that afterward he had such a great quietness of the flesh that he never afterward felt tempted to fornication. Let us imitate him and resist unlawful delights.[1]

60. To hate self-will.

The notion of hatred is rare in the Rule. We will be told later in this chapter "to hate no one" (RB 4.65), and the abbot is instructed to "hate vices but love the brothers" (RB 64.11).

To be hated, self-will must be considered a serious aberration. The term "self-will" is habitually used in a negative sense.[2] There is a single exception. In the chapter on Lent, the monk is told to offer something extra to God of his own free will (*propria voluntas*) and in the joy of the Holy Spirit (RB 49.6).[3] Saint Benedict's expectation of those who enter a monastery is that they come chiefly to avoid the peril of self-will:

> And so they seize the narrow path, of which the Lord said, "Narrow is the path that leads to life." They desire to have an abbot over them so that not living by their own judgments, and not obeying their own desires and pleasures, they walk by the judgment and rule of another and live in communities. (RB 5.11-12)

Self-will is a matter of maintaining full control over one's own life and living it for one's own advantage, convenience, and gratification. We ourselves are the only ones taken into consideration in the making of choices. It has to be said that among all the things a potential candidate gives up, the principal demand of monastic life is the renunciation of self-will. "The perfection of monks consists in setting aside self-will."[4]

Any communal existence demands the merging of individual goals with those of the group. One who joins a community must sacrifice non-concordant goals, objectives, and means. This is because affective communion depends on functional community; it is not possible to create a climate of loyalty, affection, friendship, and trust if the group is dysfunctional. But to build an effective community requires that the members accept common goals, objectives, and means, even though this may involve compromising their individual ambitions. Self-will must give way to the common will. Most of us know this in practice, but the theory upsets us in the same way that the words of Jesus cause a ripple of dread in our complacent hearts: "Whoever wishes to save his life will lose it, the one who saves it is the one who loses his life for my sake and for the sake of the Gospel" (Mark 8:35).

This is where a distinction that is at the heart of much of Thomas Merton's writings is helpful. Merton makes a sharp distinction between the outer self and the deep self. Because monastic life involves living from the heart, from the deep self, then the recognition of the false self and refusal to give primacy to its demands is a significant element in monastic growth. When we hate self-will, we are not hating or rejecting our personal reality but submitting to question the false impersonations that govern much of our everyday behavior and relationships. It is a question of uncovering the reality behind the masks we wear.

What is this false self? It is that aspect of me that is a surging sea of changing emotions, strongly influenced by whatever is happening around me. "It is like a wave on the sea blown by the wind and tossed about" (Jas 1:6); it has no stable identity but continually changes in response to influences outside itself. What is the false self? It is "the self which we observe as it goes about its biological business, the machine which we regulate and tune up and feed with all kinds of stimulants and sedatives, constantly trying to make it run more smoothly, to fit the patterns prescribed by the salesman of pleasure-giving and anxiety-allaying commodities."[5]

Basing our life on this false self can never satisfy the profound yearning of the human heart; the itch of an undefined cupidity keeps blocking our view of ultimate realities by interposing more tangible and accessible benefits on which to expend our energies. Living from the false self simply means not living from the true self, living alienated from what we are deep down, living a lie.

> All sin starts from the assumption that my false self, the self that exists only in my egocentric desires, is the fundamental reality of life to which everything else in the universe is or-

dered. Thus I use up my life in the desire for pleasures and
the thirst for experiences, for power, honour, knowledge and
love, to clothe this false self and construct its nothingness
into something objectively real. And I wind experiences
round myself and cover myself with pleasures and glory like
bandages in order to make myself perceptible to myself and
to the world, as if I were an invisible body that could only
become visible when something visible covered its surface.
But there is no substance under the things with which I am
clothed. I am hollow, and the structure of pleasures and ambitions has no foundation. I am objectified in them. But they
are all destined by their very contingency to be destroyed.
And when they are gone there will be nothing left of me
but my own nakedness and emptiness and hollowness, to
tell me that I am my own mistake.[6]

Downgrading the false self and attempting to be more
responsive to the true self is not so much the suppression of
self as the ordering of the different aspects of self: the ordering of love, the *ordinatio caritatis*, which Saint Augustine and
the twelfth-century Cistercians placed at the forefront of all
spiritual endeavor. This subordination of self-will is the engine
that drives all our efforts toward self-transcendence. In other
words, the flowering of the "deep self" necessarily requires
the taming of the "superficial self."

The strong words of Saint Benedict about self-will are best
interpreted in the context of removing a serious obstacle to
spiritual growth. They are not about devaluing the personal
worth of the individual or short-circuiting the process of "in-
dividuation" by which we attain our unique form of human
maturity. They are based on the recognition that progress in
the monastic life is the work of God and that so long as we
keep every aspect of our life in our own hands, we are liable
to put ourselves outside the path that God has destined for
us, to bring us to eternal life.

61

To obey the instructions of the abbot in all things, even if he himself should act otherwise. (May it not happen.) [Let the monk be] mindful of the Lord's instruction, "What they say, do; what they do, do not do."

The Rule of the Master reads simply, "To render obedience to the admonition of the abbot." Saint Benedict has made this verse much stronger. He has changed "admonition" to the plural "instructions" (*praecepta*), and he has reduced the lengthier phrase "render obedience" to the abrupt "obey." He has also added the rider, "in all things." In these changes we can see how unyielding Saint Benedict was in the matter of cenobitic obedience.

The most surprising addition is, however, that this obedience is not to be withheld in the event that the abbot himself does not live according to his own instructions. To support this position are added the words of Jesus about the Pharisees from Matthew 23:3: "What they say, do; what they do, do not do." In the Rule of the Master the abbot's position in the community is paramount, and his conduct is beyond the scrutiny of mere monks. The way to spiritual progress for the monks was to imitate their abbot. It was inconceivable for the Master that members of the community might be more virtuous and holier than the superior, or that the abbot's conduct might be defective in any way.

Benedict knows better. He understands that one who has the office of teaching the way to perfection will most often have to propound a doctrine that he himself has neither fully understood nor fully put into practice. His task is to teach the Gospel path to those in his charge and to explain the tradition in which the community stands. This will mean that more often he is pointing to an ideal rather than to the reality of his own life. And although the word "example" is never used of the abbot, he is encouraged to teach by deeds as well as by words: "All the things that he teaches his disciples to be wrong let him show forth by his deeds that they are not to be done, lest in preaching to others he himself is found to be reprobate" (RB 2.13). It is easy to criticize those with the office of teaching because they do not practice what they preach, but if preaching were limited to what the preacher practiced, nothing much would be said at all. Many preachers have been converted by their own words. Having pondered a matter and taken it to heart for the purpose of explaining it to others, we often find that what we are saying applies also to ourselves. Our consciences are pricked by our own words. Even though our hearers may be unmoved by our exhortations, we may often find ourselves compelled to take at least one small step in the direction that we are so eloquently pointing out to others. Benedict recognized that the same process occurs when an abbot teaches his community, "While with his exhortations he is providing correction to others, he himself receives correction for his own vices" (RB 2.40).

From this it can be seen that Benedict attributes a certain importance to the office of abbot as distinct from the character of the man who holds that office. A Benedictine abbot does not operate on his own initiative, but the authority he wields is understood within the context of the Rule: "Let the abbot do all things in the fear of God and in observance of the rule" (RB 3.11); and "Especially, let [the abbot] keep this present rule in all things" (64.20). It is not necessary that the abbot be an embodiment of perfect observance; it is incumbent on him only to take up "a difficult and arduous task" (RB 2.31). In this work there will be inevitable moments when his best efforts are not enough to perform the work assigned to him; then he will be prone to discouragement. At such times the shadow side of the abbot's personality may well emerge, and far from giving leadership by his deeds or following the example of the Good Shepherd (RB 27.8), his words and actions may give counterwitness to the message he proclaims. He is not necessarily a hypocrite; he is just a limited human being who has been stretched beyond his limits. Should such a situation arise, Saint Benedict's recommendation is that we follow the Gospel principle: "What they say, do; what they do, do not do." In this situation, it is the community's task to heal by tolerance and prayer (RB 28.4) the one who has worn himself out in their service.

The office of abbot is one of the means by which good order is maintained in the community. It is not a personal prerogative but a function or service within the total reality of the community's life. To be an abbot is not a vocation but a ministry within the abbot's vocation to be a monk, just as someone may be called to be cellarer. The nature of abbatial authority and its limitations are defined by the Rule and by canon law; the abbot serves the community in this role as long as the mandate lasts. After that, the abbot returns to the community to live as a monk, which is why he came to the monastery in the first place. Meanwhile, another serves in the office, with all the attributes described by Saint Benedict now transferred to him.

A community that has been blessed with effective abbots will, over the years, have internalized monastic tradition and will happily live the monastic *conversatio* without a great deal of intervention or intimidation from above. The monks follow the monastic way because they believe in it. In addition, to the extent that they have developed the qualities that Saint

Benedict enunciates in his chapter on good zeal, they will be tolerant and understanding with regard to the failings of others. This tolerance, if it is sincere, necessarily extends also to the men who serve the community in those offices which are more demanding on human frailty. We learn to look upon their failings also with compassion—more in pity than in blame. But as adults we know better than to imitate them.

62

Not to be willing to be spoken of as holy before he is; but first to be so that it may be said more truly.

Little children are trained to behave well through a system of sanctions. If they are good, they receive approval and are rewarded. If they are bad, they are given indications of displeasure and are punished in some way, even if it is only by the withholding of the approval for which they had hoped. The same pattern continues throughout the period of our formal education, with our every effort being labeled "success" or "failure." In an achievement-oriented society, our status is very much determined by external signifiers—rewards we have received for meeting the goals and expectations of others. Especially in the first half of our life, we quickly become adept at managing our behavior in a way that is likely to gain the maximum reward or avoid any punishment for failing to conform to accepted standards. Much of our life is lived at the behest of others; we habitually choose the path that is most likely to win approval.

There is a place for a sanctions-based formation, but it is meant to be a temporary phase. It is like scaffolding erected while good habits are being developed. Once that task is completed, the supporting structures can be removed. As we grow older, we learn the difference between right and wrong through the approval and disapproval of others.[1] The point of this learning, however, is that we may begin to discern for ourselves what is good to do and what is good to avoid. In other words, we develop an adult freedom of choice which relies more on the compatibility of an action with internalized moral principles than on the reaction or response of others.

Most of us never arrive at the point of total freedom. Whether we are fully aware of it or not, our motivations are strongly colored by the desire to win the approval of others. And not only that. A degree of competitiveness can arise so that we desire to win more approval than others. This hunger for approbation can easily give rise to jealousy and envy; the value of our own success is heightened by the failures of others, which we observe with glee. Worse still, we become so intent on winning that we allow ourselves to become complicit in the downfall of our rivals.

This desire for success and for the approval it brings also operates in the spiritual life. If possible, most of us would prefer to pass into eternal life without the necessity of being saved. We would like to think that we have, in some way, earned it by our own efforts and merits. Even if we never state this preference explicitly, we enjoy it when others notice our growth in virtue or comment favorably on the quality of our life. It may be said that "virtue is its own reward," but we like to have our good deeds noticed and praised. The other side of our desire to be held in high esteem is that we are sparing in our positive regard for others. And more than that. Unless we have been schooled in compassion by serious troubles of our own, we are overly severe in our judgments, imagining ourselves to be free of the failings we detect in those around us. We forget the warning of Cassian: "It is most certain that a monk will be subject to the same vices that in others he condemns with an unkind and ruthless severity."[2]

The Rule of the Master seems to encourage this kind of competitiveness. The Master forbids an abbot to set up any

line of succession that will prepare for the day when the abbatial office becomes vacant. The purpose of this is to keep
the monks guessing and so to motivate them to maintain a
high level of fervor with a view to becoming abbot:

> Therefore, as we have said above, let [the abbot] keep the
> order of precedence uncertain so that he may see them all
> working hard in wanting this honor at some time. Let them
> all compete eagerly to fulfill the things of God so that by
> their good deeds they may be approved for promotion. Let
> each of them show his holy works to the abbot and to God
> that so that they may expect that God and the abbot will
> look with favor on their receiving this honor. In this way
> they will more likely rival one another in their zeal for the
> good and their desire for the honor. So they are forced to
> show forth to God and to the abbot all that is holy and good
> in them, as they begin to hope to gain the [the good name]
> that is due to those who are perfect. Now, at this time, they
> must show forth in themselves by deeds what they desire
> later to teach others by words. (RM 92.48-53)

In such a system, great emphasis is placed on the external
practice of virtue with a view to winning approval. Any who
get caught up in such holy rivalry will, almost inevitably, try
to be seen as better than they are; there will be an element
of playacting in what they do. Every action will be tailored
to suit the expectations of others and little attention paid
to interior dispositions and motivation. No wonder Saint
Benedict abandoned this method of preparing for a change
in the abbatial office.

Humility, in the sense of truthfulness in the sight of God,
neighbor, and self, is the inner heart of monastic living. As
the monk grows closer to God and neighbor, he also becomes
more fully aware of his own failings and his consequent need
for mercy. At the same time, he is not stupid. He recognizes
that with the passage of years some of his vicious tendencies

have been weakened and that there has been some growth in virtue and in prayerfulness. Saint Benedict does not wish the monk to be blind to his good qualities, but he insists that he attributes them not to his own working but to the grace of God:

> Those who fear the Lord are not elated by their good ob-servance but consider that the good things in them cannot have come about from themselves but are from the Lord. And so they magnify the Lord working in them, saying with the prophet: "Not to us, Lord, not to us, but to your name give the glory" (Ps 114:1). (RB Prol 29-30)

To be overly pleased with one's progress remains a danger. In fact, it is the specific temptation experienced by those who do make progress. After a long struggle and the investment of much effort, it is natural to want to claim the credit for a successful outcome. Paradoxically, our virtue has become a barrier between us and God; once we are rid of our vices we no longer experience the same level of dependence on God. We want to assert our autonomy. Saint Aelred of Rievaulx warns against this tendency:

> You know what a struggle it is for the mind that progresses to endure. [There is a danger] that the love of human praise or flattery will cause the loss of discipline or the [pride-ful] swelling of the heart. The more the saints advance the more they are wearied by the burden of [this temptation to] vanity. In this way [the more] they lift themselves up to higher things [the more] they are sometimes dragged down to lower things.[3]

The holiness that others may perceive in us does not be-long to us; it is the effect of indwelling grace, given not for our self-adulation but in order to be a source of comfort and strength to others. If we begin to believe that this radiance is from ourselves, then, inevitably, the light will dim, and those whom it would have helped are left bereft. It is easy to convert the gifts that God has given us into fuel for our self-esteem:

> Often, the weak mind, when, for its good actions, it receives the breath of human favor, turns aside to outward delights and leaves aside what it inwardly seeks. Thus, losing discipline, it willingly lies down in what it hears externally. It delights not so much in becoming, as in being called, blessed. Because it yearns for the words of praise it leaves behind what it had begun. Thus, it is separated from God by what had seemed to make it praiseworthy in God's sight.[4]

The monk who lives in truth invests most of his energies in bringing about some improvement in the reality of his life. He is not interested in putting on a good show for others or in window dressing. He is happy to say with Saint Paul, "It is by the grace of God that I am what I am" (1 Cor 15:10).

63

Daily to fulfill by deeds the instructions of God.

Having spoken earlier about obeying the abbot's instructions (RB 4.61), Saint Benedict now adds the admonition to fulfill the instructions of God. Since the abbot is not supposed to teach, establish as policy, or command anything outside the Lord's instruction (RB 2.4), how can the Lord's instructions be different from those of the abbot? Perhaps Saint Benedict was not aware of the overlap of the verses, but maybe there is a nuance. The abbot's instructions are external and come by word of mouth. The Lord's instructions can come via the abbot, but they can also come directly through attentive *lectio divina* and from interior inspiration. Maybe we can see in this verse an exhortation to fidelity to the interior promptings of the Spirit through the meeting with God's word in Scripture and through our listening to conscience. We may note, in addition, that the verb *adimplere* indicates a more ample mode of action than mere obedience. Once we become aware of divine inspiration, we go all the way in putting it into effect.

This verse recalls what Saint Benedict had already written in the Prologue: "Having finished this, the Lord waits for us every day to respond by deeds to his holy admonitions" (RB Prol 35). Monastic fidelity is a daily fidelity, evidenced more by deeds than by words. Our vocation is to a relationship rather than to a function to be performed. Our loving desire for God is a constant factor in all that we do; we cannot simply switch it on and switch it off. To the extent that it is real, it will permeate everything we do—always, every day, and at every hour, as Saint Benedict keeps reminding us.

One of the great temptations for those who follow the monastic way is to desire to have a vacation from spiritual striving and from God: to put aside, for a time, our search for the Absolute and revert to "normal" modes of behavior. This urge may well be an indication that we have not yet attained a perfect balance in the various elements of the spiritual life. Our life is out of kilter. So much of the genius of Saint Benedict derives from the fact that he knew how to keep different polarities in suspension: community and solitariness, work and prayer, obedience and responsible autonomy, fasting and sufficiency. When our lives become too spiritual for our own good, the resultant imbalance engenders a restless tedium that augurs ill for the long-term sustainability of our spiritual pursuit. Stability is inconceivable without discretion and moderation. Of our own energies we could say, "If I make my flocks labor in walking too far, they will all die in one day" (RB 64.18).

There is a dynamic tension to be maintained in continually pushing forward while remaining within our real limits. In recent years we have become more familiar with the phenomenon of "burnout"—the complete or partial collapse experienced by those who expend themselves beyond what is prudently possible. Often enough they are victims of their own generosity. Living within a community and allowing our life to be defined by that community can offer a routine discernment about the scope and extent of our activities. Overwork is more likely for one who works alone because we are not often the best judges of how much we can do.

For those of us more inclined to take life easy, the call to an increasing level of daily fidelity is a challenge. What happens to many of us is that we set up a reasonable program of investment in religious and spiritual activities, and we remain faithful to that. The possibility of expanding the program so that we give more of our time to God and to others does not occur to us. As a result, we are liable to become so habituated to our routine that its cutting edge is blunted, and it loses its capacity to express and reinforce our spiritual desire. Our practice loses its charm and becomes a burden. The only way to prevent this is to institute some kind of review: when the new year begins, at the annual retreat, at the beginning of Lent. Whatever means we choose, we need to take a step back and consider how we may keep ourselves from going stale.

John Cassian reproduces the teaching of Abba Theodore on this point. He insists that it is not possible for us to remain for long in the same state; if we do not choose to go forward, we will certainly slide backward:

> It is necessary for the one who, in the words of the Apostle, is "renewed in the spirit of his mind" (Eph 4:23) to make progress on each day, "always extending himself to what is ahead" (Phil 3:13). If he neglects this the result will be that he will go backward and fall into a worse state. The reason for this is that the mind cannot in any manner remain in one and the same condition. It is as though someone were trying to row a boat against a strong current. If he wants to go upstream, he has to counter the flow of the current by the strength of his arms. If he drops his hands, he will be swept back by the onrush of the river.
>
> And so we must stretch ourselves with unremitting care and concern in our zeal for the virtues, and we must occupy ourselves in their continual exercise because, if progress stops, then, immediately, a diminishment will follow. As we have said, the mind is not able to remain in one and the same state, so that it neither acquires virtues nor suffers loss, for not to acquire [virtues] is to diminish because when the desire for progress ceases, the danger of going backward is present.[1]

Spiritual life is lived on a daily basis. It is to live and act mindful of present opportunities, not overwhelmed by the past or seduced by possible futures, but to do what we can in the present moment. As Saint Benedict says in the Prologue, "With eyes wide open to the divinizing light, and with astonished ears, let us hear God's voice crying out to us every day and admonishing us, 'Today, if you hear [God's] voice, harden not your hearts' " (RB Prol 9-10). Today is the day of salvation, today we are called to fulfill by our actions all the life-giving precepts of God.

64

To love chastity.

Saint Benedict wrote nothing about chastity apart from this verse, and he advises, "Let them devote themselves to loving the brotherhood chastely" (RB 72.8), though this latter instance could well mean "disinterestedly." It is not unreasonable to conclude that he considered the *Conferences* and *Institutes* of John Cassian to be sufficient instruction in this matter (RB 73.5), and it is from Cassian that we will search for a key to understand the present verse.

The monk is admonished to love the two components of monastic life that will probably give him the most trouble, especially at the beginning: fasting (RB 4.13) and chastity. The struggle against the carnal vices of gluttony and lust begin relatively early in the monastic journey. To reach the point of loving abstemious living and sexual virtue is a very high ideal, but it is one to which Saint Benedict hopes the monk will aspire. To have reached this point is to have undergone transformation. This means that it is the destination of a long journey, something attained only after the investment of many years of effort and much prayer. And the journey is different for each person: the crucial battle occurs for some right at the beginning, for others in mid-life, and for some the humiliating struggle with lust continues to the very end. "The order in which battles are fought is not the same in everybody for, as we said, we are not all attacked in a single manner."[1]

The mistake that many make is that they consider monastic chastity as something to be preserved or maintained rather than something that must be pursued. It is probably true to say that most of those who live in monasteries could be better described as being in the process of *becoming* chaste, rather than *being* chaste. If this statement causes some surprise, then it is probably necessary to remember the distinction that John Cassian makes between continence and chastity. "Sexual 'continence' is a metonymy for the whole ascetical aspect of monastic life [*vita actualis*], and 'chastity' becomes synonymous with 'purity of heart' as a way to describe the monastic goal."[2] It is by practicing continence through sexual restraint that the foundation is laid for that ultimate quality of soul by which all division and inconsistency is banished.

Saint Aelred, who was an avid reader of Cassian's writings, understands unchastity as something that destroys the integrity of the soul so that it is no longer able to make progress. Chastity, on the other hand, reintegrates the powers of the soul in such a way that forward motion becomes possible.

> The second stopping-place is chastity of the flesh at which we arrive by renunciation of the vices. In this stopping-place the soul receives [its power] of spiritual navigation. For our flesh is a kind of boat for the soul. If we are split open and torn apart by lust, then, immediately through the pleasures [of lust], as through openings, the sea comes in—that is, the bitter realities of the vices—so that the soul is no longer able to sail [*navigare*] through the waves of this world and, indeed, is submerged and drowned by its billows. But where, by the renunciation of the vices, the virtue of chastity is able to bring together [*redintegrare*] the flesh, then the soul begins to sail through this vast and spacious sea in such a way that it may be said of it: "She has become like a merchant's ship, bringing bread from afar" (Prov 31:14).[3]

Continence can be cultivated through short-term programs of self-improvement, although the effects of these may be less permanent than desired. Chastity, on the other hand, takes a long time to acquire, because its full beauty presupposes the presence of many other virtues. Thus Cassian writes, "The more someone makes progress in gentleness and patience of heart, the further he will advance in bodily purity. The further he drives away the passion of anger so will he more enduringly acquire chastity."[4] In fact, the reason Cassian regards chastity as such a lofty quality is that it cannot be attained by unaided human effort; it is the work of grace: "Even though we continually work hard [at monastic observances], we are instructed by the teaching of experience that the incorruption [of chastity] is the result of the generosity of divine grace."[5]

Cassian proposes six degrees of chastity. It is not a six-step program, but, as with humility, what he describes are indicators that spiritual progress is occurring:

1. While awake, the monk resists temptations to sexual acts.
2. He does not linger on sexual thoughts.
3. He is not incited to sexual desire by looking upon a woman.
4. While awake, he experiences no sexual stimulation.
5. He has no more interest in sex than in brick making.
6. While asleep, he is free from sexual delusions.[6]

In all these stages, we can see an emergent state of integration in which the manifold disturbances caused by sexual temptation are reduced and in which a profound sense of tranquillity takes possession of the soul. For one who, by God's grace, has arrived at such a high level of virtue, the road toward undistracted prayer is clear; union with God and selfless service of the neighbor become possible.

At this point, the practice of virtue ceases to be arduous and becomes delightful. "Whoever arrives at the image and likeness of God through this charity takes delight in the good because of the pleasure [experienced in] the good itself."[7] This is exactly what Saint Benedict says at the end of the chapter on humility: "Through this love, all that he used to observe somewhat fearfully, he will now begin to fulfill without effort, as though naturally, from habit. [He will act] no longer out of fear of hell, but out of love for Christ, from good habit itself and delight in virtue" (RB 7.68-69). Surely it is natural for all who have undertaken the monastic journey to desire to arrive at this point and so to experience for themselves a sincere and unfeigned love for chastity.

65-67

To hate nobody. Not to have jealousy. Not to give scope to envy.

These three verses overlap to some extent, although different verbs are used. To hate another leads us to withhold from them what we consider belongs to us and to wish to see them deprived of what we consider belongs to them. Taken together, they describe an attitude that is profoundly unchristian and certainly has no place in the life of a person committed to the monastic way.

65. To hate nobody.

It is possible that sociopathic personalities find their way into monastic life, but one would hope that this is a rare occurrence. The injunction "Not to murder" (RB 4.3) would certainly be relevant in their case, as would several of the other negative admonitions in the present list. Even the most skilled pastoral care generally finds itself unable to do much to help such people.

Sometimes individuals can be hated not for themselves but because they are members of a hated class or race. It is not always easy to distinguish between severe prejudice and hatred. Cliques can develop in a community whose survival depends on maintaining an active hostility toward those out-side the group. Tribal memories sometimes outweigh the good intentions of individuals. Notwithstanding Saint Benedict's call to transcend social divisions (RB 2.20), religious houses in Rwanda during the time of the genocide were not always im-mune from the internecine strife between Hutus and Tutsis.

It can happen that, after a person has been very badly treated at an important juncture in his or her life, a residual hatred of the perpetrator is later transferred to someone else. This kind of transference is not unknown in monastic life, often directed at superiors or formators, who then become the targets for a great deal of pent-up negativity. It does not always, or even usually, reach the point of hatred, but if not dealt with professionally, it has the potential to lead to an insoluble breakdown of the relationship.

A form of hatred can sometimes be mixed up with un-healthy sexual dynamics. This can happen when the person from whom some liaison is desired rejects the possibility or is indifferent. They then find themselves subjected to strong antipathy and sometimes persecuted by the frustrated swain.

There is nearly always a strong emotional component in hatred. There are those who say that complete indiffer-ence and coldness are far worse than heat of active hostility. Whether this comparison stands or not, we can be sure that there is no place for either form of uncharity in a monastery that aspires to be a school of love.

66-67. Not to have jealousy. Not to give scope to envy.

Purists distinguish between jealousy and envy, the former meaning to be over-protective of one's own goods and rights, and the latter signifying a desire to acquire what another has. Most people, including Saint Benedict, do not observe this nicety. The word used here, *zelus* (zeal), acquires its moral character from its object, as is clear from RB 72. So, in the present text, there is question of "a wicked zeal of bitterness that separates from God and leads to hell" (RB 72.1). We are dealing less with external acts than with intention, motivation, and subjective disposition. Jealousy and envy not only inspire serious wrongs but can so permeate even a good action that it becomes evil, tainted by the bitterness of the one who performs it.

Jealousy and envy stem from regarding others as rivals and adversaries. As a result, I do not wish to share with them the good things that I possess, and I resent the fact that they possess goods or qualities that I desire but do not have. Instead of belonging to a community with common ownership of goods and unity of heart and mind, I exist in a narcissistic world in which the connection to other persons is broken. So long as I can enjoy unfettered access to what is mine and go in want of nothing, what others have and are is a matter of indifference. Once I begin to feel that desirable commodities are limited, however, I begin to regard others with suspicion as potential usurpers of what is properly mine. They become my enemies. Any action of mine toward them is colored by a desire to achieve advantage for myself, even if it is at their expense.

A moment's reflection will convince us that such an attitude is highly destructive of community life, even if it was found only in a single member of the community. The danger is that jealousy and envy replicate themselves in those who were originally its targets, and so they drive everybody into a greater degree of individualism, looking after their own needs and desires and effectively standing aside from others.

Aelred of Rievaulx regards envy as the diametric opposite of charity. It is a cancer that gradually destroys the one who carries it:

> Nothing so provides a feast for the devil as envy, nothing so delights or refreshes him. Regard the countenance of an

envious man; see how pale is his face, how his forehead is
lowered and his eyes are buried; his lips are compressed; "the
skin clings to the bones and the tongue to the palate"—and
his whole outlook lacks vitality. Where is his blood? Where
is his flesh? Inside there is one who is feeding on everything,
devouring everything; he gets drunk on blood and grows fat
on flesh. Unhappy the soul on which Satan feeds. This man
has gathered so that [Satan] may scatter; he has gained so
that [Satan] may devour. Be on your guard, my dearest sons,
beware of this disease which takes a man wholly away from
himself, from his neighbor, and from God and makes him
wholly subject to the devil. Believe me, my brothers, there
is nothing that so diminishes the joys of this present life or
removes the hope of future happiness or simultaneously
undermines all the other virtues [as envy].[1]

Aelred's description of the effects of envy is striking: envy
alienates us from ourselves, from our neighbors, and from
God. It destroys happiness and hope and undermines whatever good we do. It not only poisons the spiritual life but also
progressively makes sad and ugly the person possessed by
it. Only envy, among the vices, bestows no benefit at all on
those conquered by it. Aelred would certainly have agreed
with the views expressed by a contemporary secular author:

Whatever else it is, envy is above all a great waste of mental energy. While it cannot be proved whether or not envy
is part of human nature, what can be proven, I believe, is
that unleashed, envy tends to diminish all in whom it takes
possession. Wherever envy comes into play, judgment is
coarsened and cheapened. However the mind works, envy,
we know, is one of its excesses, and as such it must be identified and fought against by the only means at our disposal:
self-honesty, self-analysis and balanced judgment.[2]

68

Not to love contention.

Many years ago a psychologist working with our community attempted to initiate us into what he termed "non-contentious dialogue." The difficulty we experienced in this enterprise was a revelation of how ingrained contentiousness can be, unless we do something to neutralize its influence. The more we have pondered a topic and arrived at some conclusions, the less likely we are to welcome alternative readings of the evidence. We are far too certain of our own observations, interpretations, and applications. We never step back to determine whether a different perspective might yield a different conclusion. We are far too certain of our slightest opinions. As a result, contention develops, polarization occurs, and there is a danger of division in the group.

The only way to avoid contention is to develop a culture of listening to others with profound respect, convinced that they have grasped some element of truth that has passed hitherto unnoticed. Taking for granted that others are speaking sincerely, we must prime ourselves to pay close attention to what they are saying. The more uncomfortable we feel as they describe their point of view, the more likely it is that up to this point we have not been taking into consideration data that they have and we do not. We want to push the discussion forward to arrive at the conclusions we have already formed, and wer are impatient with anything that delays that process. What are we doing? We are closing our eyes and refusing to take the fuller truth into consideration. We want to go ahead on the basis of half-truths. Perhaps we need to pray for the liberating grace of self-doubt.

Contention arises from a binary attitude to reality, from a belief that complex questions can be resolved by rapidly reducing them to a simple yes/no option. We forget that many different viewpoints need to be aired before arriving at a position that can claim a good level of common agreement. Avoiding the expression of alternative opinions and straitjacketing the discussion so that it proceeds to an inevitable conclusion often mean that the total group will fail to own fully whatever decision is taken. Paradoxically, the way to avoid contention is to encourage the full expression of different points of view. Expressed openly, they can be dealt with rationally; if their expression is inhibited, they remain underground as a hidden source of discontent and a reason to dissociate oneself from whatever had been too rapidly decided.

The use of the verb "love" in this verse indicates that Saint Benedict is thinking of more than the occasional, and probably inevitable, conflict. There is question of a chronic difference of opinion, openly expressed and with a heightened emotional content. This happens because some members of the community do not feel included either in the decision-making process or in the practical tasks that implement the policy adopted. In such a state of alienation, a person may begin to find further issues for complaint and dissent. Saint Aelred uses the term *litigare* for this, often linking it with murmuring and detraction. In such a state of radical discontent, nothing seems good enough, and friction develops between those who feel excluded and the others who are doing their best to provide and arrange things for the community. In the course of a lifetime, one may encounter one or another person who seems to "love contention" to the point of being unable to live without it, but, fortunately, such people are the exceptions. And in many cases, the contentiousness is merely the external manifestation of more serious problems.

The definitive way of reducing any tendency to contentiousness is detachment. Conflicts develop and relationships come under threat whenever people are so attached to their own viewpoints that common ground cannot be found. On the other hand, it is normal, as spiritual priorities gain more weight in daily life, that people lose interest in many of the trivial matters that used to cause them so much excitement. In such a state, tolerance grows strong, and the person is able to maintain equanimity even when decisions are made which are patently idiotic. A more highly developed sense of proportion enables these unfortunate outcomes to be located in a larger context, and thus their emotional content is reduced. This kind of global acceptance is especially noticeable among those seniors who have attained a mellow monastic maturity. On the other hand, conflicts and contention seem more frequent in communities lacking this top tier. Too many are so attached to their own ways to allow for the patient emergence of a common way forward.

69

To flee elation.

In the chapter on humility, Saint Benedict balances the voluntary abasement of the monk with the exaltation given by God, so that an attitude of humility is seen as the predisposition for divine exaltation.[1] Denial of self is thus understood as a means toward transcendence of self. I lower myself; God raises me up. In contrast, the vice spoken of in the present verse interrupts this process. What is being envisaged is that a person engages in self-exaltation instead of waiting to be lifted up by the action of God. It is the preference for temporal advantage over an eternal reward.

This verse is not present in the Rule of the Master; its insertion is an indication of Saint Benedict's priorities. Elsewhere in the Rule, he speaks of elation as equivalent to pride, a danger especially for those who have been elevated to a position of status (RB 28.2; 62.2; 65.18). Being pleased with oneself may seem a mild enough vice, especially if there are good grounds for satisfaction, and, after all, such secret complacency hurts nobody else. The malice of elation consists in its untruthfulness. Any spiritual progress we make is attributable not to self but to the grace of God. "Those who fear God do not allow themselves to become elated by their good observance but consider that these goods that are in themselves do not come from themselves but from God" (RB Prol 29). We might add that all their gifts and talents come not only directly from God but also from their genes, their family, their education, and from the openings provided for them by the community in which they live. We would be nothing if we had not been given the opportunities and incentives to develop ourselves.

Persons who are too pleased with themselves are forgetful of the fact that we are relational beings. We have nothing that we have not received. "Naked I came from my mother's womb and naked I will depart" (Job 1:21). Whatever I have in the interim has been given to me by others. I cannot bake a cake without the ingredients. I cannot write a book without time, talent, and technology—all of which, in one way or another, have been given to me or allowed to develop in me through the generosity of other people. When I allow myself to become overly elated at my perceived achievements, too often I forget the immeasurable contributions others have made to what has been accomplished.

There is much talk today about the problem of low self-esteem. Those who go through life unappreciated for what they are carry a heavy burden. Conversely, those who are blessed to belong to a community where people are valued for themselves and where affirmation and appreciation are generously given are usually happier and more creative. Such communities do not, of course, spring up spontaneously like mushrooms. They are the result of years of hard work. Where this effort has been spared, we will find that we are often more inclined to denounce and condemn what is wrong than to praise and applaud what is right. Positive reinforcement is not only useful in training children; adults also thrive when they are appropriately affirmed. The art we need to learn is concelebration. What a joy it would be to live in a community that not only rejoices in the "success" of others but also values and celebrates everyone for who and what they are. In such an affirmative ambience, the temptation to elation and self-exaltation would be considerably less.

Almost inevitably, elation leads to self-promotion. We instinctively understand that a private feast of self-congratulation is profoundly unsatisfying, and so we begin to look for others to recognize and affirm our good qualities. How can they celebrate them if they do not know about them? So we must find ways to keep others informed of those aspects of our life that merit praise. In a monastic community, such efforts at self-promotion need to be fairly subtle. People do not respond positively to overt boasting, and the one who is always fishing for compliments is often dismissed as pathetic. With time, we develop the skill of coating our self-advertisement with a layer of diffidence, seemingly reluctant to have others know of our eminent achievements. Such posturing would be comic if it were not tragic. The fact is, however, that there is often a dark side to self-promotion; it is often powered by envy and jealousy and, as a result, is twinned with an equal zeal in undermining the esteem in which others are held. The cruel logic is that they must decrease so that I may increase.

The only way effectively to flee elation with all its tricks is to embrace wholeheartedly Saint Benedict's teaching on humility. This Christlike quality often seems austere and unattractive at first encounter, but it is the most important element of lifelong perseverance in the monastic state. "Humility is the teacher of all the virtues, the most solid foundation of the heavenly building. It is the Saviour's special and greatest gift."[2] The Christological character of humility is of prime importance. Humility grows strong in us insofar as we have the mind of Christ, and we make progress in being reformed according to the mind of Christ by frequenting the gospels and developing a profound personal relationship with the Lord. From this relationship we derive a firm conviction that we are both lovable and loved. This personal adhesion to Christ expressed in the wholehearted desire to live as his disciple becomes the primary means by which we identify ourselves. We do not have to resort to compensatory tactics to bolster our self-esteem or win the love of others. We are known and loved by Christ, called to live in union with him, and with him to walk the road that leads to eternal life. In faith and trust, we commit our lives to him; he is the one who will raise us up to glory. Any other form of exaltation is necessarily both temporary and illusory.

70-71

To venerate the seniors. To love the juniors.

These two verses, seemingly based on Ephesians 5:33, are lacking in the Rule of the Master. The imperfect reciprocity that they suggest is a reminder that for Saint Benedict we live in "a community of unequals," to use an expression coined by Sister Helen Lombard:

> I believe that "the good zeal that monks ought to have" (RB 72) is to be exercised always in a community of unequals, a community of the weak and the strong, of some with one gift and others another, of those who need more and those who need less, of the advanced and less advanced in the monastic way of life. All are radically one in Christ (2:20), all are brothers to one another within the community. Yet the community is complex, messy, diverse. Each member has a specific place within it. Relationships are not perfectly symmetrical. There is nothing smoothly egalitarian about it at all. It is in such a community of unequals that the brothers are called to practise obedience with the warmest love (72:3).[1]

For Benedict, seniority is mainly determined by the day and hour of entry, although for reasonable causes the abbot is able to make some adjustments to rank in the community (RB 63.7-8). Beyond this formal system, there are many informal seniorities operating in most communities. Juniors may be more at home with technological advances, social changes, and new ideas than those who are still operating on what they learned decades ago. Some people are more skilled in practical tasks and need to exercise leadership when many are co-opted to participate in them. Few communities now draw their recruits from a stable and homogenous pool; as a result, there is variation in background, experience, and attitude among the various people who have entered over the years. This is not something to be lamented, but it represents the opportunity for a great enrichment of the group, even though more effort will need to be expended in the process of reaching a practical unanimity.

Adalbert de Vogüé has written about the "horizontalism" that characterizes the community in Saint Benedict's Rule and distinguishes it from the Rule of the Master. The abbot's formative influence is exercised not only directly but also indirectly. A well-formed community becomes itself a formative influence on those who enter it, so that the same message is being communicated not only from the abbot but also from all the brothers, each in his own particular way and with his own personal coloring.

> Every member of the community, by virtue of his age and seniority, plays a part in the educative role which in traditional coenobitism was reserved to the abbot and to the office-holders. The chapter "On Good Zeal" attributes even more generously to the life of charitable fraternal relationships, the purifying and sanctifying effects which the Master saw as the result of asceticism lived under the abbot's direction.[2]

As Benedict says in another context, "Each has his own gift from God, one this, and another that" (RB 40.1). The notion of seniority need not be reduced to the level of mere ceremonial or elevated into a structure of dominance. It is, most of all, an expression of fraternity by which each member of the community recognizes and celebrates the unique contribution that others make to the common life and to the attainment of the monastic ideal.

70. To venerate the seniors.

In a culture obsessed with the preservation of youth, growing old might seem to be a curse, and those who have passed beyond mid-life might be regarded as ready to be relegated to irrelevance. It is assumed that they have nothing to impart. This is one of the themes of Margaret Mead's book *Culture and Commitment*: "Whatever stand they take, none of the young, neither the most idealistic nor the most cynical, is untouched by the sense that there are no adults anywhere in the world from whom they can learn what the next steps should be."[3] Saint Benedict's injunction seems to approach seniority from a different standpoint.

It is certainly true that some functions of the brain deteriorate with age, but there are others which come to the fore. It is well known that some aspects of memory become impaired. We may be less adept in new learning, the snap processing of complex data, sustained concentration, and multitasking. It is important to note, however, that these failings are either disguised or balanced by certain gains: wisdom, expertise, competence. The ability to perceive recurrent patterns without the labor of detailed analysis means that even without a pristine brain, many persons are able to continue operating at a highly professional level even at an advanced age. "Though the brain may age and change, each phase of this progression presents new and different pleasures and advantages, as well as losses and trade-offs, in a natural progression, like the seasons."[4] "Genius (and talent) are usually associated with youth. Wisdom and competence are the fruits of maturity. . . . Wisdom and competence are the rewards of aging."[5]

While recognizing the facility that experience and competence bring to many tasks, it is important to recognize that aging does reduce energy and endurance. It may well be that human nature is drawn to show mercy to those who are growing old, but it does not always happen. Great reserves of compassion, understanding, and patience are needed in living with those suffering dementia, remembering that they were not always so and honoring them for what they gave before they ceased to be able to give and, where possible, finding honorable employment that will occupy the hours. We cannot afford to deny the limitations that aging imposes. I have seen people in monasteries left doing tasks that twenty, thirty, or forty years ago they did with enthusiasm; they are still able to perform competently and are generous in giving service to the community, but with each passing year, the doing of the work costs them more. Those who have reached eighty will tell you that they do not have the same energy that they had when they were seventy, and I can assure you that at seventy, I do not have the same physical resilience that I had ten or twenty years ago.

The skills and energies of youth are certainly to be cherished and used, but they are not the only resources that a monastic community needs if it is to flourish. The monastic journey is long, and it is not straightforward. There are many twists and turns on the road, and, often enough, the way ahead is counterintuitive. And while nobody else has ever followed the exact same path that I walk, those with years of experience can recognize and advise on certain recurrent patterns that may be baffling to me. It is possible for me to learn from others. The recognition of the value of taking counsel with an elder is strongly attested among the desert fathers and mothers and has been frequently asserted ever since. The quality that enables the elder to speak with confidence is experience; reflection on their own lives and on what others have communicated to them has given a broader insight that is, in some way, applicable to almost anyone.

It is important that we do not cut ourselves off from the voice of experience and, instead, pay attention only to maverick problem solvers. We need to keep older people in the loop, acting, as Saint Benedict foresaw, as an informal and parallel pastoral mechanism (RB 27.2). This means that we need to take care to assign to the seniors an active role in the life of the community so that their specific contributions can be garnered for the good of all. This probably means encouraging them not to retire from life but to keep mentally and physically active. "A life too settled is no longer a life but an afterlife."[6] The best way of "venerating the seniors" is to make use of the special gifts that their long years of fidelity have allowed to develop.

As with the case of showing honor (RB 4.8), treating older people with respect and reverence not only enhances the lives of those who are the recipients of such esteem but also adds something to the givers and contributes greatly to the harmony and concord of the community as a whole.

71. To love the juniors.

If the juniors are to respect the seniors and allow themselves to be influenced by them, there is a corresponding expectation that they will receive from them affirmation, acceptance, and affection. It is because of the kindliness of those more advanced in the monastic way that newcomers are willing to listen to them and learn from them. Benedict does not want the more senior members of the community to become a vigilante police force that takes upon itself the responsibility for monastic discipline (RB 70.1-7). All are brothers, from the most senior to the most recent arrival. The seniors, mindful of their own earlier struggles, are expected to be sympathetic to the difficulties encountered by those at an earlier stage of monastic maturity, looking upon their aberrations more in pity than in blame.

This is the general principle that Saint Benedict has in mind, especially with his notion of mutual obedience. In practice, however, the norms he lays down for rank in the community represent only an imperfect realization of the ideal. Mutual obedience seems reduced to a unidirectional concept. In the chapter dedicated to mutual obedience, Saint Benedict writes, "Let all the juniors obey those ahead of them [*priores*] with all charity and solicitude" (RB 71.4). This downward direction of mutuality is further reinforced in the chapter on community rank:

> Let the juniors honor the seniors and the seniors should love the juniors. Even in the use of names nobody is to be allowed to address another by the bare name, but seniors should call their juniors "Brother" and juniors should call their seniors "Nonnus," which is understood [as a term] of paternal reverence. . . . Whenever the brothers meet, the junior should seek a blessing from the senior. When a senior goes past, let the junior rise to give him a place to sit, and the junior should not sit down again until instructed to do so by the senior. In this way what is said in Scripture comes about: "In honor they give each other precedence" (Rom 12:10). (RB 63.10-12, 15-17)[7]

It could be surmised that, in Saint Benedict's time, the default position of any group was to give greater status to those who were older, and that when the Rule envisages mutuality, it does so in the context of a voluntary equality that does not disturb the acquired rights of those who have seniority. In this way, Saint Benedict maintains the shell of a well-ordered community while, at the same time, proposing a more excellent way by which the brothers will "in honor give each other precedence."

Armand-Jean de Rancé, the reformist abbot of La Trappe in the seventeenth century, was one of the few monastic writers who delved deeper into the notion of mutual obedience.

He includes in it the voluntary obedience of seniors to their juniors. He wants nobody to use seniority as a pretext for avoiding the necessary restrictions of the monastic state. Quite the contrary! The *Usages* of the Abbey of La Trappe state that whatever privileges exist should be given to the juniors, presuming that the seniors can more easily get along without them:

> It is in no way sufficient to obey the abbot in order to maintain in the monastery order, peace and tranquility if one does not also obey those with whom he shares his authority. If the commands of those who represent the abbot are not respected as coming from him, since the abbot cannot be present where he is not, each person would be left independent, in the power of his own counsel; that is to say, in confusion. The saint wants more. He wishes that the younger religious obey their elders with all possible urgency and charity. This is in order to establish among the brothers such a complete concord and understanding that it is never under threat. This is the most powerful means of creating a union of hearts. "For the rest let all the juniors obey their seniors in all charity and diligence." Finally, to cement this necessary and holy understanding, [Saint Benedict] wishes that all the brothers obey one another: the seniors the juniors as well as the juniors the seniors. "But let the brothers obey one another." And, in order to make them more faithful and ardent in acquitting themselves of this duty, he declares that it is by this road that they will go to God and open the gates of his Kingdom.[8]

72-73

In Christ's love to pray for enemies. Before the sunset, to return to peace with those with whom there has been a quarrel.

As his next-to-last topic in this long list of good works approaches, Saint Benedict brings to our attention the importance of reconciliation. He begins with love of God and love of neighbor and concludes with reconciliation with those with whom we have had difficulty and, finally, encouraging us to maintain our hope and trust in God, even in the event that we are tempted to despair.

72. In Christ's love to pray for enemies.

This verse is not found in the Rule of the Master. It parallels RB 4.31, "To love enemies." Praying for enemies is perhaps easier than loving them, although both responses to hostility are recommended in the Sermon on the Mount. The *Testament* of Father Christian de Chergé, one of the martyred monks of Atlas in Algeria, embodies this evangelical attitude, extended to the one who was to be the immediate cause of his death.[1] Most of us will never be called upon to exercise this heroic degree of love and forgiveness, but there will be many opportunities for us to let go of a grievance against someone or, if we find that difficult, at least to pray for their welfare.

Father Christian says to his killer, "In God's face I see yours." What this means is that in finding God he finds also the whole of humanity—not only his friends, but also his enemies and persecutors and murderers. Finding them in God means that they cannot be hated; they must be accepted, even in their hostility, and loved. There is no room for rejection and hatred in a heart that is drawn into God's love. It is "in Christ's love," as Saint Benedict points out, that we find the possibility of not reciprocating hostility but of meeting it with kindness, prayer, and eventually love. Instead of separation he speaks of union.

The union between persecuted and persecutor thus expresses the mystery of a shared responsibility for the objective evil that is occurring. Father Christian writes, "I have lived long enough to know that I am an accomplice in the evil which seems, alas, to prevail in the world, even in the evil which might blindly strike me down." Instead of blaming and hating the one who would end his life, he mourns his own contribution to a situation which has brought another human being to such a dire extreme. There is here another lesson for us. Before condemning those whose actions seem hostile, we need to examine our own conscience to measure the extent to which we have been complicit in the creation of the hostility. Perhaps even our self-styled "good deeds" (and our self-righteousness) have spurred the other person to reject us. We are not always as blameless as we would like to believe. Reconciliation is impossible as long as we regard ourselves as the sole injured party. Sometimes the path to reconciliation is cleared by our being willing to be the first, humbly and sincerely, to ask for pardon and forgiveness.

Letting go of our blamelessness and proactively removing any cause of complaint with regard to our enemy is a great liberation that enlarges the heart. In the love of Christ, we perceive that all are in need of redemption; in this we are more like than unlike our enemy. Together we come before Christ in need of healing; together we are healed and saved. Any attitude which would make us superior to our enemy will undermine this essential solidarity and will ultimately warp our own integrity. This is because nonforgiveness destroys any whom it possesses:

> However much we have been wronged, however justified our hatred, if we cherish it, it will poison us. Our hearts will become bitter and our vision clouded and our love will wither away. Hatred is a devil to be cast out and we must pray for the power to forgive, for it is in forgiving our enemies that we are healed.[2]

73. Before the sunset, to return to peace with those with whom there has been a quarrel.

This verse looks at the practical implementation of a policy of reconciliation. It is perhaps based on Ephesians 4:26: "Be angry but do not sin [Ps 4:4]; do not let the sun set on your anger." It is good advice. Quarrels and misunderstandings inevitably arise in community living, and there needs to be a general understanding that they will not be allowed to continue. Wiping the slate clean at the end of each day is a means of ensuring that disagreements do not assume a disproportionate seriousness.

If we allow a grievance to fester after sunset, it will interfere with our sleep. During the long wakeful hours of the night, our mind will constantly return to the source of our disturbance and reinforce our negative feelings toward any who were involved in some way. The deprivation of sleep will exaggerate our feelings of being wronged and extend the grievance from a single incident to include a wide range of hurtful situations. Instead of being able to view the matter within a commonsense perspective, we lose all proportion and our unhappiness is greatly magnified. What others may view objectively as a minor misunderstanding is now seen by us as an element in a long-lasting campaign deliberately designed to cause us suffering. The particular incident that caused the trouble has become an entry point to a wide world of grievance, and the feelings associated with it are blown beyond all reasonable limits.

What is happening is that we are allowing ourselves to be passive while our emotions rage. We do not use our reason to scale back our feelings within rational limits. We do not use our spirituality to view matters as Saint Benedict suggests in the fourth step of humility (RB 7.35-43). We have become the playthings of emotions whose real energy comes not from the triggering incident but from some deeper and more hidden source.

Jesus promised happiness to those who make peace (Matt 5:9). This seems to indicate that when a quarrel happens one or the other party has to take the initiative and move toward reconciliation. Peace will not happen of its own accord. It has to be created. All peacemaking begins in the head. We have to start thinking differently. First of all, I have to renounce all those violent imaginative scenarios in which I visit misfortune on those who have offended me. Then I have to step back and recognize some degree of complicity in any misunderstanding that has developed. Then I need to acknowledge that any continuance of war (whether it be a cold war or a more open exchange of hostilities) will be a war of attrition, which will erode the integrity of all parties, cause serious scandal, and bring impairment to the quality of life within the community. It is a no-win situation. At this point, I must begin to think about what I can do to resolve the matter peaceably and move toward reconciliation. If I am not prepared to return to peace, then the danger is that my conventional greeting of peace will be dishonest (RB 4.25).

In some cases, reconciliation need not involve much more than a willingness to let the whole matter disappear, to allow the relationship to continue as it was before the disagreement occurred. This is especially true when the cause of friction was slight and, perhaps, was unnoticed by the other person. Sometimes this normalization has to occur in stages, and nearly always it involves at least the tacit agreement of both parties. Prudence would suggest that we do not try to speed up the process but let it move forward at a natural pace. In more serious situations, a third-party mediator may be required. The context envisaged by the present verse, however, seems more concerned with bringing swift closure to trivial daily disagreements lest molehills become mountains.

In a sermon preached three weeks before being kidnapped, Father Christian de Chergé summarized his approach to peacemaking in five words. "There are five pillars of peace: Patience, poverty, presence, prayer and pardon."[3] These are elements on which we could profitably meditate when we find ourselves in a situation where peace is threatened or concord disturbed: to endure suffering, to be willing to go without, never to break a relationship, to pray for those who may have offended us, and to let go of our grievances. Learning to live thus on a daily basis will ensure that we will, in truth, return to peace as soon as possible with those with whom we have quarreled or with whom we have had a disagreement or a difference.

74

And never to despair of God's mercy.

Having proposed seventy-three practical ways in which the monk may move closer to the fulfillment of the monastic ideal, Saint Benedict relocates his recommendations in the context of grace and mercy. There are very few persons who could claim to have practiced all the precepts in this chapter, and so, at the end, most of us are probably conscious of how much more needs to be done to bring our life into conformity with the Gospel in the way that Saint Benedict envisages. We cannot do this on our own. We are totally reliant on grace, and where we have failed to live up to our ideals, we need to have recourse to God's ever-available mercy and forgiveness.

I have sometimes wondered whether the high ideals proposed in monasticism have any other purpose than to bring us to the recognition of our urgent need for the mercy of God. In other words, I sometimes doubt whether these ideals are meant ever to be realized. I have had the privilege of meeting many holy monks and nuns, but I have never been in any doubt that, were I to look upon their lives with a jaundiced eye, I could soon find plenty of evidence of fragility and failure. In the final analysis, we are all totally dependent on God's mercy, whether our lives are apparently well-ordered or seemingly inconsistent and chaotic. Exterior virtue and righteousness can sometimes disguise this innate neediness,

and a reputation for serenity can lead us wrongly to conclude that a person has no struggles. We are all sinners not
only because of the long and grisly catalogue of many moral
failures but, more especially, because we are all crippled by
concupiscence as the result of what is usually termed "original
sin." In addition, it is only with difficulty that we overcome
the distortions and bad habits introduced into our lives by
what has more recently been called "social sin." We absorb
much from ambient culture that encourages us to be false
to ourselves. Sin is much more than ethical failure. It is a
power for evil that enters our life and alienates us from God
and from one another. It is because of this prevalence of sin
that we live in a state of ontological misery. This *miseria* was
recognized by the twelfth-century Cistercians as our strongest
appeal to the *misericordia* of God. We cannot heal ourselves
or save ourselves; the human situation is such that it can only
be brought to its full potential by the outpouring of God's
generous love, forgiveness, and mercy.

Certainly Saint Benedict's recommendations stand as a
reminder of how we may live a more Christlike life, and it
is to be hoped that we will be inspired by them to do a little
better. However fervently we busy ourselves in good works,
we remain dependent on grace to do good and on mercy to
forgive what we have done amiss. If we forget our need of
mercy, we will place too much emphasis on our own efforts.
This may, for a time, seem to bear fruit, but in the longer
term it leads to discouragement and even to despair. The
spiritual life, the Christian life, is a life lived in the context
of Christ, and it is more important to dwell on what Christ
does for us than on our defective efforts on our own behalf.
Saint Bernard of Clairvaux expresses this truth with his usual
eloquence:

> Therefore, my advice to you, my friends, is to turn your foot
> aside from troubled and anxious recalling of your ways and

escape to make an easier journey by the serene remembering the good things which God has done. In this way, instead of becoming upset by thinking about yourself, you will catch your breath by looking upon God. I want you to experience what the holy Prophet advised when he said, "Delight in the Lord and he will give you what your heart asks." Sorrow for sin is, indeed, a necessary thing, but it should not prevail all the time. It is necessary, rather, that more joyful recollections of God's kindness should interrupt it, lest the heart should become hardened by too much sadness and so perish through despair.[1]

Excessive sadness makes the heart impermeable to the working of grace, and, thus isolated, it becomes prone to a despair which is not life-giving. We need trust in God and confidence in the power of God to overcome all the obstacles that bestrew our spiritual path. We build up this confidence by remembering the good things God has done and by opening ourselves in prayer to experience God's goodness. When we prefer nothing to the love of Christ, everything else slips into place, and the service we offer is done not with a sense of being burdened but in a spirit of joy. Bernard also speaks about this:

> It is only right that we should do all things with cheerfulness [*in hilaritate*] because God loves the cheerful giver. In truth, our land is in no way receptive of the seed of good *conversatio*. It will easily perish, easily take fright unless it is helped by ample waterings. So it is right that in the Lord's Prayer we ask for this kind of grace under the name of "daily bread."[2]

The Rule is a sober document, and the way of life that it imparts is serious and purposeful. This does not mean that the atmosphere of a monastery that follows Benedict's instructions will be somber and harsh. Amid all the regulations that Benedict gives, there are words that add a sparkle to what he writes. For example, he refers to delight (7.69), sweetness (Prol 19, 49; 5.14), cheerfulness (5.16), and joy (2.32; 7.39; 49.6-7) and frequently mentions the more upbeat themes of love, hope, and peace.

75-78

Behold, these are the implements of the spiritual craft. When they are used by us, unceasingly, night and day, and given back on the Day of Judgment, we will be paid the reward from the Lord which he himself promised. "What God has prepared for those who love him, eye has not seen, nor ear heard, nor has it arisen in the human heart." The workshop where we diligently work at all these is the cloister of the monastery and stability in the community.

Saint Benedict has reduced the seventeen verses of the Rule of the Master to these four. As he does at the end of chapter 7, he has omitted the Master's florid description of the rewards awaiting the good monk in the next life. Here, he simply uses a quotation of 1 Corinthians 2:9. To merit the reward which the Lord has promised, the monk has to make diligent use of the tools which are available to him, and this practice, as Saint Benedict frequently insists, must be unceasing. Unceasing in the sense of all day long; unceasing in the sense of all life long. Furthermore, putting these imperatives into effect is to be understood within the confines of the monastery and within the context of the concrete way of life that is lived there.

The theme of stability, although it is explicitly mentioned only a few times in the Rule, is fundamental for Benedict.

Before undertaking a period of probation, he requires that a candidate promise stability (RB 58.9). This means that the newcomer commits himself to stay with the process even when the way ahead is hard and puzzling. "The contract of stability rules out henceforth any feeble relapse, angry departure, aimless or curious wandering, and every vagary of fickleness."[1] The stability which belongs to integrity of monastic profession, however, is not an external canonical requirement. It is, as the present text indicates, a spiritual attitude which makes possible the perseverance in the practical business of living a good life. Its effect is that stability of mind that was referred to by Evagrius as *katastasis*: the inward tranquillity that is the prerequisite for contemplation.[2] Stability adds to the practice of all these good works the necessary concomitant of perseverance. It is not enough to begin walking along the way of virtue; many achieve that much. For definitive good to result, it is necessary to continue, notwithstanding the many difficulties and reversals usually encountered in the course of the spiritual journey.

Perseverance requires the ability to cope with the vicissitudes that mark our earthly pilgrimage, being neither too uplifted by apparent success nor strongly depressed by perceived failures. This was a theme to which Bernard of Clairvaux often returned:

> And so, on the day of your strength do not be too secure but cry out to God with the prophet and say, "When my strength fails do not abandon me" [Ps 70:9]. Further, in our time of temptation be consoled and say with the Bride, "Draw me after you and we will run in the fragrance of your ointments" [Song 1:3]. In this way let hope not desert you in a bad time, nor caution be lacking in good times. Thus amid the changeableness of prosperity and adversity you will hold fast to a certain likeness to eternity, keeping your constancy of spirit inviolate and unshaken, blessing God at

all times and, as it were, claiming for yourself—even in this wobbly world of doubtful outcomes and certain failures—an ongoing state of unchageableness. Meanwhile you are beginning to be renewed and reformed into that ancient and distinguished likeness of the eternal God with whom there is no variation or shadow of change. Indeed, as God is, so also will you be even in this world, not fearful in adversity nor lacking discipline in prosperity.[3]

Stability gives to monastic life a certain gravity, a seriousness that is not prone to the highs and lows of superficial excitement. It is this quality that enables a monk to persevere in low-impact living, quietly and without drama making use of the implements of good works. He is like the peasant who tills the soil in all weathers, in the hope of the crop which the soil will eventually yield. Or he is like the craftsmen at work on the great medieval cathedrals, investing as much painstaking effort in details that are invisible to the crowds below as in those nearby that win their admiration. Or like anyone who begins a noble task that will last a lifetime. What is needed is a zeal for excellence that does not depend for its energy on the immediacy of results or the approval of others.

A concert pianist of my acquaintance was once affronted by a review which described one of his performances as "workmanlike." It is not a very flattering description, but it is one that Saint Benedict applies to the good monk. He is simply a man doing a job (RB Prol 14; 7.70), using the tools available to him to produce a fair, workmanlike outcome but not expecting a great wave of applause as the work reaches its conclusion. Supposing he has managed to put into practice many of the tools described in this chapter, there is room for praise only to the extent that the external actions have been imbued with the inner quality of humility, and their fruits have been verified in the good effect his virtues have had on others.

If this chapter of the Rule is not to be read merely as a long list of virtuous actions, it needs in some way to be merged with the chapter on humility and the chapter on good zeal. The *conversatio* proposed by Saint Benedict is one in which a monk will engage in a lifetime of good works in a spirit of truthfulness and self-honesty, motivated by a sincere, gentle, and self-forgetful love. And undergirding everything is a faith which recognizes the call and action of grace and corresponds wholeheartedly with this divine summons. Benedict expects that the fruits of such a life will progressively become evident:

> As progress is made in the way of life and in faith, the road of God's commandments will be run with heart enlarged and in the indescribable sweetness of love. And so, let us never cease to have [Christ] as master, let us persevere in his doctrine in the monastery until death, and let us participate by patience in the sufferings of Christ. In this way will we deserve to be sharers in his kingdom. Amen. (RB Prol 49-50)

Notes

Preface

1. M. Casey, "Integrity in Interpretation: Listening for the Authentic Voice of Saint Benedict," *New Norcia Studies* 20 (2012): 51–58.

Introduction
The [Monk's] Implements: Good Works

1. The plural "good works" stands where we would expect the singular and so the phrase "implements of good works" is an example of an epexegetical genitive, a construction that is less common in English and often difficult to translate. Here the meaning is that the various "good works" are the tools of the monk's craft. See Basilius Steidle, "Das Genetivus epexegeticus in der Regel des Hl. Benedikt," *Studia Monastica* 2, no. 1 (1960): 193–203.

2. Adalbert de Vogüé, *La Régle de Saint Benoît*, SChr 184 (Paris: Cerf, 1971), 139.

3. For ample indications of scriptural parallels, see Giovanni Lunardi, *La Regola di San Benedetto "Sotto la guida del Vangelo,"* 2nd ed. (Offida: Edizioni Palumbi, 2011). For the wider monastic context, see Michaela Puzicha, ed., *Quellen und Texte zur Benediktusregel* (St. Ottilien: Eos, 2007); on RB 4 see 69–93.

4. Translated from John Cassian, *Conferences* 6.14; SChr 42, 239. See also *Conferences* 1.7; 85: "One who is zealous to acquire for

himself and make ready the tools of a particular trade does not do so merely to possess them and leave them idle. The advantage that is hoped for does not consist in their mere possession, but [it is hoped that] by their means and assistance he may acquire the mastery and fulfill the purpose of the particular craft."

5. Of these, thirty-one contain the negative *non* and the other seven contain verbs such as *odire* or *fugere*.

6. Bernard of Clairvaux, Div 42.4; SBOp 6A, 258.

7. David Hume, *Enquiries Concerning Human Understanding and Concerning the Principles of Morals*, 3rd ed. (Oxford: Clarendon Press, 1975), 270.

8. Evelyn Waugh, *Unconditional Surrender* (Harmondsworth: Penguin, 1961), 17; although originally published separately, this is the final part of Waugh's *Sword of Honour* trilogy. This very Catholic sentiment finds expression in a letter Guy Crouchback received from his father. The full quotation runs, "Quantitative judgements don't apply. If only one soul was saved that is full compensation for any loss of 'face.' " The sentence gives an interpretative key to the whole novel.

9. The theme is also in 2 Pet 3:9: "The Lord . . . is being patient with you, not wishing any to be lost, but that all will make their way to repentance."

Verses 1-2

1. Saint Benedict is following the original text; the versions given in the New Testament are verbally different: Mark 12:30 (heart, soul, mind, strength); Matt 22:37 (heart, soul, mind); and Luke 10:27 (heart, soul, strength, mind).

2. The term seems to have originated in Cicero, mimicking the Greek *antiphilein*. See his treatise *De amicitia* 14.49.

3. Thus Franz Jägerstatter: "Whoever lives in hatred of another human being cannot enter into friendship with God." *Letters and Writings from Prison* (Maryknoll, NY: Orbis, 2009), 166. Quoted in Mary Stommes, *Give Us This Day* (June 2013): 221.

4. Dil 1; SBOp 3, 119.

5. Saint Aelred of Rievaulx adds a note of realism to the discussion. In speaking of loving the neighbor as oneself, he remarks, " 'As

oneself' is an adverbial phrase of likeness not of quantity." For him, the commandment is not to love the neighbor as much as one loves oneself but simply to wish the neighbor well in the same way as one desires good things for oneself (S. 136.6; CCCM 2c, 326).

6. Romano Guardini, *The Last Things* (London: Burns & Oates, 1954), 105.

7. As a consequence, we are to withhold communion from evil-doers, not participating together with them or being in communion with them (Eph 5:7, 11).

8. SC 20.4; SBOp 1, 116–17.

9. SC 20.5; SBOp 1, 118.

10. For example, *Berakoth* 9:5; *The Mishnah*, trans. Herbert Danby (Oxford: Oxford University Press, 1972), 10.

11. "This is so because love, in its ontological sense, is letting-be. Love usually gets defined in terms of union, or the drive toward union, but such a definition is too egocentric. Love does indeed lead to community, but to aim primarily at uniting the other person to oneself, or oneself to him, is not the secret of love and may even be destructive of genuine community. Love is letting-be, not of course in the sense of standing off from someone or something, but in the positive and active sense of enabling-to-be. When we talk of 'letting-be', we are to understand both parts of this hyphenated expression in a strong sense—'letting' as 'empowering,' and 'be' as enjoying the maximal range of being that is open to the particular being concerned. Most typically, 'letting-be' means helping a person into the full realization of his potentialities for being; and the greatest love will be costly, since it will be accomplished by the spending of one's own being. Love is letting-be even when this may demand the loosening of the bonds that bind the beloved person to oneself; this might well be the most costly of demands, and it is in the light of this kind of love that drive toward union may seem egocentric. . . . The Christian religion affirms that 'God is love' and this is so because love is letting-be, and we have seen that the very essence of God as being is to let-be, to confer, sustain, and perfect the being of the creatures" (John Macquarrie, *Principles of Christian Theology*, rev. ed. [London: SCM Press, 1977], 348–49).

Verses 3-8

1. Some of the old monks used to interpret the violent invectives contained in the so-called cursing psalms as directed against these contrary tendencies within themselves. And so they were able to give voice to their opposition to the vices and strengthen their resolution to resist their attraction.

2. Richard Sipe, *Celibacy* (New York: Brunner-Routledge, 1990), 54.

3. Translated from John Cassian, *Conferences* 1.17; SChr 42, 99.

4. Walter Daniel, "Letter to Maurice," in *The Life of Ailred of Rievaulx*, ed. Maurice Powicke (Oxford: Clarendon Press, 1978), 79.

5. Since the penalty for most serious crimes was lifelong imprisonment, it is noteworthy that most medieval monastic prisons have only one or two cells. This seems to indicate that a great influx of inmates was not anticipated. It may be, furthermore, that in the course of the centuries the cells were used for other purposes.

6. EM 2.28; CCCM 138, 117–20.

7. It is believed that Dom Ambrose Bec, abbot of Melleray, who died on June 16, 1928, was poisoned to clear the way for the advancement of his prior. See Augusta Tescari, ed., *The Cistercian Order of the Strict Observance in the Twentieth Century*, vol. 1: *From 1892 to the Close of the Second Vatican Council* (Rome: OCSO Curia Generalis, 2008), 161. Another abbot is said to have been strangled by his prior as he sat alone in the chapter room preparing his Sunday conference. In both cases the affair was hushed up for fear of scandal. Perhaps such incidents gave rise to the story that a certain abbot, as part of his pastoral response in the disturbed days following World War II, kept a loaded pistol handy.

8. *Verba seniorum* 5, 5; PL 73:875C.

9. *De miraculis* 2.34–36; PL 185:1345–46.

10. John Cassian, *Conferences* 16.6; SChr 54, 228.

11. See Hugh Mackay, *What Makes Us Tick? The Ten Desires That Drive Us* (Sydney: Hachette, 2010); William B. Irvine, *On Desire: Why We Want What We Want* (New York: Oxford University Press, 2006).

12. Fydor Dostoyevsky, *The Idiot*, trans. David Magarshack (Harmondsworth: Penguin, 1965), 465.

13. Stephen M. R. Covey with Rebecca R. Merrill, "Speak about Others as if They Were Present," in *The Speed of Trust: The One Thing That Changes Everything* (New York: The Free Press, 2006), 168–71.

Verses 8-9

1. "It is called praise. It is supposed to be a small act of kindness. Next time she came past, and was right behind you, you could feel the fear from the one she had praised. Not a big fear, physical punishment did not come into it. But a subtle, little fear that would only be obvious to someone who had never received much in the way of praise. The fear of not being as good as last time; of not being worthy this time as well. You knew that, always, when Karin Ærø came up behind you, so too came a judge" (Peter Høeg, *Borderliners* [London: The Harvill Press, 1996], 46).

2. Michael Rosen, in his book *Dignity: Its History and Meaning* (Cambridge, MA: Harvard University Press, 2012), distinguishes four strands of usage for the term "dignity": status, intrinsic value, measured behavior, and respect. In Christian tradition it usually means intrinsic value.

3. Translated from Armand-Jean de Rancé, *La Régle [sic] de Saint Benoist nouvellement traduite et expliquée selon son veritable esprit*, vol. 2 (Paris: Muguet et Josse, 1689), 557–58.

4. Translated from Fernand Schwarz, "Redécouvrir l'honneur," *Acropolis* 235 (November 2012), editorial.

5. "Nobel's Greatest Prize," *The Economist* (January 20–26, 2007): 88.

6. Alain de Botton, *Status Anxiety* (Camberwell: Hamish Hamilton, 2004).

7. *Perfectae caritatis* 14.

8. See Patrick T. McCormick, *God's Beauty: A Call to Justice* (Collegeville, MN: Liturgical Press, 2012), 82–83.

Verses 10-20

1. *Abnegare semetipsum* sibi.
2. Aelred of Rievaulx, S. 175.24; CCCM 2d, 587.

3. Charlton T. Lewis and Charles Short, *A Latin Dictionary* (Oxford: Clarendon Press, reprinted 1996), 298.

4. John Cassian, *Conferences* 1.23; SChr 42, 134.

5. Aelred of Rievaulx, S. 101.17, CCCM 2c, 84.

6. Aelred of Rievaulx, S. 34.29; CCCM 2a, 285–86.

7. Aelred of Rievaulx, S. 94.2; CCCM 2c, 43.

8. Peter Brown, *The Body and Society: Men, Women and Sexual Renunciation in Early Christianity* (London: Faber, 1988), 236.

9. For what follows, see Émile Bertaud, "Discipline," in *Dictionnaire de spiritualité*, vol. 3 (Paris: Beauchesne, 1967), 1302–11.

10. See L'Abbé Boileau, *Histoire de Flagellans, ou l'on fait voir Le bon & mauvais usage des flagellations Parmi Chrétiens, Par des Preuves tirées de l'Ecriture Sainte, des Pères de l'Eglise, des Conciles, & des Auteurs profanes* (Amsterdam: Francois vander Plaats, 1750).

11. Thus, Norman Swan in *The Health Report* (April 30, 2012); www.abc.net.au/rn.

12. John Cassian, *Conferences* 2.17; SChr 42, 132. "Therefore fasts are to be moderate" (*Conferences* 5.18, SChr 42, 210).

13. Aelred of Rievaulx, S. 54.9; CCCM 2b, 69.

14. John Cassian, *Conferences* 5.11; SChr 42, 199.

15. Michaela Puzicha, *Quellen und Texte zur Benediktusregel* (St. Ottileon: Eos, 2007), 76.

16. Herbert of Clairvaux, *De miraculis* 1.13; PL 185:1291. Repeated in EM 2.9; CCCM 138, 80.

17. "Adjuvare applies to every kind of help or support; while *auxiliari* is only used of one who, from his weakness, needs assistance, and *subvenire* of one who is in difficulty or embarrassment" (Lewis and Short, *A Latin Dictionary*, 38).

18. Leo the Great, *Lenten Sermons* 2.4; SChr 49, 37.

19. Aelred of Rievaulx, S. 101.4; CCCM 2c, 79.

20. Pseudo-Cyprian, *De duplici martyrio* 33; PL 4:981a.

21. Aelred of Rievaulx, S. 43.13, CCCM 2a, 339.

22. I have written about this in "Strangers to Worldly Ways: RB 4,20" *Tjurunga* 29 (1985): 437–46. Reprinted in *An Unexciting Life: Reflections on Benedictine Spirituality* (Petersham, MA: St. Bede's Publications, 2005), 157–72. See more fully, *Strangers to the City: Reflections on the Beliefs and Values of the Rule of Saint Benedict* (Orleans, MA: Paraclete Press, 2005).

23. See, for example, Jacques Maritain, "The World and Its Contrasting Aspects," in *The Peasant of the Garonne: An Old Layman Questions Himself about the Present Time* (London: Geoffrey Chapman, 1968), 28–63.

24. Gregory the Great, *Dialogues* 2, Prol 1; SChr 260, 126.

25. Gregory the Great, *Dialogues* 2.1, 1, 2, 3; SChr 260, 128–30.

26. See, for example, Zoltan Alszeghy, "Fuite du monde," DSp 5 (1964), 1575–1605.

27. Aelred of Rievaulx, S. 106.9; CCCM 2c, 111.

28. Nicholas Carr, *The Shallows: What the Internet Is Doing to Our Brains* (New York: W. W. Norton & Company, 2010), 117.

29. "The mind is necessarily shaped during prayer by what happened beforehand" (John Cassian, *Conferences* 10.14; SChr 54, 95).

30. As recounted by Kevin Rudd, at the time of the meeting, Australian Prime Minister, on *Late Night Live* (November 6, 2012); www.abc.net.au/rn.

Verse 21

1. Cyprian of Carthage, *De oratione dominica* 15; PL 4:546b.

2. Aelred of Rievaulx, S. 106.7; CCCM 2c, 110.

3. Bernard of Clairvaux, SC 20.3; SBOp 1, 116.

Verses 22-26

1. Evagrius of Pontus, *Praktikos* 6, SChr 171, 508.

2. Aelred of Rievaulx, S. 55.7; CCCM 2b, 83.

3. Evagrius of Pontus, *Praktikos* 13 in *The Praktikos [and] Chapters on Prayer*, trans. John Eudes Bamberger, CS 4 (Spencer, MA: Cistercian Publications, 1970), 57.

4. Evagrius of Pontus, *Prayer* 24, pp. 58–59.

5. Translated from Evagrius of Pontus, *Ad Monachos* 10, ACW 59 (New York: Newman Press, 2003), 42.

6. Evagrius of Pontus, *Ad Monachos* 13.

7. Evagrius of Pontus, *Prayer* 22, p. 58.

8. Evagrius of Pontus, *On Thoughts* 37; SChr 438, 282.

9. Evagrius of Pontus, *Praktikos* 11, p. 18.

10. Evagrius of Pontus, *Prayer* 64, p. 65.

11. Paul Ekman, *Telling Lies: Clues to Deceit in the Marketplace, Politics and Marriage* (New York: W. W. Norton & Company, 2009), 329–30.

12. Aelred of Rievaulx, S. 154.19; CCCM 2c, 452.

13. There is an axiom in moral theology that states: *Irrationabiliter invito non facit iniuria* (To one who is unreasonably unwilling no injury is done).

14. *The Mirror of Charity* 3.13, 35; CCCM 1, 121.

Verses 27-28

1. Richard Sennett, *Together: The Rituals, Pleasures and Politics of Cooperation* (New Haven, CT: Yale University Press, 2012), 23.

2. Thus, Adalbert de Vogüé, *La Règle du Maître I*, SChr 105 (Paris: Cerf, 1964), 367n32.

3. Aelred of Rievaulx, S. 164.3; CCCM 2c, 512. Aelred is quoting Gaufridus Babion, *Sermo ad Sanctimonales* PL 171:902B.

4. Marianne Williamson, *A Return to Love: Reflections on the Principles of a Course in Miracles* (New York: HarperCollins, 1992), 190–91.

Verses 29-33

1. Aelred of Rievaulx, S. 166.4; CCCM 2c, 520. This sentence is a quotation from Hugh of Saint Victor.

2. John Sutton, "Electric Sheep: A Picaresque History of Twentieth-Century Memory from Twisted Molecules to Optimistic Detectives," *Times Literary Supplement* 5722 (November 20, 2012): 4. This is a review of Alison Winter's *Memory: Fragments of a Modern History* (Chicago: University of Chicago Press, 2012).

3. Dietrich Bonhoeffer, *The Cost of Discipleship*, trans. R. H. Fuller and Irmgard Booth (London: SCM Press, 1959), 78–79.

4. Joseph Cardinal Bernardin, *The Gift of Peace: Personal Reflections* (Chicago: Loyola Press, 1997), 46.

5. Bernard of Clairvaux, *Letters* 1.1; SBOp 7, 2.

6. John Cassian, *Conferences* 7.28; SChr 42, 270.

Verse 34

1. Evagrius of Pontus, *Praktikos* 14, p. 20.

2. Bernard of Clairvaux, *The Steps of Humility and Pride* 51; SBOp 3, 55.

3. Aelred of Rievaulx, S. 54.34–40; CCCM 2b, 78–79.

4. Aelred of Rievaulx, S. 166.7; CCCM 2c, 522.

5. Aelred of Rievaulx, S. 31.22; CCCM 2a, 255–56. See also S. 80.22; CCCM 2b, 326.

6. Aelred of Rievaulx, S. 54.7; CCCM 2b, 68.

7. Aelred of Rievaulx, S. 54.38.

8. That such a desire is rampant in monasteries is suggested by Professor Michael Hochschild after a prolonged exploration of several European monasteries. "A perfectly average monk constantly strives after a maximum of self-determination and at the same time for a minimum of determination by others. This means that every monk would prefer to be his own boss and where this is not possible—as in community life—the potential for conflict arises. An outside observer would expect to find humility and obedience in monastic life, but too often, in reality, individual autonomy and self-fulfillment are paramount. In all monasteries, the values associated with these latter attitudes are markedly higher than the average in society" ("Benediktiner zwischen Kontinuität und Wandel," *Erbe und Auftrag* 89, no. 1 [2013]: 33).

9. Aelred of Rievaulx, S. 54.39; CCCM 2b, 79.

10. Aelred of Rievaulx, S. 54.34; CCCM 2b, 78.

11. Bernard of Clairvaux, *The Steps of Humility and Pride* 18–19; SBOp 3, 29–30.

Verses 35-38

1. On this topic, see Francis Kline, "The First Gift: Primary Ascesis: Sex, Food and Sleep," in *Lovers of the Place: Monasticism Loose in the Church* (Collegeville, MN: Liturgical Press, 1997), 32–37.

2. Gregory the Great, *Dialogues* 2, 3, 4; SChr 260.

3. This was in his satirical treatise, *Specimen monachologiae methodo Linnaeana*. See Ritchie Robertson, "Freemasons vs Jesuits: Conspiracy Theories in Enlightenment Germany," *Times Literary Supplement* 5715 (October 12, 2012): 14.

4. William of St. Thierry, *Vita Prima Sancti Bernardi Claraevallis Abbatis* 39; CCCM 89b, 63.

5. See Michael Casey, "Moderation: The Key to Permanence," in *The Oblate Life*, ed. Gervase Holdaway (Collegeville, MN: Liturgical Press, 2008), 177–86.

6. Evagrius of Pontus, *On Thoughts* 33; SChr 438, 266–70.

7. See Hugh Feiss, "Circatores: From Benedict of Nursia to Humbert of Romans," *American Benedictine Review* 40, no. 4 (1989): 346–79.

8. *Ecclesiastica Officia* 74.4; Danièle Choisselet and Placide Vernet, eds., *Les* Ecclesiastica Officia *cisterciennes du XII*ᵉᵐᵉ *Siècle* (Reiningue: Abbaye d'Oelenberg, 1989), 216.

9. Quoted by Ian Ker, *John Henry Newman: A Biography* (Oxford: Oxford University Press, 1988), 94.

10. The classic study is Jean Leclercq, *Otia monastica: Études sur le vocabulaire de la contemplation au Moyen Âge*, Studia Anselmiana 51 (Rome: Herder, 1963).

11. Evagrius of Pontus, *Praktikos* 12, p. 18–19.

12. Aelred of Rievaulx, *De oneribus* 21.25; CCCM 2d, 195.

13. Aelred of Rievaulx, S. 43.25; CCCM 2a, 342.

14. Aelred of Rievaulx, S. 47.22; CCCM 2b, 9–10.

Verse 39

1. In my mischievously mistitled article, "In Praise of Murmuring" (*Tjurunga* 80 [2011]: 61–75), I discuss ten texts of the Rule: 4.39; 5.14; 5.17-19; 23.1-2; 34.6-7; 35.12-13; 40.8-9; 41.5; 53.18; 55.7.

2. Robert Hughes, *Culture of Complaint: The Fraying of America* (New York: Oxford University Press, 1993), 10.

3. Leszek Kolakowski, "Is God Happy?," *New York Review of Books* 59, no. 20 (December 20, 2012–January 9, 2013): 16.

4. Aelred of Rievaulx, S. 43.13; CCCM 2a, 339.

Verse 40

1. Aelred of Rievaulx, S. 54.17; CCCM 2b, 72–73.
2. Bernard of Clairvaux, SC 24.3; SBOp 1, 153.
3. Bernard of Clairvaux, SC 24.4; SBOp, 1, 154–55.
4. Bernard of Clairvaux, SC 24.4; SBOp 1, 155–56.

Verse 41

1. Thomas Aquinas, *Summa Theologiae* 2–2, 18.4, ad 2.
2. Saint Benedict has omitted the Master's injunction: "Not to hope for means of subsistence only from one's own labor, but more from God" (RM 3.49). Such a hope is for something apart from God and apart from eternal life.

Verses 42-43

1. RB Prol 29-32. I have pondered these verses in *The Road to Eternal Life: Reflections on the Prologue of Benedict's Rule* (Collegeville, MN: Liturgical Press, 2011), 104–18.
2. John Paul II, *Reconciliatio et paenitentia* 16; official Vatican translation.
3. John Paul II, *Veritatis splendor* 33; official Vatican translation.
4. A masterly description of the dynamics of temptation from first suggestion to ultimate enslavement by habit can be found in Saint Aelred's discourse for Saint Mary's purification; S. 32; CCCM 2a, 259–66.
5. On this, see Michael Casey, *A Guide to Living in the Truth: Saint Benedict's Teaching on Humility* (Liguori, MO: Liguori Publications, 2001), 123–40. See also "Confession" in *Fully Human, Fully Divine: An Interactive Christology* (Liguori, MO: Liguori Publications, 2004), 235–49.

Verses 44-46

1. John L. McKenzie, *Dictionary of the Bible* (London: Geoffrey Chapman, 1966), 300.

2. The text of Prov 16:25 is cited five times in the Rule of the Master (7.40; 10.27; 10.32; 10.46; and 90.7), usually in a cautionary context concerning self-will.

3. Thus, the *Thesaurus Linguae Latinae, editus iussu et auctoritate consilii ab academicis societatibus diversarum nationum electi* (Leipzig: B. G. Teubner, 1900–), vol. 4 (1906–1909), col. 102–4. There, Saint Ambrose is quoted as saying, "concupiscence is said both of a good thing and an evil thing." Augustine, however, states, "Nevertheless, this has been the custom of speaking that if desire or concupiscence is spoken of without mention of its object, then it must be taken to refer to a bad thing." Thus in RB 4.6, it is clear that the injunction *non concupiscere* refers to bad things, as does the reference in RB 7.25: *post concupiscentias tuas . . . non eas.* Regarding Saint Benedict's usage in the rest of the Rule, the verb *desiderare* is used positively here and at 5.12 and neutrally at 43.19. The noun *desiderium* is used negatively at RB 1.8; 4.59; 5.12; 7.12; 7.23 (twice); 7.24; and 7.31; three of these instances are in the form *desiderium carnis*. The noun is used positively at 49.7 (*spiritalis desiderii gaudio*) and at 60.8. In the Rule of the Master, *concupiscentia* and its cognates are usually negative (RM Th 3; Thp 28; 3.6; 5.10; 7.42; 7.46; 8.9; 8.20; and 10.36); RM 10.115 is positive. *Desiderium* and its cognates are more balanced; they are used negatively in RM Thp 74; 1.19; 1.55; 1.66; 53.55; 87.32; 87.34; and 91.41; and positively at RM 3.52; 7.50; 71.10; 82.13; 86.5; 86.13; 91.28; and 91.58.

4. For a general survey of this theme, see Michael Casey, "Desire and Desires in Western Tradition," *Tjurunga* 71 (2006): 62–92; and *Athirst for God: Spiritual Desire in Bernard of Clairvaux's Sermons on the Song of Songs*, CS 77 (Kalamazoo, MI: Cistercian Publications, 1988).

5. Jean Leclercq, *The Love of Learning and the Desire for God*, 2nd ed. (London: SPCK, 1988).

6. Aelred of Rievaulx, *Mirror of Charity* 2, 17.41; CCCM 1, 86.

Verses 47-49

1. Michael Casey, "A Trappist Abbey in the Nineteenth Century," *Tjurunga* 35 (1988): 81–84. The inscription is based on an incident

in the *Vitae patrum*, where one of the elders notices a young monk sinning and, instead of condemning him, says, *Ille hodie et ego cras*, "Today it is he [who sins], tomorrow it will be I." The story is found twice: PL 73:1039 and PL 74:380.

2. Aelred of Rievaulx, S. 175.21; CCCM 2d, 586.

3. Athanasius of Alexandria, *Life of Antony* 89.4; SChr 400, 364.

4. Athanasius of Alexandria, *Life of Antony* 19.2–4; SChr 400, 184–86.

5. Karl Rahner, "Some Thoughts on 'A Good Intention,' " in *Theological Investigations*, vol. 3: *Theology of the Spiritual Life* (London: Darton, Longman and Todd, 1967), 105–6.

6. Translated from Julian of Norwich, *Revelation 14* (Chapter 48); Edmund Colledge and James Walsh, eds., *A Book of Showings to the Anchoress Julian of Norwich* (Toronto: Pontifical Institute of Mediaeval Studies, 1978), 501–2.

7. Translation in Most Rev. Dr. Healy, *The Life and Writings of St. Patrick* (Melbourne: William P. Linehan, 1905), 708.

Verse 50

1. Augustine of Hippo, *Expositions on the Psalms* 136.21; CC 40, 1978.

2. C. S. Lewis, *Reflections on the Psalms* (London: Collins Fontana, 1961), 113–14.

3. John Cassian, *Institutes* 4.9; SChr 109, 132.

4. John Cassian, *Conferences* 16.11; SChr 54, 231.

5. See Michael Casey, "Radical Self-Honesty," in *A Guide to Living in the Truth: Saint Benedict's Teaching on Humility* (Liguori, MO: Liguori/Triumph, 2001), 125–40.

6. Aelred of Rievaulx, S. 136.22; CCCM 2c, 332.

Verses 51-56

1. Bernard of Clairvaux, Hum 28–30, SBOp 3, 38–40.

2. Bernard of Clairvaux, Div 64.2; SBOp 6A, 297: *per socialitatem caritas . . . acquiritur.*

3. Bernard of Clairvaux, Div 121; SBOp 6A, 399.

4. Bernard of Clairvaux, Div 17.7; SBOp 6A, 155.

5. Saint Augustine wryly notes that advancing age often reduces the power of vice so that many virtuous practices are easier to implement. *De nuptiis et concupiscentia* 1.25, 28; PL 44: 430b.

6. Aelred of Rievaulx, S. 158.14; CCCM 2c, 478–79. But note also S. 103.8 (CCCM 2c, 94) where Aelred remarks, "We do not read that Jesus ever laughed."

7. Karl Rahner, *The Great Church Year: The Best of Karl Rahner's Homilies, Sermons, and Meditations* (New York: Crossroad, 1993); quoted in Mary Stommes, ed., *Give Us This Day* (September 2012): 137.

8. Casey, *A Guide to Living in the Truth*, 175–76.

9. John Cassian, *Conferences* 14.13; SChr 54, 200.

10. Bernard of Clairvaux, *Lenten Sermons* 5.5; SBOp 4, 374.

11. Bernard of Clairvaux, Dil 22; SBOp 3, 137–38. For a discussion of Saint Bernard's teaching on the search for God, see Casey, *Athirst for God*, 81–86.

12. See Michael Casey, "*Intentio Cordis* (RB 52:4)," *Regulae Benedicti Studia* 6–7 (1977–78): 105–20. This was reprinted in *An Unexciting Life: Reflections on Benedictine Spirituality* (Petersham, MA: St. Bede's Publications, 2005), 334–58.

13. Augustine of Hippo, *On Psalm 128.8*, 4; CC 40, 1688.

14. Thomas Merton, *The Climate of Monastic Prayer* (Spencer, MA: Cistercian Publications, 1969), 37–38.

15. John Cassian, *Conferences* 9.36; SChr 54, 72.

16. John Cassian, *Institutes* 2.10.2–3; SChr 109, 76.

17. John Cassian, *Conferences* 10.14; SChr 54, 95.

18. John of Forde, *Sermons on the Song of Songs* 53.7; CCCM 17, 376.

19. Joseph Cardinal Bernardin, *The Gift of Peace: Personal Reflections* (Chicago: Loyola Press, 1997), 67–68.

Verses 57-58

1. Terrence Kardong plausibly translates *de caetero* as "for the future" and connects it with what is commonly termed a "purpose

of amendment." *Benedict's Rule: A Translation and Commentary* (Collegeville, MN: Liturgical Press, 1996), 92.

2. Bernard of Clairvaux, *Sententiae* 2.19; SBOp 6b, 29.

3. Augustine of Hippo, *On Psalm 50*, 16; CC 38, 611–12.

4. Aelred of Rievaulx, S. 54.18; CCCM 2b, 73.

5. *L'Osservatore Romano* (Weekly Edition in English) 37, no. 546 (September 14, 1978): 8.

6. Gregory the Great, *Dialogues* 3.14, 12; SChr 260, 312.

Verses 59-60

1. Aelred of Rievaulx, S. 115.11–12; CCCM 2c, 168.

2. RB Prol 3; 1.11; 3.8; 4.60; 5.7; 7.19; 7.31; 33.4.

3. For some authors there is a distinction between *propria voluntas* and *voluntas propria*, but in the Rule the two terms seem to be interchangeable.

4. Aelred of Rievaulx, S. 43.5; CCCM 2a, 337.

5. Thomas Merton, *Faith and Violence: Christian Teaching and Christian Practice* (Notre Dame, IN: University of Notre Dame Press, 1968), 112.

6. Thomas Merton, *New Seeds of Contemplation* (London: Burns & Oates, 1961), 27–28.

Verse 62

1. Some recent experiments on very young children seem to indicate that the ability to distinguish between right and wrong or good and bad is hard-wired.

2. John Cassian, *Conferences* 11.10; SChr 54, 112.

3. Aelred of Rievaulx, S. 47.28; CCCM 2b, 11.

4. Gregory the Great, *Moralia* 10.47; CC 153, 569.

Verse 63

1. John Cassian, *Conferences* 6.14; SChr 42, 238.

Verse 64

1. John Cassian, *Conferences* 5.27; SChr 42, 216–17.
2. Columba Stewart, *Cassian the Monk* (New York: Oxford University Press, 1998), 28.
3. Aelred of Rievaulx, S. 56.11; CCCM 2b, 94.
4. John Cassian, *Conferences* 12.6; SChr 54, 127–28.
5. John Cassian, *Conferences* 12.4; SChr 54, 124. See also *Conferences* 12.16; SChr 54, 145–46.
6. John Cassian, *Conferences* 12.7; SChr 54, 131–33. See Stewart, *Cassian the Monk*, 75–76.
7. John Cassian, *Conferences* 11.10; SChr 54, 109.

Verses 65-67

1. Aelred of Rievaulx, S. 55.6; CCCM 2b, 82–83.
2. Joseph Epstein, *Envy* (New York: Oxford University Press, 2003), 97.

Verse 69

1. See Michael Casey, "Exaltation," in *A Guide to Living in the Truth*, 55–68.
2. John Cassian, *Conferences* 15.7; SChr 54, 217.

Verses 70-71

1. Helen Lombard, "Mutual Obedience: An Aborted Effort?—Chapter 71," *Tjurunga* 53 (1997): 74.
2. Adalbert de Vogüé, *The Community and the Abbot*, CS 52, vol. 2 (Kalamazoo, MI: Cistercian Publications, 1988), 430–31.
3. Margaret Mead, *Culture and Commitment: A Study of the Generation Gap* (London: Granada, 1972), 110.
4. Elkonon Golberg, *The Wisdom Paradox: How Your Mind Can Grow Stronger as Your Brain Grows Older* (New York: Gotham Books, 2005), 10.

5. Ibid., 80.

6. Ibid., 8.

7. Note in this extract that the seniors are designated by three words: *priores, maiores,* and *seniores.* Terrence Kardong notes that the title *Nonnus* could well have the connotation of "grandfather." See *Benedict's Rule,* 521.

8. Armand-Jean de Rancé, *La Régle* [*sic*] *de Saint Benoist, Nouvellement traduite et expliquée selon son véritable esprit,* vol. 2 (Paris: Muguet et Josse, 1689), 556–57.

Verses 72-73

1. The text of the *Testament* is given in Bernardo Olivera, *How Far to Follow? The Martyrs of Atlas* (Petersham, MA: St. Bede's Publications, 1997), 127–29.

2. Sheila Cassidy, quoted by Margaret Malone, "Seek Peace and Pursue It (RB Prol 17; Ps 34:15)," *Tjurunga* 66 (2004): 54.

3. Quoted in Olivera, *How Far to Follow?*, 6.

Verse 74

1. Bernard of Clairvaux, SC 11.2; SBOp 1, 55.

2. Bernard of Clairvaux, *Christmas Sermons* 1.7; SBOp 4, 250. Bernard quotes the text of 2 Cor 9:7 twenty times in his writings.

Verses 75-78

1. Bernard of Clairvaux, *On Precept and Dispensation* 44; SBOp 3, 384.

2. See Michael Casey, "The Value of Stability," *Cistercian Studies Quarterly* 31, no. 3 (1996): 287–301.

3. Bernard of Clairvaux, SC 21.6; SBOp 1, 125.